MRP II:
Unlocking America's
Productivity Potential

MRP II:
Unlocking America's Productivity Potential

Oliver W. Wight

Oliver Wight Limited Publications, Inc.
P. O. Box 278
Williston, VT 05495

CBI Publishing Co., Inc.
51 Sleeper St.
Boston, MA 02210

Table of Contents

APPENDICES

Chapter Contents

A Message for the CEO

"We had too much inventory because we made more than we sold!" Alfred Sloan said it in 1921. But if it's that simple, why have so many companies since then gotten into financial difficulty because they "made more than they sold"?

The concept was simple. But until recently, we didn't really have good tools to implement management plans to coordinate production with sales. Management often felt that the only approach that really worked was the periodic edict to "cut inventories." We also got distracted for a while by the notion that economic order quantity formulae and "scientific" safety stock "decisions" would somehow "manage" inventories.

Meanwhile, a new set of management tools, made possible by the computer, was being developed through experience. And a body of knowledge about using the tools slowly evolved.

This book is about those tools and how to manage with them. It is not about computers, systems, or even inventory management specifically - I used inventories above only as an example. It is about managing production, purchasing, inventories, cash flow, and return on investment. It is about tying marketing planning, manufacturing planning, and financial planning, into a company plan that can be executed and monitored. It's about improving the effectiveness of engineering and marketing and delivery performance. It's about having more reliable financial numbers and preventing surprise inventory shrinkages. It's about productivity, better teamwork, reducing the adversary relationship between management and labor, and improving the quality of life in a manufacturing company.

As one CEO said, "At first, I couldn't 'make the connection.' Why should I be concerned about MRP II? Now that I understand it, I realize that it addresses the gut level problems I deal with every day."

This book was written to help some managers "make the connection" and use these powerful tools. It was written to help others, who already have them, to use the tools even more productively.

Oliver W. Wight

xiii

Why a "Limited" Publication

Oliver Wight Limited Publications was incorporated especially to make new books on MRP II and related subjects available sooner than would be possible through normal publishing channels. The publishing business is just entering a period of great change being brought about by the technology of computers. This book will be shipped to the first customers eight weeks after the writing is finished.

Once the regular phototypeset edition of the book is available, the printing plates used to produce this edition will be destroyed.

We believe that this approach to getting useful information disseminated more quickly in a rapidly developing field is important. We hope you enjoy this "limited" edition of MRP II: Unlocking America's Productivity Potential.

Oliver W. Wight

Foreword

Vince Lombardi: "This is a game of blocking and tackling."

Johnny Wooden: "So many kids ask me to teach them the 'tricks of the trade.' In this game you have to learn to dribble, pass, and shoot. The tricks are easy."

In our manufacturing economy, we paid little attention to manufacturing for many years. When we finally did wake up to the need to reindustrialize and improve productivity (around 1980), we grasped for "fixes" and characteristically ignored the "blocking and tackling." We failed to address the fundamental problems in a manufacturing company that hobbled our productivity, fostered fingerpointing, encouraged compartmentalization, and thwarted efforts to develop real teamwork.

This book will help you understand these problems clearly. It also explains a method for addressing them called Manufacturing Resource Planning: MRP II.

MRP II is not a new "theory" on Industrial behavior; it is all fact. MRP II is what's happening today in a number of companies.

This book does not just make some recommendations about some new "approaches"; it's a "how to" book about solutions.

MRP II is not something that the "Japanese are doing"; it evolved in American companies like Black & Decker, Cameron Iron Works, Corning Glass, Hewlett Packard, Steelcase, Tennant, and Xerox.

The computer made it possible to develop some tools to solve deep-rooted, fundamental problems. These companies learned how to solve the basic scheduling problem that most people never knew existed in manufacturing companies. (1) We learned how to build a company game plan on that base that every function could work to.

People with these basic tools have demonstrated what they can really do to improve productivity in every aspect of a manufacturing business (not just direct labor). But until these fundamentals are done well, none of the other proposed productivity solutions are likely to generate anything like the potential results. Theory Z, quality circles, CAD/CAM, etc. have great potential, but only if they are built on a solid foundation.

Anyone involved in our manufacturing economy - bankers, economists, educators, journalists, stock analysts, etc. should read at least Chapters 1 through 8, and Chapter 20. The contribution that scheduling methods have made to amplify the boom/bust cycle needs to be understood by people in all of these categories. They will also learn more about what productivity really means and how to better judge a well managed manufacturing enterprise.

Manufacturing company managers should read the whole book. Some, in specialized functions, may wish to skim several of the chapters in Parts III and IV, and return to them later for reference.

This book isn't primarily about the tools of MRP II: Manufacturing Resource Planning. (2) It isn't just about how to use these tools. It is really about a more professional approach to managing a manufacturing enterprise.

Oliver W. Wight
Blodgett Landing
New Hampshire
October, 1981

Footnotes

1. Of all the articles written on CAD/CAM, the only one
    that ever recognized the scheduling problem appeared
    in Fortune, "A New Industrial Revolution is on the
    Way," October 5, 1981. "In every plant in the
    country, you see foremen running around with hot
    sheets in their hands - a list of parts that are needed
    immediately on the assembly line. Some plants have
    more expeditors than people making things."

2. In this book, the term "MRP" will be used as a general
    term in most instances. MRP itself means Material
    Requirements Planning. When this is expanded to
    include capacity planning, shop floor control, and
    purchasing, the correct term for it is Closed Loop
    MRP. When the financial functions are tied in and it
    is used as a company game plan, it is called Manufac-
    turing Resource Planning or MRP II.

    In normal conversation, we speak of New York without
    defining whether we are referring to Manhattan, the
    greater New York City area, or New York State. The
    context of the conversation usually conveys the mean-
    ing clearly. So the term "MRP" will be used without
    defining whether it is Material Requirements Planning,
    Closed Loop MRP, or MRP II; unless that is required
    to clarify the meaning of the text.

Acknowledgements

Every author owes a lot to a great many people. I wish to thank in particular, Walter Goddard (my most demanding critic), Darryl Landvater (Editor and Publisher), and my wife, Joan. Their help with this book in discussing ideas, helping with the editing, and their patience and understanding, is beyond my gratitude. Mike Rowan, Editor and Assistant Publisher of Modern Materials Handling magazine also provided his usual outstanding input. And there are many others whose thoughts have helped so much along the way. Working and writing a book together with George Plossl in the 1960's was a mutual learning experience. Working closely with Joe Orlicky as MRP evolved in the 1970's was also a great opportunity to learn and exchange many ideas. In recent years, those whose thinking has influenced me most include these experienced professionals: Dick Alban, George Bevis, Roger Brooks, Jim Burlingame, Dave Garwood, Dick Ling, Andre Martin, John Schorr, Al Stevens, Bernard T. Smith, and Tom Wallace. And I'd also like to thank the executives in the over 1,300 manufacturing companies I have visited in the last 30 years, as well as the thousands of executives who have attended our Top Management classes and our executive conference for the insights they have provided on the many facets of managing a manufacturing business more professionally. These people, from some of the best managed manufacturing businesses in our country, have passed on many of their observations on subjects like Japanese manufacturing and have greatly stimulated my thinking.

Of course, I owe a great deal to the people in our offices who helped me: Peggy Jordan (who worked hard to insulate me from the day-to-day problems, as well as proofreading), and, in particular, Anne Hilton, Sandy Perry, Dana Scannell and Jennifer Snyder (in charge of production) all of whom worked so hard to get this book out. Finally, I would like to thank Linda Mansfield for her work on the figures.

Oliver W. Wight

PART I
The Missing Link in Productivity

Chapter 1
Our Manufacturing Economy at a Crossroads

Section 1
It IS a Manufacturing Economy

A high school teacher made this observation:

"Maybe we should get out of the automobile manufacturing business. Maybe we just can't compete with the Japanese. Maybe we should get out of manufacturing altogether!"

The lack of fundamental understanding betrayed by these comments is stunning! This is no reflection on the school teacher; his thinking is probably fairly typical for even well educated people in our society who don't understand a fundamental principle of economics:

PRODUCTION IS THE PRIMARY SOURCE OF WEALTH

It is our factories and our farms (and our farms would not be what they are without our factories), it is construction, and it is mining, that creates the wealth. It is not created by banks, insurance companies, schools, stock brokers, politicians, or any other service functions. Some say, "But better than half the gross national product is in services now, not in production." That may be. But ask anybody in a town like Youngstown where the manufacturing companies are shutting down about that. The dry-cleaners aren't too busy and the people who service swimming pools are wondering what other businesses to get into. This is not to say that these services are not important - nor that some of them are not essential in the support of production - but they themselves create no wealth.

Wealth is created by the "producers." Without them there wouldn't be any funds to pay for education or any of the other important services that we consider the necessities of life today.

Manufacturing is "the goose that laid the golden egg." But where do we stand in American manufacturing today? It is no secret. We're slipping badly.

Productivity in the United States in the period 1968 to 1978 went up 23.6 percent. In Japan it went up 89.1 percent. (1) Part of the result is inflation, and that affects everyone. We know it affects people on fixed incomes, but even the most militant labor unions are not usually able to win annual wage increases to match an inflation rate that has gone as high as twenty percent.

The implications go much farther than that. As Senator Frank Church said on "Face The Nation" (CBS, Sunday, April 13, 1980) in discussing the lack of respect shown toward the United States abroad:

> We have lost our economic clout. We have lost our place in the international marketplace, and we haven't lost it to the Russians, to the Chinese, or to any part of the communist world. We have lost it to the Germans and the Japanese, our so-called trading partners. And that is where we should be concentrating and rebuilding on the American position in the world, rejuvenating the American economy.

Time Magazine put it into even more basic terms:

> For all capitalism's proven success in producing material prosperity, the ultimate justification for the system does not rest on it's output of cars or cosmetics. Capitalism's fundamental rationale is that it permits and promotes freedom by enhancing the rights of the individual and limiting the power of the state. While some capitalist countries are not democracies, no communist or totally socialist economy has remained a democracy for long. The reason is clear: political freedom is impossible without economic freedom. (2)

Time went on to quote Hilaire Belloc, the British writer, "The control of wealth is the control of human life itself."

We cannot duck the issues:

1. Much of what we have in our culture, as well as material things, comes from the wealth that comes largely from manufacturing. The industrial revolution did not start in an insurance company!

2. We are rapidly losing our position as the world leader in manufacturing.

Why are we slipping? For one thing we have not recognized how important manufacturing is in our economy. How many college students want to study manufacturing and make it their career when they can have more prestigious and rewarding jobs as stock brokers, bankers, consultants, or real estate developers? As one professor of business management pointed out, "It's difficult to keep them interested in manufacturing when they find that a job in Wall Street will pay twice as much to start."

We have an <u>attitude</u> problem. Denis Healey, the former Chancellor of the Exchequer in Britain, said in an article in <u>Newsweek</u>, August 22, 1977, "In Britain we must change attitudes in the educational system so that people aren't looked down on if they go into a factory rather than an office, or work in industry rather than banking." That's the kind of disdain for manufacturing that has helped reduce England to a second rate industrial nation.

Here is a quote from Rupert Murdoch given in a London luncheon speech, "In Britain the Industrial Revolution was not followed by a revolution in social values. Aristocratic and rural attitudes and values were maintained - Merrie England and all that. Industry was vulgar. Social prestige could only be gained by using the wealth acquired in industry to escape it. How many first-class graduates from the best universities dirty their hands in industry? Practically none. It is going to take a lot to break down the snobbery and shibboleths to reverse the gentrification of Britain. We must understand the business of Britain is <u>making things</u> and <u>selling things</u>". (3)

Consider this quote from Antony Pilkington, Chairman of Pilkington Brothers Limited, the glassmakers: "I had no great vocation for a particular job, so it seemed fairly natural for me to go into the family business." Incredible! No "vocation" so he joined a manufacturing company, and after some "on the job training" became chairman. Later the article (4) goes on to say that the Pilkingtons, like most of the old industrial families of England, keep a low profile. "England has traditionally been a land owning aristocracy," noted Antony Pilkington. "We rather play down our industrial life and successes." (One has to wonder just how much wealth that can be circulated throughout the economy is actually being produced by the "land owning aristocracy.")

That is not an indictment of Mr. Pilkington. It's an indictment of the attitude the English have about the requirements for professionalism in running a manufacturing business. This attitude is a luxury no industrial nation can afford. America <u>must</u> get that message!

We can see this attitude in the other members of the team in a manufacturing company. Even the term "Manufacturing Resource Planning" tends to be looked upon as something that affects the manufacturing people only. Marketing, finance, and engineering people rarely think of themselves as part of the team in a manufacturing company, but in most companies they think of their functions as separate entities. This is not to say that manufacturing is more important than marketing. Without marketing, manufacturing wouldn't have anything to do. Without engineering, there would be no product for marketing to sell or manufacturing to make. Without finance, there would be no money to pay for these activities. But we have, in the past, done a great job of compartmentalization in the typical manufacturing enterprise.

Small wonder! We have colleges of finance and marketing and engineering; but where in our manufacturing economy is a school on how to run a manufacturing business in all of its facets? What about the subject of manufacturing itself? If it is taught at all at the college level, it is typically, to quote Wickham Skinner (5), "Generally taught in graduate schools of business administration as a combination of industrial engineering (time study, plant layout, inventory theory, etc.) and quantitative analysis, (linear programming, statistical safety stock calculations, queuing theory, etc.)"

There is not even a well defined body of practical knowledge on the subject. There are virtually no college textbooks that address the subject from a practical view point. As Professor Jerry Harvey, George Washington University, said: "Why aren't management textbooks funny? It's because they don't have much realism to them. If they had much realism to them, they'd be funny as hell."(6)

It's about time we recognized that every function in a manufacturing business is important and interdependent, as well as recognizing the tremendous responsibility we have in managing our manufacturing businesses more effectively.

There are few activities in our society that have more impact on more people than managing a manufacturing enterprise. Consider a company in trouble, like Chrysler. Workers lost their jobs, management people lost their pay, independent business men who had automobile dealerships with all their money tied up in them went out of business.

Customers ran the risk of losing part of their investment by buying a potentially "orphan" car. Even the taxpayers had to bear some of the risk by underwriting loans to try to keep Chrysler in business.

Another problem we see in our manufacturing economy is the boom/bust cycle that we typically go through. Even our economists are generally unaware of the real causes of this amplification in our business cycles. In our manufacturing economy much of this is caused by the fundamental way we schedule our own factories and our vendors' factories. More will be said about the specifics of this problem later, but certainly anyone who was working in manufacturing in 1974 remembers how commodities like electronic components were almost impossible to get in August, and yet were a glut on the market in December. This, of course, contributes to inflation and recession. Once again, the social impact is far reaching.

We have the tools today to reduce this boom/bust amplification dramatically. We have the tools to run our manufacturing businesses far more effectively. We must recognize that:

1. We have a manufacturing economy.
2. Those who manage our manufacturing businesses have a profound social as well as business responsibility.

A solid body of professional knowledge on running manufacturing businesses is developing today. A great deal of this knowledge is the result of business managers developing skills with the new tools that are available. Some of it has come from observing our competition.

Section 2
Our Worthy Competition

If any country has demonstrated an ability to use manufacturing to create wealth effectively, it's Japan. Many people today can remember the old cliches about "cheap Japanese copies." Today there are not many German cameras around, there are not many English sports cars around, and there are not many American television sets.

The United States is beginning to look like an economic colony of Japan. The classic colonial relationship is one where the colony ships raw material to the mother country and buys back its finished products.

What's their secret? Cheap labor? Hardly! The Japanese have found it very profitable to build factories in the United States to take advantage of our labor in building their products!

Another excuse we give for Japan's emergence at the top of the industrial world is the Japanese "work ethic." Robert Cole, Director of the University of Michigan's Center for Japanese Study (7), has worked in Japanese factories. He says that "The Japanese work ethic is a myth."(8) He agrees that the Japanese worker often does a better job of identifying with the company, but attributes much of that to management attitude and says "A great deal of Japanese industrial success has to do with management priorities."

An article in the Cincinnati Enquirer (Sunday, March 30, 1980) titled "U.S. Workers Perform Better Under Japanese Bosses" discussed the Savin Copier Company's three factories; one in Japan, one in California run by American management, and one in California run by Japanese management. Result: the productivity of American workers under Japanese management is as great as the productivity of their Japanese counterparts. We can blame labor, and we can blame government (with some justification); but the facts point to one unavoidable conclusion: we need to upgrade our professionalism in managing our manufacturing industries if we are going to compete internationally.

What DO the Japanese know that we don't know? They know that:

1. THEY HAVE A MANUFACTURING ECONOMY.
   They are not ashamed of it. They nurture it.
   We tend to hide our heads in the sand and look
   at manufacturing as some kind of "dirty finger-
   nail" activity, certainly less prestigious than
   banking, insurance, selling stock, etc., etc.

2. PEOPLE ARE THE KEY TO EVERYTHING. The
   typical American executive would be insulted to
   be told that they needed continuing education.
   That simply isn't the way it's been done in the
   past. Education ended at college and was
   punctuated by a few "seminars"; but it was not
   really looked upon as a prerequisite to professionalism. The Japanese know that education is
   fundamental and continuing.

3. THE COMPETITION IS OUTSIDE THE COMPANY.
   American companies are usually very functionally
   oriented. Engineering thinks that people in
   marketing are irresponsible, marketing thinks that
   the people in manufacturing are unresponsive.
   The Japanese recognize that they have to play
   team ball to compete.

4. THE COMPETITION IS OUTSIDE THE COUNTRY.
   We've been complacent. We assumed that we
   would always be the leaders in the world in
   manufacturing. Yet we've let our leadership
   erode. While our management failed to reinvest
   the funds required to keep our television
   industry efficient, and our labor concerned itself
   with getting better wages and fringes, both
   forgot about the competition, and we wound up
   losing most of our television industry.

5. MANAGEMENT IS A LONG TERM PROPOSITION.
   We've had too much short term orientation. Too
   many managers are concerned only with this
   year's results, and they motivate other people in
   their companies to do the same. Management is
   stewardship. Yes, we must have short term
   results, but responsible managers must be concerned about long term results also. Trading
   tomorrow for today is one of the reasons that
   American companies have lost their dominance in
   the world markets.

If we had to sum up the Japanese success in a word it would be <u>teamwork</u>. The Japanese culture is entirely different from the American culture. Some years back, IBM tried to hold a sales contest in their Tokyo office. This resulted in the poorest sales month ever. No Japanese salesman would try to win the contest and embarrass his fellow salesmen! Being a part of the team was far more important than being an outstanding individual. Just the opposite approach that an American would have! But, when they held a sales contest between the Tokyo office and the Osaka office, the contest was very successful.

In many Japanese companies today, the workers sing the company song before the beginning of the shift. The company in Japan is an extension of the family, and the country is an extension of the family too. There's a great feeling of identity with the company objectives between management and labor, and people work together to get the job done.

So we have much to learn from our competition and three messages seem particularly clear:

* They know that they must manufacture to survive.

* They take a very professional, long term approach to managing their manufacturing businesses.

* They know that the real key to productivity is people. People working as a team with clearly identified competition, and with clearly understood company objectives foremost in their minds.

Section 3
Some Proposed Solutions to the Productivity Problem

Nineteen eighty was the "watershed year" for American manufacturing. We suddenly realized that we had to do something about productivity in our manufacturing industries. Articles on the subject appeared in virtually every magazine.

Newsweek (Special Report, 9/8/80) talked about "The Productivity Crisis." Business Week talked about the "Reindustrialization of America". The Atlantic featured an article titled, "American Industry - What Ails It - How to Save It" (Volume 246, September, 1980, pages 35-50). Time Inc. had a special theme in all of its magazines on American renewal, and followed up with a series on "Working Smarter" in subsequent issues of Fortune in 1981. Many articles on "How the Japanese do it" appeared in various publications. Even television picked up the theme: American manufacturing had slipped and had to do something. NBC, in a prime time program in the summer of 1980, asked "If Japan can, why can't we?"

But while agreeing on the problem and agreeing that we must learn from our competition is a beginning, the real need is for solutions. At a meeting at Harvard in the spring of 1980, 150 "business men, academics and congressmen" concluded that solutions to the productivity problem were: more labor - business - government dialogues, tax cuts, less regulation, and a program to "educate Americans about the problems and the need for solutions."

The people that attended this conference apparently believed, as so many do, that the problem was really labor and government. And they apparently believed that the solutions existed only in better, more efficient, production equipment: more modern machine tools, more automation, more use of robots.

There is no question about the productivity potential of more efficient machines. But, for many people, that is the beginning and the end to improving productivity. This quote from Denis Healey, from the same article mentioned earlier, (Newsweek, August 22, 1977) is indicative of that thinking: "We must also re-equip our manufacturing industry so that it's fully competitive worldwide, against the time the oil runs out."

This is a common, but very narrow, view of productivity and its causes. Not that more modern and efficient machinery can't help, but there is far more to productivity than machines alone.

Still others were recommending more use of computer technology like CAD/CAM (Computer Aided Design/Computer Aided Manufacturing). CAD would typically involve putting the equivalent of an engineering drawing into a computer, "digitalizing" it, and then being able to manipulate it; producing (CAM) bills of material, routings, and, ultimately, a tape for running a numerically controlled machine tool from this data, and then using it for inspection.

CAD/CAM has made great progress recently and has even greater potential. But people were still looking for productivity primarily from using <u>machines</u> more efficiently.

<u>People who really understood the productivity problem began to direct their attention toward management.</u> <u>Business Week</u> talked about "Management's Drag on Productivity" (<u>Business Week</u>, December 3, 1979, page 14), <u>The Wall Street Journal</u> reported "Poor Productivity Gets Blamed on Managers - By the Managers Themselves" (<u>Wall Street Journal</u>, Tuesday, January 6, 1981, page 1), <u>Fortune</u> suggested that "What business does to correct one particular management oversight - could turn out to be far more decisive than government favors in restoring U.S. industrial vigor and competitiveness" (<u>Fortune</u>, July 13, 1981, page 52, "Rediscovering the Factory").

The "one oversight" mentioned in this <u>Fortune</u> article is recognizing the importance of the manufacturing function in a manufacturing company. Professor Wickham Skinner of the Harvard Business School - long a champion of manufacturing even when it was out of favor in academia - contends that much of our trouble in manufacturing today exists because "Manufacturing is generally perceived in the wrong way at the plant level, managed in the wrong way at the corporate level, and taught in the wrong way at business schools."

In the meantime a few companies were making great inroads into the problem of product quality. The statistical sampling procedures that were the "rage" in the quality control field in the 1950's and 1960's can be used to determine that a process is out of control. But the real problem is: <u>making the product right the first time</u>. Getting the workers involved directly in fixing the causes of the problems through "quality circles" has had great success. And making the product right the first time means less scrap and more productivity.

The emphasis was swinging toward better management and better use of our human resources to improve productivity. Not _just_ more efficient machines!

Theory Z (9) is an approach to managing people by having a clearly understood management philosophy, and emphasizing teamwork based on trust and mutual respect. Theory Z uses much of the best of American and Japanese management approaches, while recognizing that Americans are culturally different and can't just mimic the Japanese. And this is a point well made. Quality circles without a foundation of trust between management and labor will just be a charade.

Good solutions all of these; especially the emphasis on people and more participative management. But all of these solutions assume that a manufacturing company operates the way it should, when in reality it doesn't.

There is a problem in manufacturing. A serious problem:

SCHEDULING DOESN'T WORK

But this problem is so deeply imbedded in our experiences and so universal that no one seems to notice it.

As Paul G. Hemmen, Corporate Manufacturing Manager of Uniflite, Inc., said in commenting on a series of articles on productivity that were published recently, "You'll find that not one of the prominent business, education, or political leaders writing articles on productivity seems to know anything about the problem. Incredible! How many plants in this country have people standing around waiting for parts and foremen fighting against poorly integrated master schedules, and manufacturing systems either non-existent or not operating."

Is the solution to the productivity problem then to use more efficient machines and techniques to make more of the wrong parts at the wrong time?

Will we ever get other members of management to respect manufacturing, or get young people to go into the field, when in the real world, the manufacturing people are expeditors and whipping boys because they can't meet "schedules" and don't have real facts to answer marketing's constant demands?

Will more participative management attain its potential in manufacturing when the people don't have the tools to do their jobs, tools like valid schedules?

Or will all of this good thinking go the way of MBO (Management By Objectives)? MBO was great theory and looked like it was going to revolutionize our approaches to managing a manufacturing business. But one of the prime objectives of a manufacturing company is to <u>ship</u> products. When shipments aren't made:

The assembly foreman says, "I didn't have the parts."

The production control people say, "Nobody works to the schedule."

The shop foremen say, "The schedule is a joke - we work to the shortage list; and anyway we don't have the material we need from purchasing."

Purchasing says, "We bring material in when somebody expedites it. If we actually worked to the dates on the purchase orders and brought in all of the past due material tomorrow, you wouldn't know where to store it."

MBO? How can performance really be measured? Who is really accountable? One of the reasons Management By Objectives didn't work as well as it should have in manufacturing was lack of a valid plan: <u>a valid schedule</u>.

Not that a valid schedule is the panacea. We need to take all of the good thinking on productivity and integrate it into an overall approach. But if scheduling doesn't work in a manufacturing company, the other good things that can be done simply won't produce the potential results that they should. (10)

Section 4
A New Perspective on Productivity

Virtually all of the things that have been said and written about productivity dwell on the productivity of direct labor. And even then the impact of poor scheduling on productivity has largely been ignored.

But the inability to schedule well in a manufacturing business has far deeper implications. One of the problems is the lack of a company game plan that everyone can work to. As a result, a great deal of effort is expended, but isn't well integrated and it isn't directed toward well defined goals. This means the productivity of the entire organization is affected. And that's particularly significant since most productivity solutions dwell on the productivity of direct labor and ignore the fact that it is a relatively small percentage of the overall cost of running a manufacturing business. Figure 1-1 shows the way the sales dollar breaks down in a small sample of manufacturing companies. The sample companies were placed in three categories:

	Component Manufacturer	Equipment Manufacturer	Consumer Products Manufacturer
Labor	.11	.07	.04
Material	.28	.43	.25
Overhead	.20	.21	.10
Factory Cost	.59	.71	.39
Operating Cost	.25	.15	.40
Total Cost	.84	.86	.79
Profit	.16	.14	.21
Sales	$1.00	$1.00	$1.00

Figure 1 - 1. Sales Dollar Breakdown

*   Component manufacturers who make parts for other companies such as manufacturers of electric motors.

*   Equipment manufacturers who make products like industrial machines or tractors.

*   Consumer product manufacturers who make products like pharmaceuticals, toiletries, etc.

Obviously, many companies would fit between two of the categories rather than falling neatly into any one.

The important thing in Figure 1-1 is the small percentage of labor that constitutes the total sales dollar ranging from a high of eleven cents to a low of four cents (that is not to say that some companies don't have higher or lower figures than these averages from the sample companies). In an equipment manufacturing company, for example, if purchased costs could be reduced seventeen percent, that would be the equivalent of eliminating all direct labor cost!

What about the cost of research and development, engineering, manufacturing supervision, marketing, and advertising? These are buried in factory overhead and operating costs - once again, these costs are larger than direct labor. Anybody who's worked in a manufacturing company could cite examples where engineering, marketing, manufacturing, and financial efforts were not coordinated in the introduction of a new product. The financial people were surprised by the additional inventory required; marketing insisted on product release before it was fully engineered; manufacturing had to spend excessive amounts of money in overtime to get the product out and make up for lost engineering time. In addition, the productivity of the entire organization was affected when the new product was introduced but wasn't well tested and, as a result, got a poor customer reaction. That is a productivity problem as much as the problems in the direct labor area.

This is not to say that we shouldn't be concerned about the productivity of direct labor. But it does say that we've got to look at the bigger picture too.

Peter Drucker said it well (11) in speaking about the attempt to get the quick "trade offs" (trying to buy machines to get rid of people). He said, "Capital investment creates the need for more knowledge work," and this is, obviously, more expensive work. He pointed out that the days of the easy "trade offs" are behind us. He went on to say, "From now on, all resources will have to be managed better for greater productivity."

And that is the theme of MRP II: managing all of the resources of a manufacturing company more productively. And the first problem that must be addressed is scheduling, because in a manufacturing company:

SCHEDULING IS FUNDAMENTAL

Footnotes

1. Bureau of Labor Statistics, United States Department of Labor, December, 1979.

2. "Capitalism: Is it Working?," Time, April 21, 1980.

3. "Other Comments," Forbes, October 26, 1981.

4. "The Pilkingtons of Britain," New York Times, Sunday, July 27, 1980.

5. Wickham Skinner, Manufacturing and the Corporate Strategy, (New York: John Wiley and Sons, 1978), p. 27.

6. "The Money Chase," Time, May 4, 1981, p. 58.

7. Author of the book, Work, Mobility, and Participation; A Comparative Study of American and Japanese Industry.

8. The Boston Globe, Saturday, October 8, 1980, p. 20.

9. William Ouchi, Theory Z, (Reading, Massachusetts: Addison - Wesley Publishing Company, 1981).

10. In Chapter 20 the integration of all of the approaches to more professional management of a manufacturing business will be discussed.

11. Peter F. Drucker, Managing in Turbulent Times, Harper and Row Publishers, 1980.

Chapter 2
Understanding the Scheduling Problem

Section 1
Why Scheduling Doesn't Work

Perhaps the single most difficult thing to explain to people not familiar with manufacturing and distribution scheduling is the fact that the environment is one of constant change. Schedules have to be made for a few hundred items in some companies, or as many as thousands of individual components, raw materials, and finished goods items in other companies.

In most companies these schedules start with a forecast, and the forecast is usually wrong. With each passing day as actual sales materialize, the true "need dates" for material are changing in the real world. One job is being moved ahead of another, another is being pushed back (often by default!). Customers need jobs in a hurry because of breakdowns in the field. In the aircraft supply business, for example, an AOG (aircraft on the ground) means that "all stops must be pulled" to get the needed material to the aircraft as soon as possible. In the oil field support industry, a blowout at an oil well (not in the "forecast" of course!) means that the needed parts must be made on an emergency "rush" basis and flown to the spot.

Many companies whose primary products are made to customer order operate off a large order backlog. It would appear that they have no forecasting problem and consequently can use the backlog as a schedule. But it doesn't work that way in reality. Customer specifications are changing, there are engineering changes; and even though the end delivery schedule may not change, there are many changes in the supporting schedules that are required to cope with change and still meet the delivery schedule.

And forecasts aren't the only problem. In a typical factory there is scrap, rework, machines that break down, tooling that doesn't work properly, processes that go out of control suddenly - often for no apparent reason! Engineering changes are required to keep the product up to date and the process up to date, but most of these engineering changes will cause reschedules somewhere in the factory. Every time there is a key person in the factory absent, it can affect a schedule.

Every change in a production schedule means potential changes in the supporting schedules in the factory and changes in the vendors' schedules. Vendors often have delivery problems of their own - after all, they are manufacturing companies too! If a purchased component is going to come in late, that may mean that a factory schedule or several factory schedules will have to be changed to reschedule the product to a later date than when it was originally intended to be built. And something else will probably have to be rescheduled to an earlier date so that people can be kept working, and product will be shipped at the budgeted rate.

Most companies have <u>interdependent</u> component priorities. If one item is not going to come in on time, related items will have to be reviewed to see if they should be rescheduled. But some of these items are usually common to other jobs, and that makes rescheduling even more complex. Some of these components may still be needed on the original date for other products, even though they will be needed at a later date for this particular job.

These changes don't occur once a month or once a week, many of them occur several times in the same day. And just about the time that manufacturing management is trying to cope with a rush order they need out quickly, they are likely to find that there's going to be a transportation strike, a shortage of a vital commodity, or some other serious problem. Just as one set of changes has been factored into the schedules, a dozen more are occurring because:

THE MANUFACTURING ENVIRONMENT
IS ONE OF CONSTANT CHANGE.

<u>There is no way</u> for a manual system to cope with the constant changes. The scheduling system must be able to answer the question, "When do we <u>really need</u> that material?" It must be able to establish and maintain valid need dates.

The standard approach before the computer was available was to have a formal system, the inventory control system, that was used to order material. The "informal system" was the shortage list. It overrode the dates that the inventory control system placed on shop and purchase orders and did establish better "need dates" than the inventory control system did. This "order launching and expediting" approach generated a great deal of scheduling confusion because in reality it turned out that the dates on shop orders and purchase orders were the lowest scheduling priority in the shop and with the vendors. These dates were constantly being overridden by expediting.

The shortage list itself - while it did give better need dates than the order launching system - had its own set of problems:

1. The planning horizon didn't extend out far enough. Typically material was "pulled" from the stockroom to cover the next two to three weeks of production in order to make up the shortage list. But, in the typical manufacturing company, two to three weeks time doesn't give purchasing and manufacturing enough time to get all of the material delivered. One company addressed this problem by pulling material out of the stockroom to cover the next six weeks of production. They wound up with an immense shortage list because virtually every part that they carried was needed during the next six weeks and they didn't know which parts were needed first, second, third, etc.!

2. The shortage list didn't state the requirements in small enough time increments. It simply said that all of the material was needed. Since it can't all be produced at once, it's important to know what material is needed in what priority sequence.

3. Physically pulling material out of the stockroom to cover future schedules is an extremely inflexible approach. Even if, for example, it could be physically stored in different locations to indicate the week in which the material was needed, the shortage list still can't cope with change. One company that used physical pulling of material to generate the shortage list several weeks in advance ran into a serious problem when they had some dramatic schedule changes. They literally had to take all of the material, put it back into stores, and re-pull it to cover the changed schedule! It was a monumental task. If they had MRP, a simple change in the master schedule would have enabled the computer to simulate putting all of the material back into stock and repulling it to meet that schedule without having

to physically do it. This is because MRP really is a simulation of the shortage list.

4.   The shortage list approach makes no provision for unexpediting. There is no "longage list," there are no unexpeditors. Figure 2-1 shows what happens.

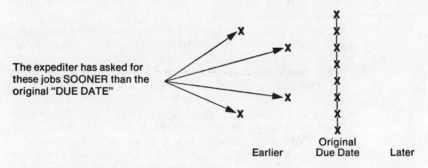

Figure 2 - 1.   Order Launching and Expediting

Dates are established by the order launching system. The expediting system says that some of the material is needed sooner, but none of the material is needed later! With order launching and expediting there is no provision for unexpediting. That not only means that there will be too much material in inventory, it also means that the wrong material will be in inventory. One company, for example, making a highly engineered product, had a job that was three months past due that couldn't be shipped because the engineering design had not been completed for the drive unit. Their best estimate was that it would be another three months before they could have the parts made for the drive unit if they got the engineering documentation at once. Another job couldn't be shipped for lack of an electric motor. It was only one month past due. An electric motor that was wound to a different specification, but undoubtedly made using the same production facilities, was sitting among the parts that were available for the job that was three months past due! The vendor had worked to the earliest due date and sent the motor that was on the purchase order for the job that was supposed to be shipped three months ago. Actually that motor wouldn't be needed for another three months, but now the customer couldn't get the motor that was needed for the job that was one month past due. Had they rescheduled properly, the vendor would have made the right motor, one job would have been shipped, and inventory would have gone down, not up. It certainly wasn't the vendor's fault that they got the wrong motor, it was theirs. And this is an important principle of scheduling:

UNEXPEDITING IS AT LEAST AS IMPORTANT AS EXPEDITING BECAUSE ANY MATERIAL RECEIVED BEFORE IT IS REALLY NEEDED WILL NORMALLY BE RECEIVED INSTEAD OF MATERIAL THAT IS REALLY NEEDED.

Order launching and expediting also generates a phoney backlog because material is not unexpedited. This results in many past due shop and purchase orders, some of which are needed, but many of which are not really needed; and that causes massive confusion which will be discussed in more detail later in this chapter.

Why did it take so long to develop computer systems that could keep schedules up to date? Part of it, of course, was having computers that were fast enough and had enough file capacity to manipulate massive amounts of data, time phase it properly, etc. But that was a minor part of the problem. The real reasons were:

1. There was a great deal of confusion generated by the formal and informal systems in use in most manufacturing companies. Since the formal system is the one in the book of procedures, it was natural that this was the one first put on the computer. After all, when systems people put the payroll system on the computer they simply took the system in the book of procedures, enhanced it a little bit, and mechanized it. When they did the same thing with the formal scheduling system, they mechanized a system that didn't work manually and consequently didn't work when it was put on the computer. A good indication of the kind of confusion that existed

for many years is the fact that most of the books that talked about inventory management discussed it as a way to determine the answer to the question "When to order?". They saw the order launching system, assumed that order launching was the right thing to do, and proceeded to put that system on the computer when, in fact, it had little or nothing to do with the real scheduling system.

2. Even though computers that had enough speed and capacity were available for many years, people in manufacturing didn't know what to do with them to improve schedules. It's easy to take an existing system and put it on a computer (and that, by the way, usually doesn't pay off very well because if the system works manually, putting it on a computer offers little benefit). But having valid schedules was something that was not possible before the computer came along. There was no way to maintain valid need dates in the complex and ever-changing manufacturing environment. Since the computer made it possible to do what couldn't be done before, it took many years to learn what should be done and how to do it.

3. Even the people in the typical manufacturing business didn't identify the problem as a scheduling problem. The formal and informal system generated too much confusion in the heat of battle. As people struggled to do their jobs with bad scheduling information, they were more likely to blame other people for the problems than to recognize that the problem was really a lack of valid schedules.

When scheduling doesn't work well in a manufacturing company there will be many problems. Some of these problems - indeed the most serious ones - seem rather far removed from scheduling itself. Yet lack of valid schedules is at the root of many of the difficulties that most manufacturing companies experience today. And it's important to understand why because:

IF PEOPLE DON'T UNDERSTAND THE PROBLEM,
THEY WON'T UNDERSTAND THE SOLUTION.

Section 2
The Effects of Invalid Schedules

When, because of scheduling problems, the right material is not made or purchased at the right time, there will be too much inventory, and at the same time, customer service will suffer. Productivity of direct labor will be affected by shortages of material in fabrication and assembly, and constant expediting will require the jobs that are currently being run to be stopped while others are run to cover shortages. These job interruptions and extra machine set ups result in lost production.

Poor scheduling shows up in overtime. Overtime is often a way to cope with problems after they've occurred because they couldn't be seen far enough in advance to prevent them. Chronic overtime results in lost productivity because the pace of workers slows down after they have worked regular overtime for more than a few weeks.

When schedules aren't valid, purchasing people are constantly operating in expedite mode. Expediting is compelling. It must be done at once. It is higher priority than making money for the company through value analysis, negotiation, developing annual contract agreements, working with engineering to standardize the product, etc.

When scheduling doesn't work well, additional traffic costs are incurred to bring material in and ship product out.

Many companies experience high obsolescence costs. Much of this could be eliminated if they could schedule better and phase in engineering changes properly - since much obsolescence is caused by engineering change.

These are some of the problems that are fairly obvious by-products of scheduling that isn't effective.

But there are a number of less obvious, insidious side effects of the informal system which are not well recognized, although they are visible in most manufacturing companies:

1.   There is chronic finger pointing.

The assembly foreman knows that he's doing a good job, but the shipments aren't going out the door, so it must be somebody else who's falling down on the job. The production control manager is convinced that people are simply irrational in their refusal to work to his schedules. It seldom crosses his mind that the schedules aren't right - he sees that virtually everything on the shortage list is past due and assumes that if people would work to the schedules, these problems would go away. The machine shop foreman knows that schedules aren't valid. There's no sense working overtime to produce a job that is two months past due when nobody's looking for it. He will wait until the expeditor asks for it. The purchasing manager knows that if all the material that is past due was actually brought into the company, there wouldn't be enough room to store it. And the company would be running out of money paying for material it doesn't need.

But to each of these individuals, the only real comfort in this exasperating situation is the conviction that "I am doing my job well, but they aren't." Without a company game plan that can be translated into detailed schedules that everyone can work to, there will always be finger pointing.

2.   Management doesn't have the numbers to run the business.

When a company operates with an informal system, the numbers that they use to run the business will usually be contradictory and conflicting since virtually all of these numbers are generated by the formal system that isn't really being used!

The purchase commitment report is a case in point. It is intended to show how many dollars the company is committed to spend with its vendors. This report is made by taking the open purchase orders, costing them out, and then adding them up by time period.

In one company, their purchase commitment report, when added up, showed a total "past due and due in month 1" of $3.1 million (much of this, of course, was "phoney backlog" from order launching and expediting). Their normal monthly receipts of purchased material typically ran about $1.7 million!

The financial executive can't really use this kind of information to estimate cash flow. Yet, the amount of money that is spent on purchased material is usually the biggest single dollar expenditure in a manufacturing company.

Typically, the financial executive learns to take a report like this and adjust it with a "fudge factor" that says something like, "Normally, the amount of material that is likely to come in is about 60 percent of what it shows on the purchase commitment report." This amounts to approximately $1.8 million. Is that too high? Is that too low? The only benchmark at all is historical comparison: "It's higher than last month!" In the world of order launching and expediting, there are very few real financial control systems, particularly at the detailed level. Most of these systems consist of "FUNNY NUMBERS" adjusted by "FUDGE FACTORS" and measured by "HISTORICAL COMPARISON."

The reconciliation of inventory is a good example of the kind of problem that the financial people have to cope with when the manufacturing people don't use the formal system and don't actually run the business with the numbers. About one year out of four, the typical manufacturing company finds, after they've taken their annual physical inventory, that they have an inventory "shrinkage." There is a substantial amount of inventory shown in the financial figures that simply isn't there. This money has to come out of profits, and of course, seriously affects profit projections. Because this happens so frequently, in many manufacturing companies they set up an "inventory reserve" to keep from having to take this money out of profits when the inventory shrinkage inevitably occurs! This is a good example of "institutionalized error." If the manufacturing people were using a formal system and kept their inventory numbers correct, the only time there could be an inventory discrepancy is if the cost figures being used were incorrect.

3. <u>There is very little real accountability</u>.

Perhaps the most serious problem of all with the informal system is the fact that it is very difficult to measure performance and, as a consequence, there is little real accountability. Surely the assembly foreman cannot be blamed for the failure to hit the shipping budget when he doesn't have the parts. Can the production control manager be blamed when nobody works to his schedule? (For that matter, in most companies, the production and inventory control people don't have MRP and couldn't possibly produce valid schedules! Management has not provided them with the tools.) Certainly no one could blame the machine shop foreman for not working to a schedule he knows is invalid. And surely the purchasing manager can't be blamed for expediting shortages rather than expediting overdue material that isn't really needed.

The problem is basic:

A COMPANY CANNOT MEASURE PERFORMANCE AGAINST THE NUMBERS FROM THE <u>FORMAL</u> SYSTEM WHEN THEY REALLY RUN WITH AN <u>INFORMAL</u> SYSTEM.

In fact, <u>true accountability in the world of the informal system exists only at the top</u>. The general manager <u>can</u> be held accountable because whether or not the shipping budget has been achieved <u>can be measured</u>!

Section 3
The Phoney Backlog and our "Boom and Bust" Economy

The last section explained the purchase commitment report and the effects of the phoney backlog due to order launching and expediting. The machine load report is a similar report for the factory. Figure 2-2 shows the typical machine load report in a company that uses order launching and expediting.

Work Center No. 1000
(All Figures in Standard Hours)

Weekly Capacity – 240 hr.		
Week	Load	Over/Under Load
Past Due	824	+584
Week – 1	286	+46
Week – 2	150	—90
Week – 3	90	—150
Week – 4	39	—201

Figure 2 – 2. The Overstated Machine Load

The weekly capacity in work center 1000 is 240 hours. The past due equals 824 hours! Much of this, of course, is orders that are late that aren't actually needed. When the foreman has a job that's three months old that nobody's looking for, he is not likely to bring someone in and pay overtime on Saturday to get that job produced. Order launching and expediting completely destroys the credibility of the machine load report in the eyes of shop supervision.

The informal system causes plenty of confusion within a manufacturing company. If anything, it causes more in the dealings of manufacturing companies with their vendors. To understand this better, let's look at a commodity like castings. It could as well be electronic components, bearings, or virtually any other purchased commodity because they all have the same problems.

Here's a typical example of what happens:

1. The foundry has a six-week backlog of work and is quoting a six-week lead time.

2. The foundry's customers are using that six-week lead time to determine "when to order." One of their customers using an order point system computes it as follows:

   Order point equals demand during lead time plus safety stock. Demand (estimated) is 100 a week, times a six-week lead time plus 250 safety stock. Order point equals 850. When the inventory on hand and on order equals 850, more must be ordered.

3. Business picks up slightly. As a consequence, more work goes into the foundry than goes out. They don't see enough work behind them to add to their capacity, but their backlog builds from six weeks to eight weeks.

4. The customer complains about the longer lead times and is told that he must "plan for lead times of at least eight weeks." He consequently changes his order point like this:

   100 times 8 plus 250; order point equals 1050.

5. Having raised the order point by two weeks, an additional two weeks' worth of material is below order point and must be ordered, thereby generating two more weeks' worth of input to the foundry.

6. The foundry, recognizing that they now have a ten-week backlog and cannot possibly deliver in eight weeks, quotes a ten-week lead time and the customer, in turn, responds by increasing his order point and generating more input to the foundry!

This is the way we get fifty-week lead times for castings, sixty-week lead times for bearings, etc.! Everybody knows that the lead times aren't realistic, but the backlog has forced the customer to order earlier.

The "lead time syndrome" is not confined to companies that use order point. Consider a company using material requirements planning, like so many companies do, as an inventory <u>ordering</u> technique.

Figure 2-3 shows the kind of thing that happens with material requirements planning as lead times increase.

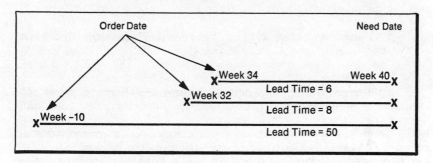

Figure 2 – 3.   Responding to Lead Time

When the need date is week 40 and the lead time is six weeks, the item must be ordered in week 34. If it's eight weeks, it must be ordered in week 32. If it's fifty weeks, it should have been ordered ten weeks ago!

The increases in lead time certainly present a problem for purchasing and production control people. But that problem is nothing compared to the problems created by the "phoney backlog." It is little understood and completely confuses the issue. It isn't hard to see how enormous phoney backlogs can be generated as lead times extend to forty or fifty weeks. Due dates put on orders that far in the future are likely to be wrong under the best of circumstances. Real "need" dates are always changing. Jobs needed earlier show up on the shortage list. The ones needed later simply go past due. The longer the situation exists, the greater the level of phoney backlog that accumulates.

Once the phoney backlog has been built up, the stage is set for it to collapse. And that will occur when the business community gets word that a recession is coming. Consider, for example, three Wall Street Journal issues on three consecutive days in 1979. The front page articles were titled:

Wednesday, June 13, 1979 - "The Prime Rate Was Cut - As Investors Grew More Certain That the Economy is in a Slow-Down Which Would Cut Credit Demand."

Thursday, June 14, 1979 - "As Recession Looms, Money Managers Try to Protect Portfolios."

Friday, June 15, 1979 - "Global Gloom - Oil Prices and Shortage May Cause a Recession and World Inflation."

And another that day - "Looming Recession Promises Scant Relief for Carter's Inflation Fighters."

Whenever there is talk about how the leading business indicators are "pointing downward," the typical financial executive rightfully gets concerned. The natural reaction is to take a hard look at current purchase commitments and current inventory and compare them with current needs. Lack of good information - like an accurate purchase commitment report - makes this difficult, but the fiscally responsible executive will be sure to do it when faced with a business downturn.

When an executive finds that the amount of material on hand and on order is much more than is needed to support current production rates (as is always the case with order launching and expediting), pressure is put on to push out dates on purchase orders and start living "hand to mouth."

Meanwhile, back at the foundry, where they had a fifty-week backlog of work, many customers have rescheduled orders into later time periods because of the pressure from financial people in their own companies. They aren't ordering as much, and they aren't ordering as soon.

Sales people at the foundry notice that orders aren't coming in as fast as they were. They assume that this is due to the long lead times. They put the pressure on to cut lead times. Production people, seeing that they have some open time in their schedules, reduce their quoted lead times. Their customers drop their order points, reduce the lead times in their material requirements planning systems, and don't need to order as soon.

This reduces input to the foundry which, in turn, reduces backlog. In no time at all, the foundry finds itself looking for work. Consequently, it reduces lead times.

Customers reduce the planning lead times they use in their order points and material requirements plans. The backlog evaporates as if by magic.

L. J. Burlingame, Manufacturing Vice President, Twin Disc, Inc. and International President of the American Production and Inventory Control Society in 1979, made the astute observation: "In American industry we build inventories on overtime and reduce them on unemployment compensation."

Figure 2-4 shows a chart that was kept by a foundry superintendent over many years. The chart shows the backlog at the foundry, and it's interesting to note that in more recent business cycles, backlogs have gone up higher each time.

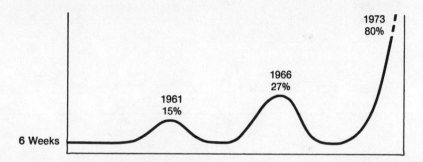

1973
80%

1966
27%

1961
15%

6 Weeks

Figure 2 – 4. Foundry Backlogs

The figure also shows the results of a survey taken by the American Production and Inventory Control Society. One of the questions on the survey was, "Do you use computers in inventory control?" In 1961, 15 percent of the companies responding were using computers. In 1966, 27 percent were. By 1973, 80 percent were. There is little question that the availability of computers to increase lead times faster and easier than ever before has greatly enhanced our capability to build a phoney backlog faster and higher than ever before. Changing lead times with a manual system was an onerous task that took weeks and even months to implement. With a computer, it can be done overnight, and, of course, it just feeds upon itself.

Will MRP fix this "boom and bust" amplification problem? Is it "miracle requirements planning"? No, it certainly is not miracle requirements planning, but it's a simple, common sense way to schedule properly. With MRP properly managed, particularly at the master schedule level, need dates are moved in AND ALSO MOVED OUT. There is no need to wait for the financial executive to put the pressure on to move material out of the schedule because this backlog doesn't develop to start with. There is no question that MRP - properly managed - can reduce the boom and bust amplification in our manufacturing economy. Because the phoney backlog won't be there to fuel a recession as it is with order launching and expediting. We may already be seeing signs of this happening.(1)

Section 4
A Misleading Phenomenon

It's little wonder that the people who were talking about productivity didn't recognize the scheduling problem in manufacturing. Even those closest to it didn't. The evidence that they saw simply didn't tell them that scheduling was the real problem. Like the people who lived before Columbus, they had little reason to question whether the Earth was round or flat. The misleading evidence was overwhelming.

Consider the company with order launching and expediting. The assembly foreman blames his problems on other <u>people</u>. Production control blames their problems on other <u>people</u>. Purchasing blames their problems on other <u>people</u>. The foremen blame their problems on other <u>people</u>. <u>Virtually nobody recognizes that the problem is the lack of a valid schedule, and for that matter, the lack of the tools to make a valid schedule!</u> One vice president of materials management for a large corporation (who was always a proponent of order points, the most flagrant form of order launching and expediting) (2) said just before his retirement, "I had hoped to work long enough to see a factory where people would work to a schedule, but it never happened." And it never crossed his mind that the prime reason was that the schedules were never valid!

Most of the solutions proposed for production control problems failed to recognize what the real scheduling problem was:

1. In the early years, priority rules like work to the shortest operation time, least slack time between operations, earliest due date, etc. were tried in computer "job shop simulation" programs to see which would give the best results.(3) Yet no one ever thought to ask whether the due dates used in the simulations were valid and what the value of the simulation was if the due dates didn't reflect actual need dates.

2. During the 1960's many companies tried to install shop floor control systems (to "make those shop people work on the right jobs") before they put in MRP systems to make a valid schedule! The symptom that "the shop isn't working on the right

jobs" was misleading. It wasn't the perversity of the people in the shop, it was the fact that they didn't know what the right jobs were because the schedules weren't valid.

3. Automatic load leveling programs to optimize factory scheduling have been developed repeatedly over the years. These programs take the schedule dates and revise them in order to level the load. But if these schedule dates aren't valid - and they aren't in most manufacturing companies - what value can possibly come from this kind of exercise? Programs of this type have generally had a very short life span.

4. Materials management - an organizational approach to putting purchasing, production control, inventory control, and other materials functions under the same manager was proposed as a solution to the problems. The theory was that now people in purchasing, production control, and inventory control would work together rather than constantly battle among themselves. There is nothing wrong with the materials management form of organization, but the idea that changing the organization around would solve "the problem" when the real problem was lack of a valid schedule that everybody could work to was just one more assault on the symptoms.

5. One writer said in an article,(4) "This author has always regarded the main contribution of MRP as being at the input end of the system. Many authors take the view that a major benefit of MRP is its ability to manipulate the due dates of work in process batches in order to maintain correct, relative priorities." And further, "This in itself includes an assumption that the dispatching rules, which one expects to be employed on the shop floor, must be directly related to due dates." Here is one of the leading authorities on requirements planning from England, unaware of the fact that MRP's value is in keeping schedule dates valid in the manufacturing environment of change! And evidently assuming that there are some kinds of scheduling rules that <u>do not involve dates</u> in the real world!

These quotes concerning a major aircraft manufacturer are a classic example of the symptoms of order launching and expediting and the lack of recognition of the fundamental problem:

1. "The primary condition affecting our ability to deliver aircraft is that over fifty percent of our fabricated parts are past due when completed ... We have opened a new flight hangar ahead of schedule to provide more room to handle the backlog of unfinished aircraft ... All employees in the fabrication departments, certain small parts assembly areas, and normal production support functions are being scheduled for a standard six day work week for the next six weeks."(5)

2. "The plane builder's manufacturing got so fouled up that half of its fabricated parts were being completed behind schedule, creating shortages on all assembly lines. The division started to miss delivery dates and customers began to cancel orders. The situation got so bad that they had to open a new hangar ahead of schedule just to accommodate the backlog of unfinished planes."(6)

3. The company "went ahead anyway keeping its assembly lines moving, although it was producing incomplete aircraft and letting them pile up outside the plant," and "short term debt jumped by 60 million in six months to 92 million."(7)

    "High inventories have forced them to lay off workers and temporarily close the plants and divisions." They had about fifty executive jets "in various stages of production, most of which are 98% complete, but they are sitting in the fields waiting for parts."(8)

4. The company "soon ran short of 150 critical parts. By early 1980 incomplete aircraft worth $40 million were sitting outside the Wichita Plant while borrowings to finance grounded inventory had ballooned to $92 million." They "belatedly closed the production lines until the parts bins filled up again."(9)

Fifty percent of the parts were past due when they came out of manufacturing, yet the shortages turned out to be on only 150 items! They scheduled six weeks of over-time to get material through, and then laid people off because they had high inventories! This is the kind of misleading picture that order launching and expediting presents. This is what happens when schedules are not valid, and there are many past due orders that aren't really needed. But the picture is confusing to everyone involved. Note that not one article quotes management as recognizing - nor do any of the authors of the articles point out - that the real problem was scheduling. No one says, "They didn't really need all of the parts they worked overtime to make. But they didn't know which parts they really did need!"

A lack of understanding of the real scheduling problem exists with purchased material as well as manufactured material. During the most recent experience we had with the lead time syndrome, a company in Pennsylvania com-plained bitterly about the bad service its foundry was giving. It could show many open orders that were past due. At the same time, the number of castings in the yard was increasing dramatically. Because the company order launched and expedited, most of the orders from the foundry were past due, especially after lead times had gone up to one year. And no effort was made to reschedule the ones that weren't needed. As a result, the casting inventory was increasing at the same time as casting short-ages in the factory were increasing. The past due orders for castings made it look as though the problem was that the foundry was "behind schedule," when the fact was that the foundry was working on the wrong items. When every-thing is "past due" at the foundry, they are bound to work on the wrong jobs.

(Incidentally, two years later, this same company was trying to figure out what to do to get rid of all of the castings that they had built up in inventory - during the period when they were claiming that the foundry was behind schedule!)

The following quote, typical of many comments that have been made after a period of "boom and bust," shows how even high level business executives have trouble understanding what is really happening. This is from the senior vice president and chief financial officer of one of the largest corporations in the United States who obviously does not understand why the phoney backlog happens. "In 1974," he said, "shortages caused many firms to receive only fifty percent of what they would order. Hence, they ordered twice what they actually needed. When the down-turn came, so did cancellations of what were inflated orders to begin with, making the slump worse."(10)

When people do not understand what is really causing the problem - order launching and expediting - they come up with interesting explanations for the backlog that, in retrospect, was obviously phoney. The fact of the matter is that people were not doing much "double ordering" during the period discussed. And when they did it - if they did it at all - it was only _after_ backlogs had extended out 12 months or more. Double ordering was not the _cause_ of the phoney backlog. Order launching and expediting was.

It certainly is no wonder that it took so long to solve the scheduling problem when it was so difficult to under-stand. The executive who wishes to address the scheduling problem - and the next chapter will talk about the solution to it - should be sure that his people understand what the _real problem_ is. This is one of the obstacles that contri-buted to the long gestation period for MRP and MRP II.

Footnotes
_____

1. See Chapter 4, Section 1 for some quotes on the subject from Fortune.

2. See Appendix 4, The Order Point Inventory Model, if this point is not clear.

3. R.W. Conway, W.L. Maxwell and L.W. Miller, The Theory of Scheduling, (Reading, Massachusetts: Addison-Wesley Publishing Co., 1967).

4. Colin New, "MRP and GT: A New Strategy for Component Production," Production and Inventory Management, Third Quarter, 1977, p. 54.

5. From an internal company newsletter to the employees, February 9, 1979.

6. "The Trick of Material Requirements Planning," Business Week, June 4, 1979.

7. Wall Street Journal, April 8, 1980.

8. Wall Street Journal, April 8, 1980.

9. Fortune, June 1, 1981.

10. Industry Week, November 27, 1978, p. 115.

Chapter 3
From MRP to MRP II

Section 1
Formalizing the Informal System

It isn't unusual to hear people say, "We were using MRP twenty years ago!" From their point of view, that may seem to be true. But the chances are very remote that they were using MRP twenty years ago as it is understood today because MRP has changed dramatically. The techniques haven't changed as much as our knowledge of how to use the techniques has developed from experience. There were four steps in the evolution of MRP:

1. A Better Ordering Method.
2. Priority Planning.
3. Closed Loop MRP.
4. Manufacturing Resource Planning: MRP II.

There are two fundamental methods for ordering material: the order point, and material requirements planning. All other methods are variations of these two.

The order point establishes "when to order" based on average usage for the planned replenishment lead time plus a "safety stock" to protect against greater than average demand. Material requirements planning typically determines "when to order" based on schedules for the items that use the material. MRP is obviously superior to ordering based on average usage - but in practice it was a difficult method to use.

Before the computer was available companies took six to thirteen weeks to calculate the requirements manually - or with some help from tabulating equipment. They typically "ordered" once every thirteen weeks (this was called the "quarterly ordering system"). This didn't work a lot better, in many applications, than order points.

The computer made it possible to calculate requirements over a weekend! This was a great step forward that facilitated ordering more frequently. It became common practice to order monthly and break the time phasing down into monthly time periods.

The computer made MRP a workable technique. It became more widely used as a better ORDERING METHOD than order points.

As computer capabilities increased, some companies recalculated requirements as often as weekly and broke the time phasing down into weekly time periods. The fundamental capabilities of replanning frequently enough, and breaking the time phasing down into fine enough increments to establish and maintain real "need dates," were there. But before this scheduling capability could be used, the concepts of "rescheduling" and "master scheduling" had to develop. This occurred over a ten year period. "Rescheduling" simply meant that each time requirements were recalculated, the need dates for open purchase orders and shop orders would be checked, and reschedule messages generated, if changes caused them to be needed sooner or later.

The notion that there should be a master schedule - a statement of what was going to be produced - was as old as MRP. But it wasn't until 1971 that people recognized that this master schedule had to represent what was really going to be made! If the master schedule contained more product than could really be made, contained products that couldn't be made because of genuine shortages that existed, or was in any way unrealistic, MRP would not generate valid priorities based on real need dates. And until that could happen, the shortage list - with all its shortcomings - was still the real scheduling system.

But as people learned how to manage the master schedule properly, MRP evolved from an ordering system into a PRIORITY PLANNING SYSTEM. (1)

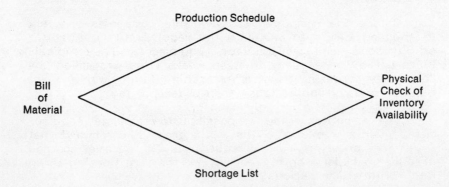

Figure 3 - 1. The Logic of the Shortage List

The logic of the shortage list is fundamental. It is shown in Figure 3-1. To make a shortage list, the expeditor looks at the production schedule to find out what is going to be made, gets a bill of material to find out what material is required to make the product, physically checks inventory availability in the stockroom (often by "accumulating" or by "staging" the components that are needed), and makes up a "shortage list" of the components that are not available. MRP, in a computer, uses exactly the same logic. The master schedule is a statement of what products are to be produced. This is put into the computer program along with the bill of material, and inventory records, and the material requirements plan results. Figure 3-2 shows this.

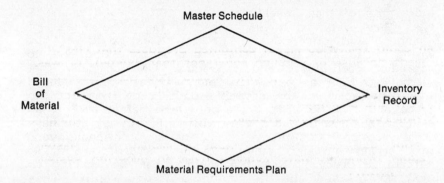

Master Schedule

Bill
of
Material

Inventory
Record

Material Requirements Plan

Figure 3 – 2. The Logic of MRP

The material requirements plan overcame the shortcomings of the physical shortage list discussed in Chapter 2:

A. The planning horizon could be extended out as far as necessary. Typically companies planned one or two years in advance.

B. The planning could be time phased into weekly or even daily time periods.

C. The system was extremely flexible since any time the master schedule was changed, MRP would simulate putting components that weren't required back into stock, and pulling components that were required out of stock.

D. With MRP, reschedule messages to move material "out" into future periods, as well as "in" to earlier periods, would be generated. There was still, of course, the psychological problem of teaching expeditors the value of rescheduling material to a later date. The message that <u>unexpediting is the most powerful form of expediting</u> is emotionally difficult to come to grips with, even though every expeditor has seen it in practice. When there was only one job with a red tag on it in the factory, it moved through quickly. When every job had a red tag, nothing moved through any faster than anything else.

The shortage list had been the real scheduling system in virtually every manufacturing company. Now shortages could be predicted a year or more in advance in very fine increments of time, weekly or even daily. Even if shortages were predicted a year ahead of time, the element of change would still exist. The schedules would still be wrong. But that was MRP's strong suit: being able to repredict, repredict, and repredict. One company that introduced MRP as a priority planning technique reduced their shortages in the assembly department from between three and five hundred items per week before MRP to an average of three to five a week with MRP. (They still have some occasional quality problems, and an occasional inventory error; although their inventory records are at 98 percent accuracy.) Now the foremen can be working on next month's shortage the beginning of this month. They can be working to prevent the shortages in the future, rather than working to fix the shortages after they happen. Now the formal system <u>could</u> establish and maintain need dates. The company mentioned above eliminated the need for a shortage list. They work to the schedules generated by MRP.

The shortage list dealt with the fundamental manufacturing equation:

A. What are we going to make?
B. What does it take to make it?
C. What have we got?
D. What do we have to get?

That fundamental equation exists in every manufacturing company whether they are making biscuits or battleships. It's the equation for the shortage list, it's the equation for MRP. MRP is simply the logic of the informal

system - the shortage list - developed into a formal scheduling system.

Section 2
Closing the Loop

Now that the priority planning could be made work-able, it became evident that priority planning by itself was not sufficient. Knowing what material was needed was fine, but if the capacity wasn't available, the proper material couldn't be produced. Keeping priorities up-to-date was fine, but if these schedules couldn't be transmitted to the factory and to vendors, they didn't have any great value. Having solved the problem of priority planning, the users of MRP took another giant step forward by incorporating it into an overall system called: CLOSED LOOP MRP.

Figure 3-3 shows the schematic of the Closed Loop MRP system.

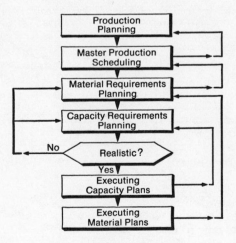

Figure 3 – 3. The Closed Loop Diagram

The production plan establishes production rates for product families. It answers the question, "How many model 30 pumps per week will we build?" The production plan in a make-to-order business is established by looking at the current order backlog, the desired backlog, and the sales forecast to determine the production rate. This is the beginning of the fundamental manufacturing equation that says:

A. What have we got? (in <u>inventory</u> for a make-to-stock product family or in <u>backlog</u> for a make-to-order product family)

B. What are we going to sell?

C. What are we going to make?

The master schedule takes that production plan in units for a product family and breaks it down into specifics which would be individual stockkeeping units in a make-to-stock business or group of components like pump housings, impellers, bearings, etc. in an assembled-to-order business. This is where the rest of the fundamental manufacturing equation takes over to determine, "What do we have to get?"

The capacity requirements plan does the same thing in standard hours. It looks at the shop schedule (this is the released shop orders and planned order releases generated by the material requirements plan) and uses a routing file to determine how many standard hours will be required at each work center; once again, addressing the fundamental manufacturing equation, only this time in standard hours. Once material and capacity plans have been made, it has to be determined whether or not they are realistic. If they are, then the actual standard hours produced by each work center must be monitored to be sure that the plans are being executed. And schedules for vendors and for the factory will have to be issued and updated regularly in order to execute the material requirements plan.

Before MRP worked, it was hard to see the relationship of the various techniques. Strange as it may sound today, people talked about capacity planning without thinking about doing material requirements planning first. They installed shop floor control systems without making sure that the need dates were valid. Once material requirements planning could really be made to work, it was easy to see how everything fit together. In fact, the first closed loop diagram (shown in Figure 3-3) was drawn in 1969 at the Markem Corporation in Keene, New Hampshire. Markem was the first company to use a software package to install MRP. Once the heart of the system - material requirements planning - became a usable priority planning technique, it became apparent how the rest of the tools fit together into a closed loop system.

The term "Closed Loop" really has two meanings. It means that the missing elements in a system, like capacity planning, shop scheduling, and vendor scheduling were filled in. It also means - and this is shown by the arrows in Figure 3-3 - that there must be feedback from the vendors, from the factory, from the planners, etc. whenever there is any problem in executing the plan. This feedback will be discussed in more detail in Chapter 19.

Section 3
MRP II

<u>There is a basic law of systems</u>: poor systems breed more systems.

In most manufacturing companies several systems exist to answer the basic question, "What do we really need when?" There are dates on shop and purchase orders. There is a shortage list to override those dates, an expedite list for service parts, another one for interplant material, another one for the export department, etc., etc. Because there isn't one simple system that answers the question, "What do we really need when?", there are many systems. And none of them tend to work very well

The closed loop MRP system solved the problem of having redundant scheduling systems. If the master schedule, in particular, is managed properly, there can be one system to answer the question, "What do we really need when?", rather than many conflicting systems.

The same situation existed in accounting. Because the operating systems didn't work effectively, a separate system dealing with the same basic numbers was used by the financial people. Accounting posted their own inventory records in dollars for financial purposes. The inventory control people kept a separate set of records. The last thing most cost accountants would have considered was to use inventory control's figures for cost accounting since their accuracy was highly questionable.

There was a business plan that top management used. It said:

What are we going to sell?

What do we have? (in <u>inventory</u> in a make-to-stock company, or in <u>backlog</u> in a make-to-order company)

What do we have to make?

Down in the factory in the production planning department there were production plans that addressed the same questions. They worked in units instead of dollars.

But the business plans and the production plans were made separately. In many companies, the people who made the production plans were unaware that the business plans even existed and the people who made the business plans never did see the production plans! Yet the business plan in its basic form (omitting research and development and other parts of the business plans not directly related to production) is simply the sum of the production plans expressed in dollars.

When MRP came along, the operating system finally could work. People using it successfully as a closed loop system quickly realized that they could tie in their financial systems. If the inventory records are good enough to support MRP, why not cost them out? If the material requirements plan represents what's really going to be made and purchased, why not use it as the source of a valid purchase commitment report? If the production plans represent what's really going to happen, why not express them in dollars to keep the business plan up-to-date at all times? As manufacturing companies developed systems that really worked, they were able to eliminate the redundant systems. When we understood what we were really trying to do, everything became simpler. Tying the financial and the operating system together was the big step from closed loop MRP to MRP II.

From the days when the master schedule began to be recognized as the key input to MRP, everyone said that marketing's forecasts would be a crucial input to the master schedule. In many companies, marketing ignored MRP. They thought it was a production control technique. In some they provided a forecast because they were required to. But they didn't really get involved in the master scheduling function. In a few of the companies where closed loop MRP really was working, marketing recognized that the master schedule was the best marketing tool that had yet been devised. By working closely with manufacturing, a master schedule that best met marketing's requirements, within the constraints of what manufacturing could actually do, could be worked out. Manufacturing now had the ability to translate these plans into detailed plans. A discussion between manufacturing and marketing could easily result in a change in the master schedule, and a change in the sequence in which jobs were to be run in the factory the very next day.

Engineering, which had always seemed like a function far removed from the day-to-day activities in a manufacturing company, became part of the team also. In a company making a highly engineered product, introducing a lot of new products, or with a great deal of engineering change (or all of the above!), engineering activities need to be coordinated with manufacturing, marketing, and finance. But in the past, they typically weren't very well coordinated. Now that there was a way to have valid schedules, scheduling engineering and relating that schedule to the other schedules was a natural step. Now that there was a formal system requiring valid data, engineering people in design engineering and manufacturing engineering became the source for providing - and maintaining - accurate data for the information system. The bill of material, for example, in the past was a reference document. With MRP it became a control document. And the role of engineering in keeping this data valid became critical.

Once the operating system in a manufacturing company could be made to work - and the closed loop MRP system did work in a good many companies - making MRP a whole company system was the next logical step. MRP II is a system that includes manufacturing, finance, marketing, engineering, purchasing, distribution - and certainly changes a lot of things for the data processing people. Figure 3-4 shows the business plan as the beginning of an MRP II system. The other financial interfaces have been omitted to keep the diagram simple.

MRP II evolved from the closed loop system. Manufacturing Resource Planning has these characteristics:

1. The operating and the financial system are one and the same. They use the same transactions, they use the same numbers. The financial figures are merely extensions of the operating numbers.

2. It has a "what if" capability. Since a good system is basically a simulation of reality, it can be used to simulate what would happen if various policy decisions were implemented.

3. It is a whole company system now, involving every facet of the business because the things that MRP II is concerned with - sales, production, inventories, schedules, cash flow, etc. -

are the very fundamentals of planning and controlling a manufacturing or distribution business.

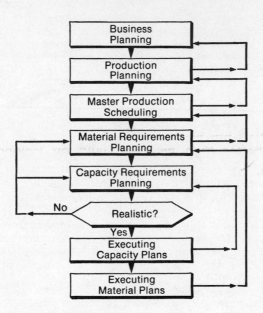

Figure 3 - 4. MRP II Diagram

MRP II results in management finally having <u>the numbers to run the business</u>. One set of numbers, valid numbers, and everybody using the same set of numbers. And perhaps even more important than that, MRP evolved into a company game plan. And this is not theory. This is <u>what is happening</u> today in the companies that have learned to use MRP II.

If someone were to say, "What, then, is MRP II?", the answer would be, "Technically, it's not much different from closed loop MRP. It does include the financial numbers and a simulation capability." The technical differences are small compared to the real significant difference. And that is the way management uses the system. The techniques for providing the company game plan have been made possible by modern computers and the knowledge that has been developed in practice over the last 30 years. How effectively these techniques are put to work is up to the people who run a manufacturing business.

Section 4
The Standard System

A system is just a simulation of reality. A good example of simulation is the instruments in an airplane that simply represent reality. The pilot can look out the window and see a thunderstorm ahead and know that he should go around it. But if he sees two thunderstorms with darkness beyond, should he go through? Or if it's night and he can't see the thunderstorms very well, what does he do? Weather radar in an airplane can look far ahead into the night and show him how he can get around these dangerous storms far better than he ever could by looking out the window.

MRP II is a simulator. It simulates material requirements far enough in advance so that shortages can be predicted and prevented, rather than fixed after they happen. It simulates capacity requirements far enough in advance so that capacity problems can be prevented. R.D. Garwood, one of the top professionals in the field of MRP, makes the statement, "Manufacturing can do anything given enough time and enough money." Because MRP II is an effective simulator, it gives management the information so that they have the time, and it's then up to them to decide whether or not they want to, or can afford to, spend the money.

MRP II simulates reality. Reality in a manufacturing company revolves around the fundamental manufacturing equation. This equation doesn't change from company to company. It is a standard logic. Consequently, there is a standard logic for systems to be used for planning and control in a manufacturing company.

Reality in a manufacturing company cannot be changed. The fundamental manufacturing equation exists. Some people say, "What is the alternative to MRP?" MRP, by definition, is a simulation of the fundamental manufacturing equation. The alternative is not to simulate that equation in the formal system. A company that does not have a formal system that simulates the equation will have an informal system, a shortage list, that does. The fundamental manufacturing equation is like the law of gravity. It cannot be changed, it can only be dealt with.

If there is a standard system and a standard manufacturing logic, why is it then that we hear phrases like, "We
had to develop our own systems to meet our special requirements"; or that ultimate parochialism, "We're different,
we're unique!" The reason systems were different from
company to company in the past was very simple: they did
not work!

A young corporate systems man for a major automotive
company was lamenting the fact that the divisions all wanted
their own systems, each unique and different. He had
documented how each of these systems worked and indeed
they all were different in detail. But, of course, these
were the formal systems, and the informal systems were the
real systems. In fact, in that company the foremen and the
expeditors really did their scheduling the same way in each
division. They looked ahead a few days to see what they
were going to make. They determined what was required to
make it. They looked around and saw what material they
had, and then they determined what material they needed
and expedited it. The formal systems all looked a little
different because, they were not the real systems! The
informal systems all looked the same because they were the
systems that people really used.

In the early years of the computer age, the users
tended to think that their problems were unique and
systems people were taught that their job was to "design" a
system to fit the unique "needs of the business." To
enhance the illusion of "uniqueness," systems were given
names - usually acronyms like SMART (Scheduling Material
and Reporting Techniques), and GIRP (General Instruments
Requirements Planning). One of the most innovative names
for material requirements planning was MUTT (Materials
Utilization Timing Tables). Of course, everybody was
simply reinventing the wheel - because the systems that
worked were all fundamentally the same.

Before the airplane flew, there were many interesting
opinions on what an airplane should look like. Some
designers showed them with wings that flapped, others
sketched a machine with paddle wheels on the side driven
by a steam engine. Today the airplanes that fly look
remarkably similar to each other. The biggest difference
today is that one has an airfoil that is stationary in relation
to the aircraft, while the other has an airfoil that whirls
through the air overhead - the helicopter. In a similar
way, the MRP output reports can be printed horizontally or

vertically without any serious problems. Although, once again, people will tend to see that their system is different if this minor technical distinction isn't clearly explained.

If it doesn't matter whether the system works or not, its designers are entitled to unlimited creativity. If, however, the objective is to have a system that actually works, it will have to simulate the universal manufacturing equation. And its fundamental logic will be the same as all the other systems that work. (Manufacturing Software Systems, P.O. Box 278, Williston, VT 05495, publishes reviews of computer programs that are doing MRP II. Part of this service is a thorough documentation of what constitutes, from a software point of view, a "standard system.")

Companies using MRP successfully tend to have systems that not only are the same, they even look the same. The output reports from a company manufacturing spices, another one manufacturing power tools, another one manufacturing turbine driven generators, another one making chemicals, another one making oil drilling equipment, another one making fork lift trucks, another one making pharmaceuticals, etc., etc., all look alike. They should look alike because they _are_ alike. If they weren't, they wouldn't work.

Today we recognize that the logic of manufacturing is universal. The more we can do to demonstrate that by showing how standard systems are, the better off we will be. The more unique a system looks, the more difficult it is to educate people because they will see the differences rather than the things that are the same.

Moreover, any system at some time or another will get challenged. Someone in sales, for example, who has not been educated will blame the system when things can't be done, rather than recognizing that the system is just generating the information. When the system is challenged, however, the best possible response is, "This is MRP II; the same thing everybody else uses. Let's stop blaming the system and figure out what we need to do to manage better!" Financial people don't usually challenge the standard cost system if they are not making a profit. They try to use the information to find out where the problems are so that they can be fixed. Standard systems tend to take the focus off the system and on to what really counts: action to solve the real problems.

A financial professional moving from one company to another would look for the standard tools of the trade: accounts receivable, accounts payable, general ledger, budgets, standard cost, etc. He wouldn't expect to see a "unique" system, nor would he expect the system to be given some acronym that conveys a false impression of uniqueness for a name. Manufacturing didn't have tools that worked before the computer came along. Now the tools for running the operations of a manufacturing business have been defined. They are universal in application and any executive moving from one manufacturing company to another should expect to find tools like production plans, master schedules, capacity requirements plans, etc. Like the financial tools, we should be able to audit them to see that they are all in place, operational, and being used effectively.

The time for playing games with acronyms is over. We now have the standard tools and the standard body of knowledge available that is the foundation of any profession. These apply in virtually every manufacturing business - large or small.

Section 5
MRP II in the Small Company

The fundamental manufacturing equation exists in manufacturing companies of every size. But MRP has been slow to catch on in small companies ($2 - $10 million) for three major reasons·

1. The high cost of computer power in the past.

2. Lack of available software.

3. The lack of understanding.

For many years, a computer big enough to do the massive data manipulation required by MRP cost 15 to 40 thousand dollars a month to lease. Today, there is almost always a way to get computer resources at an affordable price for the small company.

A small company in Vermont produces and distributes video taped education programs. Sales in 1981 are about two million dollars. They lease a small computer to do MRP. They must inventory video tapes, notebooks, books, and articles. They have several hundred part numbers. The cost of their computer and the computer program to do MRP? Under fifty thousand dollars a year. Their CEO comments on the results, "We began to suffer from shortage problems, which resulted in delivery problems, and our inventory started to climb. We didn't have the funds to finance too much inventory so that we could later come back and use that as a justification! Nor could we afford to get a bad reputation for customer service. And with a projected growth that will take us to twelve million dollar sales in 1985, we needed the control. With MRP we have practically eliminated shortages. We can respond far better - we delivered well even last October when our sales were 600 percent of forecast! Our current inventory, we feel, will support about twice our present volume because so much of our material has to be ordered in minimum quantities because our volumes are low. Like any new business that is concerned with conserving cash, this is particularly critical to us."

Note that the cost of the computer in this company is about 2½ percent of the sales dollar, which is a fairly high percentage but not a great deal of money even in a small company, especially one that is growing rapidly and could easily stifle that growth for lack of controls.

The biggest reason that small computers haven't been used in small companies was the lack of available software for the computer. However, today software is starting to be offered for very small computers.

Another alternative would be to have MRP done by a service bureau. Here, again, costs would have to be checked very carefully because they tend to escalate very rapidly in the service bureau or teleprocessing environment.

One of the most important things for the CEO of the small company to keep in mind is that he must provide the leadership to make sure that the system is being approached as a business project. This is particularly critical in the small company where people have to wear many hats. Too many <u>small companies</u> try to imitate <u>big company inefficiencies</u> when they install computer systems, rather than <u>running lean, tight, and hard and keeping it simple</u>.

Whether or not MRP is needed in a small company is much more a function of the complexity of the scheduling than the size of the company itself. A company doing several hundred million dollars in business a year that turns out potash and only has a few reactors in operation at any one time and uses a small number of raw materials, doesn't need MRP on a computer. They will still perform the basic functions, but most of these are capable of being done manually. A small electronics company that purchases several hundred components and has constantly changing customer demands and engineering changes should definitely look into MRP, but they should only use it if it can be justified as a business proposition using the criteria covered in Chapter 16.

The good news for small companies is that MRP, being basically a system that is built around people, is much easier to install in a small company because there are fewer people involved. As computers become less and less expensive and software more readily available, the application of MRP will become far more widespread in small companies.

Section 6
Applications of MRP II

The major difference among companies' applications of MRP will be in the handling - not the design - of the master schedule. To a great extent, the handling will be a function of their delivery lead time to their customers.

From a lead time point of view, products can be broken down into three general categories:

1. A company making a make-to-stock product - Example: A manufacturer of power tools or a manufacturer of industrial drills.

2. A company making a short delivery lead time make-to-order product - Examples: A manufacturer of fork lift trucks that custom assembles them to customer order. A manufacturer of forged rings that stocks them to a rough outside and inside diameter and then machines them to size required by the customer.

3. A company making a long delivery lead time make-to-order product - Example: A manufacturer of extruders that are custom designed for each application.

Obviously, very few companies fall neatly into these categories. Most companies have some make-to-stock items like service parts and other make-to-order items such as assembled machines. Some product lines are somewhere between make-to-stock and make-to-order. Customer orders are accumulated and then a batch of a product is made to cover these orders and to put a few in inventory to last until such time as enough orders have been accumulated to justify running another batch.

In a make-to-stock product line, the master schedule contains defined items that will be put into inventory. MRP will be used as a planning tool for the finished goods inventory and the planned order releases will be compared with the master schedule to make sure manufacturing schedules are in line with current sales activity.

In the short delivery lead time make-to-order product line, the master schedule will probably be stated in terms of components or groups of components rather than a defined end item like the make-to-stock company has. The fork lift truck company, for example, would show a master schedule with engines, transmissions, masts, wheels, cabs, etc., and as customer orders came in, they would be matched up against these components or groups of components in the master schedule to determine when the order can be delivered. The master schedule, of course, is the vehicle for planning material and capacity and, consequently, it's also the vehicle for making realistic customer delivery promises. The assembly schedule will show the final configuration of the product actually being made for the customer.

A company making forged rings would show the master schedule in terms of semifinished forgings. Customer orders would be matched up with these forgings that are available or planned to be available just the same way they were for components of the fork lift truck.

In a long delivery lead time make-to-order product line, material must be ordered for the specific customer order, rather than from a forecast. The biggest problem in this type of business is that the product is being designed while it is being built.

Many companies making a highly engineered long lead time product tend to feel that they can't use MRP because they don't have fully defined bills of material for most of the procurement and manufacturing cycle. This simply is not true. Since the computer is merely simulating what really happens, it's important to ask "what really happens?" in a manual system. Purchasing typically calls engineering to ask for some information on the basic types and sizes of stainless steel, for example, that will be required for the product. This allows them to get a reservation in the steel mill schedule even though they don't have a complete bill of material. Making a highly engineered product requires working with partial bills of material and scheduling the development of the bills of material to coincide with the lead times for procuring and manufacturing material as well as possible. This, in fact, is what was done in the informal system. And this is what the formal system will have to do also.

The highly engineered product is one where change is constant. Problems in meeting schedules are also a normal way of life because the product is being designed as it is being built. Nowhere is MRP needed more than in this type of business. If a project is held up because a customer has not yet approved the design of a pressure vessel, for example, that's the time to reschedule this project to a realistic later date so that the materials and resources can be used for other projects instead. Certainly in this kind of business, engineering will be scheduled - using the basic MRP type logic - as well as manufacturing.

Many companies making a highly engineered product find that material and capacity don't tend to be the bottleneck as much as engineering and supervision time. While there are not usually standards that are readily available for planning capacity, even estimates can be very useful for planning to make sure that the company is not accepting projects that will greatly overtax its resources and thus put it in a position where it cannot deliver on schedule.

The examples used above were companies making products out of metal. But the problems are certainly no different in a company making apparel, pharmaceuticals, chemicals, textiles, food, or cosmetics. The primary differences are terminology and emphasis as opposed to significant logical differences in the way these manufacturing companies actually operate.

The pharmaceutical industry is highly regulated, and the FDA (Food and Drug Administration) requires that they operate to a series of good manufacturing practices (GMP) and document very closely how their products are actually produced. This is similar to companies in the space or nuclear fields that must have the same type of information on how the product was made as well as configuration control to tell when changes were introduced, etc.

In the cosmetics industry, most of the cost is in design, packaging and marketing. Nevertheless, it's important to coordinate the activities of marketing, manufacturing, purchasing, and design, to make sure that a product is on the shelves when the advertising program goes on television, for example. Otherwise, a great deal of money will have been wasted through the lack of coordination of these activities. MRP in this situation is more important as a company game plan than just as a manufacturing plan because the manufacturing cost is usually such a small percentage of the total cost.

In the chemical industry, products proceed through stages of "intermediates," "batches," and "bulk" to finished packaged product. But the problems are still the same - having the right material in the right place at the right time to make the product that's needed now.

Certainly anyone who's worked with the apparel, textile, or food industries knows that they have these same problems. Unfortunately, because the people who make machines - who pioneered MRP - use terms like "parts" instead of speaking of things like "greige goods" (undyed textile material), the differences are easier to see than the similarities.

A large segment of manufacturing is concerned with making a product that has an "upside-down bill of material." In a wire and cable company, once a given size of wire is extruded, it can follow many different paths in manufacturing depending on whether it is or is not tinned, how it is stranded, the color and compounding of the covering, whether or not, or how, it is to be cabled. But the fact that one item becomes many items - as it typically does in a steel mill - doesn't change the complexities or network scheduling involved. And MRP applies just as it does when many parts become one product.

Some companies make a one-piece product. But even in the simplest of situations, they must make a production plan, a master schedule, plan capacity, and execute the material and capacity plans. A foundry appears to be a simple type of business to run, and it is usually true that the material planning function is nowhere near as difficult as it is in a company making an assembled product. Never-theless, proper scheduling of the melting and pouring with the molding, shakeout, and snagging, becomes quite complex. In a foundry that makes castings using a great many cores, scheduling of cores and core box repair - not to mention the making and maintenance of patterns - can get very complex from a scheduling point of view, even though the logic is very straightforward. In a forge shop or a stamping factory, the material planning per se can often be straightforward, but the capacity planning - and especially the scheduling of tool maintenance in the die shop - can be a very challenging scheduling problem.

Some companies rebuild products rather than making new ones and it's easy to believe that this is a "unique" business. But, in fact, it's virtually identical logistically with a company that makes an assembled product with many options. For the company making an assembled product, there are certain common parts that will always be in the product. Then there are options that will be required in various percentages of the total production. A small car, for example, will always have the same frame, the same front and rear bumpers, and the same four cylinder engine. Sixty percent of the output will be with the standard transmission while forty percent will be with the automatic, etc., etc. A company rebuilding a product will also have a group of common parts that will be applied to one hundred percent of the master schedule. Every machine to be rebuilt will get new gaskets, seals, and vacuum diaphragms. Sixty percent will get new bearings, etc.

PERT (Project Evaluation and Review Technique) and CPM (Critical Path Method) and LOB (Line Of Balance) have been used and still are used as network scheduling techniques. MRP is a very straightforward network scheduling technique that is just a simplified form of PERT.

Today MRP is being used to schedule activities like engineering. The computer doesn't know that a number represents an activity rather than a part. And why not use MRP rather than PERT or PMS (Project Management System). Why not have one universal system that's used in all applications rather than a lot of systems that appear to be different, when their fundamental logic is the same.

MRP applies wherever there are network schedules concerning materials and production. It applies wherever there are scheduling networks to contend with.

When people ask, "Does MRP apply?", the first question should be, "Are you talking about material requirements planning or closed loop MRP?" The functions of closed loop MRP apply to every manufacturing business, even though the material requirements planning may not be a great challenge in a company like a foundry or a forge shop.

In fact, MRP and MRP II apply whether or not they are being done by computer. The functions in the closed loop MRP system are just a logical way to run a manufacturing business. Because we lacked the massive data manipulation capability the computer finally made possible, redundant systems became confusing and complex. But even if a company does MRP on the back of an envelope, one way or another they will have to do the fundamental functions of the closed loop MRP system and even MRP II whether they recognize it or not.

The less things worked and the less we understood, the more things looked different. The better we were able to do the fundamental scheduling of a manufacturing company, the more we realized that the differences were superficial. The better we understand, the more things look the same.

Before we had the MRP tools, people established dates on shop orders and purchase orders and assumed that these would remain valid with very few changes. They complained vehemently about the fact that the "forecast" was wrong, that the "engineers made too many changes," they struggled hard to get the world to hold still. But the world of manufacturing would not. The computer made modern MRP possible, and MRP gave management a set of tools for planning that could cope with the one constant in the manufacturing environment: change. With powerful tools like this to address the scheduling problems that have always existed in manufacturing, company after company demonstrated that dramatic results could be achieved.

Footnotes

1. Any reader not familiar with the mechanics of MRP, should refer to Appendix 1 at this point.

Chapter 4
The Impact of MRP II on Productivity

Section 1
Productivity in our Manufacturing Economy

Surveys and estimates by professionals would indicate that, as of mid-1981, there are approximately 8,000 manufacturing companies in the United States that are using some form of MRP. Probably 5 percent or less of these companies could be classified Class "A" or "B." (A Class A company is one that uses MRP to schedule so well that they don't have to use a shortage list at all. In a Class A company, MRP is a company game plan involving marketing, manufacturing, finance, and engineering. A Class B company is one that has a very good production and inventory control system, but hasn't extended it into a whole company system. They probably need a little "boost" from the shortage list from time to time also. A Class C company is one that uses MRP as a better inventory control system. They use it primarily for better order launching. A Class D company is one where it is primarily a data processing system that has little impact on operations. For more about Class A,B,C, and D, see Appendix 2, The ABCD Checklist.) This isn't surprising. MRP is a new technology. It isn't just exploding bills of material or inventory ordering anymore, and it takes time for people to learn how to apply a new technology.

But even with the small penetration of MRP in American industry, the results may already be starting to show in the area of better inventory management. (Remember that even a Class "C" MRP user does a better job of ordering inventory.) An article in <u>Fortune</u> concludes that the 1980 recession was the shortest on record, because it was not fueled by the abrupt inventory liquidation that characterized previous recessions:

"Both its brevity and mildness were almost entirely due to the unusually stable behavior of inventories. An important reason for that stability was the successful use of computerized inventory controls.

"Many businessmen close to the action contend that what happened last year was a result of permanent changes in the way inventories are managed." (1)

If this is really true, it is good news. It indicates that even with the limited progress that has been made to date in applying MRP in American industry, substantial results are beginning to show. The boom/bust cycles that were discussed in Chapter 2 are beginning to be tamed. The rise in unemployment during the 1980 recession went from 6.2 percent to 7.6 percent of the labor force, when it normally would have been expected to reach 9.1 percent, according to the article quoted above.

Later, the article - attributing the bulk of this success to wider use of MRP - goes on to say, "Machinery manufacturers increased their stocks and materials in the 1973 - 1975 recession almost 20 percent in constant dollars, but reduced them almost 4 percent in the 1980 recession."

Reducing the boom/bust cycles in our manufacturing economy can have dramatic impact on: 1. Unemployment that happens during the "bust" part of the cycle. 2. Inflation that is a normal by-product of the "boom" part of the cycle. 3. Overall productivity that comes from stabilizing production levels and dramatically reducing the waste that results when industry is constantly struggling to increase capacity, and then decrease capacity to respond to the boom and bust cycles.

That's the big picture on productivity. One that is almost never recognized in the articles about productivity. The following sections will talk about specific areas within a manufacturing company and their contribution to productivity.

Since MRP was originally thought of as a way to reduce inventory and improve customer service, those are the best documented gains in most companies. The contribution that good scheduling could make to productivity because of fewer material shortages and more time for supervision to do their job has also been recognized for some time, and considerable information is available about improvements in these areas. There are other areas like reduction of obsolescence, the productivity of engineering, and improved market penetration that haven't been well measured. That doesn't mean that gains haven't happened and people haven't recognized them. We simply haven't been aware enough of the broad implications of better scheduling and having a company game plan in a manufacturing company to have been looking for these improvements.

In the following sections, the contributions to productivity from the most significant areas will be discussed along with the reasons for these improvements and some specific references from specific companies.

Section 2
The Productivity of Money

When money doesn't have to be tied up in inventory, when inventory shrinkage can be reduced, when cash flow can be improved, the productivity of money can be increased. This is the same money that would be used to buy better machines, to invest in better controls like MRP II, and, in other ways, improve productivity.

Here are some of the proven areas for increasing the productivity of money:

1. INVENTORY REDUCTION

    Typical Gains: Between 20 and 35 percent.

    Why: Better Scheduling. Inventory management is a by-product of scheduling. Getting the right material at the right time.

    Reference: A survey of MRP users indicated, "The average increase in annual inventory turnover was an astounding 50.3 percent." (This would be a one-third reduction in inventory.) (Reference #1)

    Ilsco: Since installing MRP has been operating with "30 percent less total inventory." (Reference #2)

2. LESS RISK OF INVENTORY SHRINKAGE

    Typical Gains: Not able to quantify, but there is no known example of a company that really has MRP II working at a Class "A" or "B" level where there has been a surprise inventory shrinkage. It could only happen because of an error in the cost figures.

    Why: When the financial numbers for inventory are a by-product of operating numbers that are correct, when manufacturing actually uses "the numbers" to run the business, the financial inventory figures will be the same as the actual inventory.

    Reference: At least two companies (not identified by request) had serious inventory shrinkages before installing MRP and have not had shrinkages since.

3. IMPROVED CASH FLOW

    Typical Gains: Receivables reduced by ten days or more.

    Why: More even shipments week by week instead of the bulk of the product going out the door in the last week of the month. Product that goes out the first week of the month will normally be paid for the first week of the following month. Product that is shipped the last week of the month, typically won't be paid for until after the following month.

    Reference: Di-Acro in 1976 shipped 78 percent of their product in week 4. In 1981 they shipped approximately 25 percent of their product every week of the month. (Reference #3)

    At Hill-Rom, for example, the shipment rate at month's end used to exceed the rate at the beginning of the month by 30 to 50 percent. Now, with MRP, the variance does not exceed 5 percent. (Reference #4)

4   BETTER FINANCIAL PLANNING

    Typical Gains: Not quantified, but users report results.

    Why: The ability to simulate what will happen in the operations in a manufacturing business and convert this readily to dollars.

    Reference: "It makes budgeting so much simpler", (vice president of finance and administration, Ohaus Scale). "You can cost out materials and labor for an entire year. When unanticipated periods of heavy purchasing come along, it is simple to calculate how much money in excess of budget will be needed. Accounting can be based on actual cost instead of estimates because every job is done under MRP." (Reference #4)

    "One of the most powerful benefits of an integrated MRP and financial system is that you can predict the impact of changes and operations performance on the financial aspects of the business. We can say that in our first year our shipping plan technique predicted the product mix so well that production cost at standard came out within one percent of the projection," division manufacturing manager, Hewlett Packard, Colorado Springs. (Reference #5)

Section 3
The Productivity of Labor

Specific labor productivity increases can be expected from these areas:

1. DIRECT LABOR OUTPUT INCREASED

   Typical Gains: Average 5 to 10 percent in fabrication areas, average 25 to 40 percent in assembly areas.

   Why: Fewer shortages, less frequent interrupted short runs because of expediting.

   References: Haworth, "Better availability of materials has given us a 50 percent improvement in productivity. In our company where we had a 35 percent growth rate in 1979, the dollars saved on direct labor alone amounted to $1,260,000. (Reference #2) Wright Line, "In final assembly, for example, productivity rose 40 percent." (Reference #2)

2. INDIRECT LABOR

   Typical Gains: Not many companies have quantified this, but users report results.

   Why: Less paperwork, less confusion, less redundant effort, and less expediting.

   References: American Sterilizer's indirect labor cost "Has come down 24 percent since 1975." (Reference #2) Indirect labor productivity improvements were also experienced by Ilsco, but were not specifically quantified. (Reference #2)

3. REDUCED OVERTIME

   Typical Gains: Fifty to ninety percent.

   Why: Better planning, fewer shortages, making more of the right things at the right time, better ability to plan capacity requirements further in advance. Most companies work too much overtime today, yet have too much inventory indicating that they are building inventory on overtime. Chronic overtime - when a company works four or five Saturdays in a row, for example, is a dramatic case of reduced productivity because, by the fifth Saturday, they will be paying for six days of work but only getting five.

References: Tennant reduced overtime from "14.5 percent of total work time to just 4 percent." (Reference #4) ITT Courier cut their overtime from 52,000 hours a month to 3,000. (Reference #2)

4. IMPROVED QUALITY CONTROL

Typical Gains: No specific data available yet - difficult to quantify, but users report results.

Why: When there are constant shortages and material substitutions, this will affect quality. The end of the month "push" definitely affects quality. One manufacturer (not identified by request) that keeps records of their warranty claims shows a direct correlation between the end-of-the-month push and the number of warranty claims. When supervision spends much of its time "firefighting" instead of doing the tasks that are in the job description, one of the results will be quality problems.

References: Vice president of manufacturing at Tennant (speaking at an Executive Conference May 18, 1981), when asked about the impact of MRP on quality, said, "Of course it has an impact. When management has the time to work on the real problems rather than fighting fires, every area of the business can be improved."

Quality control manager of Di-Acro, "Prior to MRP, the 'crunch' was responsible for some things being missed in the rush such as manuals, documentation, etc. Getting the last machines out meant working excessive overtime. Now our employees can go home, morale is better, and quality is improved. Basically, now everyone cares, and they are taking the time to do it right." (Reference #3)

Section 4
The Productivity of Purchasing

Typical Gains: Average 5 percent additional reduction in purchased costs.

Why: Less paperwork and less expediting for purchasing people means more time for value analysis, negotiations, working with engineering on standardization, working with vendors on annual contracts, etc. One buyer indicated that 50 percent of the requisitions coming across his desk either said "at once" or "confirming phone call." Certainly, that doesn't give purchasing much time for vendor selection or negotiation.

References: Tennant reduced expediting in purchasing from four hours a day to one hour a day after MRP. (Reference #6)

Steelcase, before MRP, had a total cost reduction result of $592,326. After MRP, two years later, the total was $5,341,320. (Reference #7)

Section 5
The Productivity of the Marketing Effort

Better customer service means more productivity of salesmen's time. Less time apologizing for the last order that hasn't been shipped yet and more time getting the next order. It means better coordination between marketing and manufacturing - many companies waste a great deal of their marketing and advertising dollars promoting products that manufacturing does not yet have the capacity to produce. Better customer service means increased market penetration. Very few companies have measured this, and very few, of course, would attribute it to MRP alone. One apparel manufacturer has gone from an estimated 20 percent to an estimated 60 percent market penetration, since they've installed MRP. It wasn't the total answer, but they say it helped greatly.

The most significant other areas for improved productivity in marketing are:

1.   BETTER CUSTOMER SERVICE

Typical Gains: Dramatic improvement with most MRP users reporting customer service at 95 percent or more.

Why: Making more of the right product at the right time. Better customer service and inventory reduction go hand in hand. The best way to reduce inventory is to ship it! Make what the customer wants, and send it to the customer.

Reference: American Sterilizer, "Before MRP, the percentage of orders delivered to customers on the first date promised was 70 to 72 percent. Now it runs between 90 and 97 percent." (Reference #2)

President of Ilsco, "We've been able to achieve a 98 percent level of customer service defined as the availability of stock items off the shelf or of make-to-order items when scheduled; and we've been able to support this service level with 50 percent less in process inventory and 30 percent less total inventory." (Reference #2)

"Products delivered by the promised date was below 80 percent in pre-MRP days; today, Wright Line averages 95 percent." (Reference #2)

Vice president of manufacturing, Steelcase, "Customers are happy when they get a quality product delivered on schedule. Before MRP, the Chair Plant completed 80 percent of its orders on time. With MRP, we currently have over 65 consecutive weeks of 100 percent schedule completion. File Plant number 2 has over two years at 100 percent completion, and the Panel Plant has 91 weeks of 100 percent completion." (Reference #8)

"At Hill-Rom, MRP's big payoff has been in customer deliveries. The hospital bed makers used to miss one of three. Now the manufacturing vice president says he thinks his operation is doing a terrible job if it misses one delivery date in ten." (Reference #4)

2. BETTER CUSTOMER INFORMATION

Tennant's materials manager points out, "MRP simulation made it possible to give marketing a prompt and accurate answer, and Tennant's customers got reliable delivery dates." (Reference #5)

Also, with this better data, according to the vice president of sales and marketing at Wright Line, "Marketing and manufacturing can communicate more effectively at the strategic planning level as well as in their day-to-day operations." (Reference #2)

Section 6
The Productivity of Engineering

Very little has been done to quantify the improvement in productivity in engineering yet, due to MRP II, but there are some definite indications that this is happening. Having a common data base means that engineering spends less time retrieving and maintaining data. Because this data is used in finance, manufacturing, and marketing, it is easier to keep one set of numbers correct than it is to try to maintain several sets of numbers. The use of techniques like "modular bills of material" can substantially reduce the amount of time engineering must spend creating and maintaining bills of material, particularly for custom-assembled products. Because MRP II lends itself to good configuration control, this cuts down the amount of time that engineering must spend searching for data for warranty claims, product liability problems, or field service questions. Because MRP facilitates time phasing of engineering changes, this can result in substantially reduced obsolescence.

Where there is a great deal of new product being introduced, MRP can be of great value.

References: Material control director, American Sterilizer, "Four years ago, 85 percent of the products on the floor were ten years old, today 85 percent of them are less than 3 years old. The MRP system helps us get new products into production much faster; our research and development is more productive." (Reference #2)

Engineering manager at WEMCO Division of Envirotech, "Now that we are using MRP for scheduling engineering, our on time performance consistently exceeds 95 percent. Prior to MRP, we were continuously past due. Now we know our priorities. Within 15 minutes I can go over my scheduling report and know where we are in trouble and do something about it. We now run the company in a much more relaxed atmosphere and operate much more effectively. Managers now have time to work into the future. Now it's fun on the job. We are in control and have much closer communication between departments throughout the company. MRP has now touched everyone. It has permeated through the ranks in the organization. It's a pleasure to watch the people now working for me, enthusiastically doing the job that I used to have to do." (Reference #9)

When engineering integrates their activities with the rest of the company and uses MRP for scheduling, backlog can be reduced, delivery performance can be increased, and engineering can be a far more productive part of the company team.

Section 7
The Productivity of Leadership

A good manager's job is primarily to be a good leader. When people see that the leaders are in conflict with each other, that they are unable to plan well, that they too are overwhelmed with day-to-day problems, the effectiveness of that leadership is seriously eroded. When managers have more time to manage, when they have better tools for planning and monitoring performance, when they are better able to perform as members of the team, this leadership - the most important function of all in running a manufacturing company - can be far more effective. This, again, is a very difficult area to quantify, but substantial results have been experienced by MRP II users in the following areas

1. MORE EFFECTIVE MANAGEMENT

Why: Better planning (MRP II is a simulator that allows management to look further ahead).

References: "Ohaus Scale has found that MRP allows it to run 'what if' simulations that can help in planning capacity, scheduling new products, and many other management decisions." (Reference #4)

The president of Wright Line, "We are now able to function more as a team and work toward one goal. With MRP, we focus all our energy in one direction, sort of like a laser beam, in a coherent, disciplined process. We have eliminated the confusion that unruly and undefined management functions bring about." (Reference #2)

Manufacturing manager, American Sterilizer, "My personal productivity has risen at least 90 percent. I'm doing what I ought to be doing as a manager. Before, all I could think of was, 'Where are the parts we were supposed to have at four o'clock that afternoon'. I was the highest paid expeditor we had." (Reference #2)

2. TEAMWORK

Why: With a company game plan, all functions can work together far better.

References: Materials manager, Ohaus Scale, "Suddenly everyone is playing off the same sheet of music." (Reference #4)

Materials manager, Di-Acro, "Additionally, a new level of mutual respect between marketing and manufacturing has come from MRP. They know we will meet the delivery dates." (Reference #3)

3. MORE EFFECTIVE SUPERVISION

Why: About 60 percent of the average American foreman's time is spent looking for material, in attending shortage meetings, expediting, planning emergency overtime, shifting people around within the union contract and seniority rights, and, in general, frittering away time because of poor scheduling.

References: "A major benefit of the program in American Sterilizer is that people are able to do what they are paid for without having to chase parts. This is true of the foremen who now can concentrate on their supervisory activities. But it's also true at higher levels." (Reference #2)

Operations manager, Sealol, "Supervisors have time to actually manage the work force." (Reference #8)

Section 8
The Productivity of Profits

The chairman of Steelcase, in addressing an SME Conference, said, "You can't talk productivity without talking profits. Profits create the capital needed to invest in improved productivity. We often hear of profits through productivity - when we should really be thinking about productivity through profits. No one can sustain increased levels of productivity without capital investment, and capital is created from profits. The three factors - capital investment, productivity, and profits - cannot be separated." (Reference #10) This is an excellent and long-needed statement. Profits and productivity feed upon each other.

There are so many things involved in company profitability that it would be presumptuous to attribute all of them to MRP II. The best MRP II users are typically the best managed companies because they recognize the value of tools that help management to run a business more professionally. Nevertheless, the correlation of profitability and successful MRP II users is not a coincidence.

Reference: President, Di-Acro, "We are a privately owned company and do not divulge profit information, but profits have improved substantially since MRP." (Reference #3)

"Cameron Iron Works placed tenth in growth among companies with $500 million and over in sales in fiscal 1980. Having grown 9 years in a row, earnings per share have risen from 1969's 13 cents to $2.61 in fiscal 1980." MRP is, according to the vice president and general manager of the Oil Tools Division, "more than just a material requirements program; it's a great management tool. Working through the master production schedule, you can judge performance, improve operating efficiency, and put order back into the shop. There's been a tremendous amount of spin off beyond the advantages of better inventory control, improved deliveries, and customer satisfaction." (Reference #11)

Section 9
The Quality of Life

Virtually every company that uses MRP II in Class A or B mode comments on the improvement in the quality of life. It's almost as if this were a bonus, a payback that they didn't expect.

<u>Why</u>: Better teamwork because of a better company game plan.

<u>References</u>: "The system provides us with tremendous flexibility to respond to market demand. Today we are much more orderly and are experiencing improved quality of life in manufacturing. There are fewer frustrations, and we spend our time executing the schedule rather than reacting to exceptions," operations manager, Sealol. (Reference #8)

Vice president of manufacturing, Wright Line, "It's much more enjoyable to support an agreed-upon, attainable production plan than to expedite madly with one that is unattainable." (Reference #2)

Section 10
Tools for Top Management

After Xerox had been operational with their MRP system for several years, some of their executives were asked, "What was the greatest benefit you got; reduced inventory, improved service, improved productivity, etc.?" Their answer was, "All of the above, but more important than all of that, we got the tools to control the business!"

Why: MRP II makes it possible to translate overall management plans as expressed in the business plan and the production plan down to the detail level plans that everyone else will be working to execute. Before MRP, plans weren't particularly well connected to each other or responsive to change since much of what was done was done with informal systems.

References: President, Di-Acro, "Operating a manufacturing company with a fully functioning MRP system compared to one without MRP is like night and day. In fact, having a functional MRP system - in both good times and bad - gives us control that's so good it's like cheating. It's very exciting to operate a company with MRP. The thing that is so exciting is the degree of control, and that makes a difference in how I spend my time. I used to have to arbitrate between marketing and manufacturing making operational decisions, and this took up a sizable part of my day. Now I rarely get involved. I spend less than part of a day over a period of months on this problem. I can review the plans made up by the manufacturing group looking only for basic logic flaws. Once we've resolved the plan, I can literally wash my hands of it. This gives me the time I must have to run the division." (Reference #3)

Former senior vice president of Tennant, "We had created something that theoreticians have been speculating about for years. In our MRP system, tied in with finance and other functions, we had created a computer model of the business. We could now simulate almost any part of the business and test the impact of new plans or, indeed, any changing conditions." (Reference #5)

Vice president, corporate manufacturing, Uniflite said; "Since we last saw you, an incredible set of circumstances has affected our company. Business began to fall off, and by February 1980, with interest rates at an all time high, our orders practically stopped, banks actually refused to finance boats just when we had introduced our new 48 foot Sport Fisherman at $325,000 per. At times like this, MRP is a must. Cash flow and resource management becomes intensely important to survive. Some companies in our industry have gone under, and I have to blame their mismanagement where I know they simply overextended into Chapter 11.

"We were having a rough enough time as it was, but on April 8 Uniflite had a major disaster when a fire completely destroyed our main laminating and assembly building. We were wiped out. One of the most important experiences has been our recovery. I realized very quickly an unexpected value and asset of MRP. An MRP system can recreate everything that was in place at a given instant. We were faced with the task of proving our losses to the insurers. I could cite one example after another where we were able to fix the loss precisely on every item in inventory, work in process, etc. (our records were near 95 percent accurate at the time, and our computer was located in another building). We knew exactly what tooling molds were lost and the open orders affected. Within 60 days, new molds were made for every major part lost, and on 15, July, we took the challenge of recreating the 48 foot Sport Fisherman for the Norwalk, Connecticut boat show in mid August. A company just could not have achieved this without MRP." (Reference #12)

Vice president and controller at Abbott Laboratories, "MRP makes possible a change from reactive management to a planned and controlled management." (Reference #4)

Section 11
Productivity in Other Areas of the Company

In 1979, the American automobile industry spent over $100 million on premium air freight, most of that due to scheduling problems. And that figure does not include the use of their own airplanes or what their vendors spent! In an automobile manufacturing company, they cannot afford to shut lines down because of part shortages. As a consequence, the cost of poor scheduling and inaccurate inventory records shows up in the incoming freight bill. The cost of poor scheduling will also show up in the outgoing freight bill in many companies. When a company is behind schedule or has a penalty contract, they may have to spend extravagant sums of money for premium freight.

Like so many other areas that MRP has affected, people weren't originally looking for results here, and as a consequence, few have quantified them. Nevertheless, the potential is there.

And the potential exists in many other areas. One pharmaceutical company reduced obsolescence by 80 percent after they installed MRP and reduced distribution (including traffic) costs by 15 percent using DRP (Distribution Resource Planning).

Perhaps the best common perspective on the potential of MRP is to consider, once again, the earlier quote from the vice president of manufacturing at Tennant, "When management has the time to work on the real problems rather than fighting fires, every area of the business can be improved."

With all the talk about productivity today concentrating on the direct labor area, it's well to remind ourselves that this is typically only 10 percent or less of the total cost of a product in any company. Productivity should be looked at in a much bigger context: the productivity of all of the members of the team - especially management.

Section 12
Productivity Through People

There are three very important things to remember about the potential productivity improvements from MRP:

1. They can be very different from company to company. A manufacturer of tobacco products, for example, is not likely to see great productivity improvements in purchasing when they own their own tobacco fields and paper factories. They could probably get their return in areas like distribution and reduced inventory.

2. None of the results above <u>are due to MRP</u>. They came about because of people who made MRP work. "Successful MRP came from the planners, foremen, shippers, in other words, the people here at Di-Acro." (Reference #3)

3. Undoubtedly, the greatest productivity improvements of all will come from using our human resources better. From taking the obstacles away from people so that they can do their jobs more effectively. "Can we do as well in realizing our potential as the Japanese can do in realizing theirs? To answer that question we have to look beyond technology and beyond capital investment; we have to look at people. The real secret of Japanese productivity is people." (Reference #13)

And that's the most important message of all. The productivity improvements don't come from the tools, they come from the people using the tools to do a more professional job. And, of course, some of the most important people are the team leaders, the members of management. Teamwork is a powerful way to improve productivity; with MRP, the members of the team have a way to work together better which will help them get more accomplished and respect each other far more than they did before they had a common game plan.

MRP is also an important element in improving trust, not just among the leaders of the team, but between management and labor. When production rates can be stabilized, when there is less overtime, when there is less crisis and firefighting in the factory, labor has far more respect for management and they can work together far better to improve productivity.

Fortunately, today labor is developing a far more positive attitude toward productivity. Once the unions looked upon any steps taken to improve productivity as a threat to jobs. But today it's recognized that this simply isn't true. This quote from The Economist makes the point:

In Britain the ten industries that have increased productivity fastest in the past two decades have raised their employment by 25 percent although employment in British manufacturing as a whole has fallen.

In the United States, high technology industries have increased productivity twice as fast as low technology ones - and expanded employment nine times as fast.

Unions should be asking employers to increase productivity faster, not slower. The best job prospects are those in industries that improve productivity fastest. (Reference #14)

References
_____

1.   Lewis Beman, "A Big Payoff From Inventory Controls,"
     Fortune, July 27, 1981, pp. 76-80.

2.   "Productivity: Out of MRP - A New Game Plan,"
     Modern Materials Handling, January 6, 1981.

3.   "Class A MRP II at Di-Acro," Oliver Wight Video
     Productions, Inc., 1981.

4.   "The Trick of Material Requirements Planning,"
     Business Week, June 4, 1979.

5.   "MRP II: Manufacturing Resource Planning," Modern
     Materials Handling, September, 1979.

6.   "MRP Breaks With Past Patterns of Failure,"
     Purchasing, July 24, 1980.

7.   "MRP and Purchasing at Steelcase," presentation made
     by John Ruhl, Director of Production Planning and
     Procurement, and John Schorr, Manager of Purchasing
     at Steelcase, Incorporated, at the 1975 APICS National
     Conference.

8.   "MRP - What Does it Take to Make it Work For You,"
     Production, June, 1981.

9.   Letter to R. D. Garwood from the engineering manager
     at WEMCO Division of Envirotech.

10. Modern Materials Handling, Management Newsletter
     quoting Robert C. Pew, Steelcase Chairman and
     President, speaking to the Society of Manufacturing
     Engineers Conference, February 20, 1981.

11. "Continued Growth Isn't Accidental - It's Managed,"
     Iron Age, November 12, 1980.

12. Personal letter from vice president corporate
     manufacturing, Uniflite, Incorporated, September 27,
     1979.

13. "Productivity Growth - What Can We Learn From
     Japan," Modern Materials Handling, May 6, 1980.

14. Dethrone King Ludd, The Economist, August 23, 1980.

Footnotes

1. Lewis Beman, "A Big Payoff From Inventory Controls," <u>Fortune</u>, July 27, 1981, pp. 76-80.

PART II
A New Set of Values

Chapter 5
The New Principles of Systems

Section 1
Focus on People

When computers were new, we thought that they would be used to mechanize clerical work. The classical question was, "How many people will we get rid of with this computer system?" Actually, very little that man has ever invented has created more jobs than computers. Eliminating clerks by putting their work on computers has not been a highly profitable application in most instances.

Then, during the late 1950's and 1960's, the computer "system" became the focus of attention. People tried to build as much sophisticated logic into the computer system as they could, and the general attitude that prevailed back then is conveyed by this quote from some 1960's promotional literature about a computer program: "(The system) will take complete charge of the planning, scheduling and control of the inventory and production process in a job shop. It is truly remarkable in the manner in which it performs this function, eliminating the need for the human decision where ever possible..."

Unfortunately, computers don't do an effective job of expediting vendors. Computers don't add capacity, that requires a person to buy a new machine, hire more people, decide to work overtime, subcontract, or use an alternate routing. And, ironically, the more logic that is built into the computer system, the more difficult it is for a person to know what logic was left out; and until such time as a logic built into a computer system can be one hundred percent right one hundred percent of the time, putting more logic into the system simply makes it more difficult for people to understand the system and use it intelligently. Computer systems can best handle simple, repetitive, consistent logic that must be done over and over thousands and even millions of times. During the '60's there was great talk about putting "management decisions" into the computer and one business magazine went so far as to ask, "What will become of middle management when their decisions have all been programmed into the computer?" The answer is clear today, they're still here - working harder than ever. Because the computer simply processes information, people make decisions.

Another false start was in the direction of "management science." This was really a quantitative, analytical, mathematical approach to business "decisions." It was hardly "scientific" at all since the scientific method says:

1. Observe.
2. Hypothesize.
3. Test the hypothesis to see if it works.
4. Revise the hypothesis to correct it until it does work.

Mathematics is not a synonym for science. Mathematics is simply one of the tools to be used; one that has some application, but nothing like the amount of application in the real world of business management that mathematicians imagined. Inventing tools, and then looking for problems to fit them is hardly being "scientific," and if mathematical, analytical approaches are used while ignoring the scientific method, people have lost sight of fundamentals. A truly "scientific" approach to management, when built around the testing of the hypotheses to see what really works, has made the direction of successful systems, present and future, very clear:

THE GREATEST VALUE OF THE COMPUTER AND COMPUTER TECHNIQUES IS IN HELPING US TO USE OUR HUMAN RESOURCES MORE PRODUCTIVELY.

We had to develop a whole new set of systems principles and a new approach that was far different from what was envisioned in the early days of computers.

Section 2
The Four Systems Principles

Once it's understood that systems are just tools for people, the systems principles emerge. The four most important systems principles are:

1. Accountability.
2. Transparency.
3. Data Integrity.
4. Validity of the Simulation.

The principle of <u>accountability</u> is fundamental. A computer cannot be held accountable; only people can. Yet it is not unusual to see someone installing an "automatic purchase order system." A system where the computer will generate purchase orders and send them out to the vendors "untouched by human hands." Will something go wrong someday? Certainly. There will be a bill of material error, a mistake made in the master schedule, a problem with an engineering change. That something will go wrong is <u>inevitable</u>! When the general manager sees some power supplies on the receiving dock that he knows were meant for an order that has been canceled, the question will be, "Who was the imbecile who let that happen?" And the answer will be that famous refrain, <u>"Don't ask me, the computer did it!"</u>

There is nothing wrong with having the computer generate a vendor schedule - but the planner should be held accountable for approving the schedule. This doesn't mean that the planner will do a great deal of research on all items, but it does mean that the planner should look for any obvious mistakes and that the planner will at all times be held accountable whatever happens.

The planner should be given a very simple message, "You are not the computer's slave; the computer is your slave. The computer is doing all the drudge work - making the recommendations - so that you can use your human intelligence."

The principle of <u>transparency</u> involves several facets:

1. The planner can see <u>through</u> the computer system to the simple logic being used.

2. The system is simple.

3. Users understand the logic of the system.

4. Users can see from one "level" of the system to another.

5. It meets the test of transparency: "Why did the computer tell me to do that this time?"

American Airlines SABRE reservation system was one of the most technically sophisticated and advanced computer systems of its day. It was developed in the late 1950's and was one of the first "on line - real time" systems. For all its complexity and sophistication, however, the airline reservation clerk used the system intelligently because the system simply showed what the reservation clerk always needed to know: what seats are available on what flights? To the user, the complexity and sophistication of the technical part of the system was irrelevant. The logic was simple and straightforward. This is a fundamental principle of good systems design in an environment where people will have to use the system intelligently:

1. Make the logic obvious.

2. If a system is to be used intelligently, simplicity is the very cornerstone of understanding and, consequently, accountability.

One large manufacturing company was putting in a shop floor control system. In the office of all the systems people there was a little sign that said "KISS" (Keep It Simple, Stupid). But their idea of simplicity was to develop six different scheduling algorithms for the factory. This made an excellent article for one of the technical journals, but in fact, did nothing to improve scheduling in the factory. It only made it more difficult for the foremen to understand the priorities and use the system intelligently.

This is the basic rule that should be followed: Always use the simplest techniques that will work. Anything more sophisticated should be justified totally on the basis of operational effectiveness in the hands of the users.

Many people believe that mathematical decision rules, operations research, and other sophisticated techniques are the tools of "scientific management." Unfortunately, these people are the enemies of simplicity, and consequently, they tend to destroy the transparency of the system, and that, in turn, destroys accountability. We have a re-education job to do to teach people that:

SIMPLICITY IS THE ULTIMATE SOPHISTICATION.

The issue is <u>understanding</u>. If people do not understand the logic in a system, they cannot be expected to use it intelligently. The simpler the system, the easier it will be to understand the system. The better they understand it, the better they will use it.

Figure 5-1 shows the closed loop MRP system again. In a well designed system, the user can easily see from one part of the system to another to answer the question, "Why did the computer tell me to do that this time?"

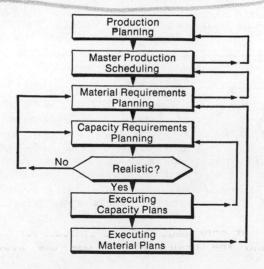

Figure 5 - 1. Closed Loop MRP

If, for example, there is a capacity problem in one work center, the planner can identify the jobs causing the capacity problem by part number, reference back to the material plan, and follow the material requirements plan up from one level to another right to the master schedule level if necessary (this is done through a technique called pegging described in Appendix 1).

One company came up with a computer output for material requirements planning that was the ultimate in brevity. It simply showed the planner a part number and quantity to be ordered by a given date or rescheduled from one date to another. The planners had absolutely no idea why the computer was telling them to order or reschedule. Half of them followed it blindly, and when asked a question about an order or a reschedule, typically said, "Don't ask me, the computer told me to!" The other planners ignored the system completely. These were the more intelligent people. Transparency had been designed out of the system.

There is an important distinction to make here. The user may well understand how a formula or algorithm works without being able to pass the test of transparency, "Why did the system tell me to do that this time?" Knowing how the formula works and knowing why it came up with a particular answer at a particular time are two different things. If the user has to do a lot of research to determine "why" and that takes too much time, the user won't usually do it and consequently will not be able to be held accountable.

Second order exponential smoothing - a moving weighted average with a trend calculation - is a good case in point. It is easy to explain the formula and how it works. But if a user wants to know why a particular answer came out of the system, a great many calculations must be made to go back and reconstruct the history to find out how the system came up with a particular answer today. Most users simply won't do it, and while they "understand the formula," the system does not pass the test of transparency.

Data integrity is a problem in a manufacturing company for a very simple reason: the people in the company are used to operating with informal systems where numbers don't mean much. If they are to run with formal systems where the numbers are used to run the business, then the numbers will have to be right. Virtually every company that installs MRP has a major task in getting information correct and keeping it correct.

The problem of data integrity will have to be addressed using the principles of management discussed in Chapter 6. Chapter 6 shows how they would be used to develop inventory record integrity. One of the key elements in getting people to keep numbers right is, of course, education. If they don't understand why accuracy is now important, they simply aren't likely to put in the effort to do it.

The subject of data integrity will be discussed in the various chapters where it applies, such as: Chapter 10, concerning manufacturing; and Chapter 13, that discusses engineering. The real problem here is in changing the way people think, and that is a problem in management which will be discussed in Chapter 7 because it must all start with the chief executive officer.

A system must be a valid simulation of reality or it simply won't work. Figure 5-2 shows an example where material comes into receiving, goes through receiving inspection, and into stores. One of the questions posed by the systems designers is, "When should we add the material into the on-hand balance - when it goes into receiving or when It goes into stores?" If material is added to the on-hand balance when it goes into receiving, the planner could well schedule a foreman to use the material that receiving inspection would reject and send back to the vendor. If the material is added into the on-hand balance only after it's gone through receiving inspection, the planner would be likely to expedite purchasing who, in turn, would expedite the vendor only to find out that material was already sitting on the receiving dock.

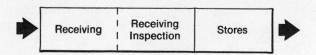

Figure 5 – 2. Receiving Logic

The system must work the way the real world actually works. The system must represent the movement that is actually taking place. In this case, it would be essential to know that material went into receiving and also that it moved from receiving into stores. Without this information, the planner would have no recourse but to spend a good deal of each day down on the receiving dock and in the storeroom checking to see where material actually was.

The test of the valid simulation is: How does it really happen?

The system is just a representation of the way it really happens - a simulation. And if the simulation does not represent the way it really happens, it cannot be used.

In one company, a raw material inventory clerk - a veteran of 32 years in the company - would not post his inventory records regularly in spite of a great deal of pressure from his boss. Looking into the situation, it was found that, among other problems, the system didn't simulate the way inventory was actually stored in manufacturing. There were seven different starting departments where material could be stored at the mixing operation. The inventory record was a simple in/out balance system as shown in Figure 5-3. When material came in, it was added into inventory. When it went out, it was deducted. An in/out balance system is merely a simulation of a stockroom. But, in this company, there were really eight different stocking locations. As material moved from the warehouse into a given department, the movement was not recorded in the system. It was only deducted from inventory when it was reported as used by a production department. As a consequence, the raw material inventory control clerk could look at his records and know how much material was on hand, but he would not know where it was. This is the well-known "wall-to-wall inventory record." The raw material inventory control clerk couldn't do his job without being able to tell the foremen where the material was. And consequently, the inventory control clerk, had he used the formal system, could only say to a foreman, "We have the material, but I don't know where."

Date	In	Out	Balance
			1850
10/11/80	110		1960
11/24/80		780	1180

Figure 5-3. Inventory Record Card

This is a good example of two points:

1.   When the system is not a valid simulation of reality, the users will not keep information correct.

2.   It's important to ask the question: How <u>should</u> it really happen, before making the system a simulation of reality today?

It might well be in the example of the raw material clerk discussed above that material should <u>not</u> be stored in the mixing areas of the starting departments. Perhaps material should be issued only to a manufacturing order rather than letting the foremen requisition material. It would be wrong to design a system that represented the way things actually happen when that's not the way they should happen.

These are the principles, then, that are involved in developing systems that people can use. Systems developed observing these principles can be very practical, usable systems. When the principles are violated, the systems probably won't work in practice.

It took a lot of learning and a lot of experience before we were able to develop computer systems that could be used to produce results consistently. We learned the hard way that companies approaching MRP as one more computer system are going to be very disappointed with the results. Above all, we learned that the magic is not in the computer and the magic is not in some mathematical formulas. The magic is in people - the same people who have been running our business for years - who now have the tools to enable them to do their jobs more professionally. We have learned that what is needed is:

<u>A PEOPLE ATTITUDE TOWARD SYSTEMS RATHER THAN A SYSTEMS ATTITUDE TOWARD PEOPLE.</u>

Chapter 6
The Old Principles of Management

Section 1
Management Principles

Today, because of the massive data manipulation powers of the computer, we have the capability to generate valid plans. We have the capability to manage with a formal system, but it's going to require a new approach to management. We must take some principles that we understood in theory and put them into practice. MRP II provides management with tools to manage more effectively. Now the principles of management will have to be applied not only to use these tools, but to make these tools work well enough so that they can be used. It's worth reviewing these principles briefly.

There are six basic principles involved in managing anything, be it a manufacturing company, a public library, or the United Fund Drive. They are:

1.   Defining Objectives.
2.   Assigning Accountability.
3.   Developing Understanding.
4.   Providing the Tools.
5.   Measuring Performance.
6.   Providing Incentives.

One of the most difficult challenges for any organization is to establish and maintain the proper <u>objectives</u>. One company that sells primarily through distributors had a credit manager who felt that his objective was to have no bad debts. Whenever a new distributor opened up, the sales people for his company had little chance of signing them up because their credit record had not been established. As a consequence, the company got very little new distribution. But the credit manager bragged at the monthly credit managers' association meeting that he had "virtually no bad debts" at the end of the year. It would have been far more intelligent in this company to set an objective for the credit manager: "You can write off up to $X-thousand a year, but, in return, you and the sales department should work closely together to try and get us at least a million dollars worth of new distribution every year." In this particular company, the credit manager set his own objectives because no one else told him what the objectives were. A classic example of "management by objectives by default."

Peter Drucker said that efficiency is doing things right while effectiveness is doing the right things. One of management's prime responsibilities is to assign proper objectives to each function in the organization so that each function is working to the overall objectives of the organization.

While this sounds straightforward, it requires some very clear thinking if it is to be done properly. Very few people, for example, understand the real objectives of production and inventory control as it was called in the past. They are often told that it is their job to "get the right jobs out to the customers at the right time." This, of course, is simply not true. It is the responsibility of manufacturing people to get the right jobs shipped to the customers at the right time. It is the responsibility of production and inventory control to make valid attainable schedules that manufacturing can use to meet this objective.

The dictionary makes little distinction between "responsibility" and "accountability." But there certainly is a difference in the real world. Responsibility means that someone has been given a job to do. Accountability means that they have the tools to do the job and that their performance in doing the job will be measured. Accountability means that no avenue has been left open for making excuses for not doing the job.

Implicit in any assignment of accountability to meet objectives is understanding. The credit manager mentioned above did not understand his job and the overall context of the company objectives. He saw only his personal objective of having no bad debts.

People cannot be expected to do their jobs if they don't have the tools. The production and inventory control function discussed above is a good case in point. Their job is to provide realistic schedules that other people will be held responsible for executing. Without MRP, production and inventory control people could not generate valid schedules. They simply did not have the tools to do the job properly.

Measurement of performance is fundamental to accountability. Without valid plans, there is no real measurement because there is nothing to measure against. The existence of the plans does not, by itself, mean that performance will improve. The plans are merely the prerequisite to measurement. And when performance is measured, it almost always improves. One of the reasons the credit manager in the example above tried to have no bad debts was that management themselves complimented him on that! That was his de facto measurement! They did not really measure him on his contribution to <u>overall</u> company performance.

The sixth principle of management is <u>incentives</u>. The most typical approach is to set objectives for each manager. To measure performance against these objectives and to have a performance review several times a year. This performance review determines what level of performance the manager has attained. Many companies then rank their employees as "A," "B," "C," or "D" performers. The "A" performers get the largest raises and bonuses. The "B" performers get somewhat less. The "D" performers are typically on probation in their present jobs and considered for other jobs where they can make a greater contribution.

The methods for providing management incentives are beyond the scope of this book. Suffice it to say that there must be incentives for people to do a professional job.

These were the principles of management in theory. Peter Drucker wrote about them, George Odiorne wrote about them; perhaps not exactly as they have been expressed above, but with the same basic message. The idea has been to get the focus off "What are we doing?" and on to "What are we trying to accomplish?" Some call this management by objectives; it is really just plain common sense. But, unfortunately, this logical approach to managing a manufacturing business didn't work very well in practice in a manufacturing company.

Section 2
Making the Principles Work

The principles of management by objectives <u>could not</u> work in the environment of the informal system. For one fundamental reason:

There was little real accountability.

Accountability implies measurement, and a prerequisite to measurement is valid plans. In the manufacturing environment, the plans were not valid because scheduling did not work. This problem was discussed in Chapter 2.

Today the massive data manipulation capability of the computer makes it possible to have valid plans. But now people must be taught how to operate with a formal system, a system that relies on the numbers being <u>right</u>. In order to make this work:

1. New <u>objectives</u> will be required. In the past, for example, the bill of material was used as a reference document. With a formal system, the bill of material must represent the way the product is made.

2. Managers must be held <u>accountable</u>. Making accurate bills of material that can be used by the entire organization for planning and control now becomes a function that engineering must perform.

3. People must <u>understand</u> why and how to meet these new objectives. The people in engineering are bound to ask, "What's in it for us, why should we have to go to so much trouble?" The real question should be, "Isn't it amazing that engineering did not provide the right kind of usable documentation to the other functions in the business in the past?" But this was not their fault, the informal system didn't require it. The people in engineering will also have to understand how to structure bills of material so that they can be used throughout the company.

4. <u>Performance</u> must be measured. The accuracy and usefulness of bills of material for the rest of

the organization will have to be measured before MRP is started. And after MRP is operating, it will have to be measured on a continuing basis. The methods for measuring bills of material accuracy will be discussed later in this book.

Today, we have an opportunity to really use professional tools like management by objectives to run a manufacturing business more effectively. But this is going to require a new set of objectives for people in the company, or the tools that the computer has made possible will be of little value.

Section 3
The Principles Applied to Inventory Accuracy

Stockroom inventory record accuracy will be discussed later in Chapter 10, but it is an excellent example of the application of the management principles discussed earlier in this chapter. In most companies, inventory records are not accurate. In fact, in some companies <u>management</u> doesn't even understand what inventory record accuracy <u>means</u>! When asked if their records are accurate, the reply is, "Sure, we took the annual physical and it came quite close!" That simply means that the pluses and the minuses canceled each other because they found as many as they lost. That is not the kind of accuracy that is acceptable if a formal system is to be used for scheduling.

The problem of data integrity has plagued companies trying to use computer systems since computers came along. Many solutions like the following have been proposed:

1.   One of the early books on computer systems lists "file clean up" as one of the steps in installing a system. Cleaning up the computer file is not the solution to the problem; the source of the problem isn't in the computer files, and the day after they have been "cleaned," they will get dirty again.

2.   One company added about a dozen people to their staff in a "data input control" group. These people took the input data and screened it to try to pick out any errors before they went into the computer system. This led one author to state as an axiom his belief that "file maintenance costs will significantly exceed original estimates."

3.   Some companies thought that the way to fix the inventory records was to take an annual physical. Most companies have taken an annual physical inventory once a year. None of them corrected the fundamental problems of record accuracy in the past, why should another one do it?

To solve a problem it must be understood, and the fundamental problem was that the shortage list did not require accurate inventory records. When a company operates with an informal system, the numbers don't have

to be right.   When it operates with a formal system, they
do have to be right.

One large manufacturing company with seven plant
locations and several stockrooms in many of the plants
achieved inventory record accuracy using this approach:

1.   They established the <u>objective</u> of 95 percent
     inventory record accuracy in each of their man-
     ufacturing locations. (The means for measuring
     this and the rationale for 95 percent will be
     explained in Chapter 10.)

2.   They established <u>line accountability</u> for meeting
     this objective.   The general manager made the
     vice president of manufacturing accountable, who
     in turn made each of his plant managers account-
     able.   They, in turn, made the materials manager
     accountable (since stores reports to him), and
     stores managers were made accountable for meet-
     ing this objective.

3.   Everyone concerned was educated so they would
     <u>understand</u> why this new objective was important
     to support the formal system.   When the on-hand
     inventory balance is incorrect, the net require-
     ments for every future time period will be incor-
     rect; and if these are exploded down through a
     bill of material, the lower level requirements will
     be incorrect!   They were also told <u>how</u> to achieve
     this objective.

4.   They were provided with the <u>tools</u> to do the job.
     A work simplification program was instituted to
     make it easier to handle transactions going in and
     out of the stockroom properly.   Forms were
     reduced from thirteen to three.   Each stores
     manager was given a "limited access stores" area.
     Without limited access, the stores manager cannot
     be held accountable for making sure that a trans-
     action takes place every time material is moved.

5.   Daily "cycle counts," discussed in Chapter 10,
     were instituted in every storeroom as a method of
     <u>performance measurement</u>.

6.   Performance against the inventory record accur-
     acy objective became an important part of the

merit review for each of the people accountable
for inventory record accuracy in this company.
This was how <u>incentives</u> were applied.

So MRP provides management with an opportunity to
use some more professional tools. But even before MRP is
operating, a more professional approach to a number of
fundamentals will have to be taken or the tools won't work
well enough for management to get the real benefit from
them

Section 4
The Missing Link in MBO

"Where should the stockroom report?" is a typical question from the inventory manager. He wants it to report to him because the plant manager doesn't care about accurate inventory records. And that is the problem, the plant manager doesn't care because no one has made the plant manager accountable for inventory record accuracy because it didn't matter in the past. Giving the proper person the proper objective is a far better answer than changing the organization chart.

One company has one machining division supplying three assembly divisions, and originally had the machining division reporting to the general manager of the largest assembly division. The other two general managers complained that he always got his parts but they didn't get theirs. Management put a new, independent manager in charge of the machining division to solve the problem, but he lasted just over a year before he was fired. They didn't have MRP, and with order launching and expediting, the three assembly managers could always blame any problem in getting shipments out the door on the fact that they didn't have the parts, and point to the big backlog of past due orders in the machining division. Another company with MRP has a plant manager for their machining facilities and a plant manager for assembly - and no finger-pointing. If the plant manager in the machining division hits his schedule, the assembly facility will hit theirs because the schedules are valid.

A classical question is, "Who is accountable for inventory?" The inventory manager says, "Not me, what if the sales forecast is wrong?" The sales manager says, "Not me, what if manufacturing doesn't make what we tell them we need?" The manufacturing manager says, "Not me, I only make what they tell me to make." When no one else can be held accountable, only the general manager can. When a valid planning and scheduling system exists, each member of the team has a plan to meet, and it becomes readily apparent who did not meet the plan when there is too much or too little inventory.

One company had a continuing squabble between the purchasing department, the inventory control department, the production control department, and the factory. They all blamed each other when schedules weren't met. Their solution was to put a materials manager in charge of production control, purchasing, inventory control, and the other materials-related functions. He reported at the same level as the plant manager for the brief period of time he spent in the job. When product didn't go out the door, the plant manager had no problem proving that the planning wasn't being done properly. And it wasn't! Because the materials manager didn't have the proper tools. Had that fundamental problem been addressed, there would have been no need to have changed the organization chart. Illustrating one more time the principle that:

WHEN PEOPLE JUGGLE THE ORGANIZATION CHART IN THE HOPES OF "OSMOTING" THE PROPER OBJECTIVES TO THE RIGHT PART OF THE COMPANY, THEY WILL NORMALLY EXCHANGE ONE SET OF PROBLEMS FOR ANOTHER.

Now that we have planning systems that can work so that performance can be measured and accountability can really be assigned, the emphasis in the future will, undoubtedly, be less on fiddling with the organization chart and more on setting the proper objectives.

Chapter 7
The CEO's New Priorities

Section 1
The Prime Responsibility

In the early days of computer systems, people liked to say that top management "support" was needed if the system was to succeed. But support implies that there are "good guys" and "bad guys," and that management must support the good guys against the bad guys. Moreover, support without understanding is a liability. The top manager who signs off on an MRP II systems project without understanding it is sure to question the system when the miracles don't happen, and is sure not to do the things to make the results really happen.

Then people said that management must be "involved." That turned top management off. They are already involved in more things than they can handle in most companies; and involvement isn't the real issue, the amount of extra time that's required of top management to implement an MRP system is really minimal. It's a case of doing the right things rather than putting in a lot of time.

The real issue is top management leadership. Without the leadership to establish and maintain a new set of values in an organization so that they can operate effectively with a formal system, a company will never achieve the potential of MRP. Any company attempting to install MRP without top management understanding and leadership would be well advised to stop.

What then does the CEO - the Chief Executive Officer - need to know if this type of system is going to work? What does the CEO need to know to enable the company to use these new tools to operate at a higher level of professionalism?

Undoubtedly, most important of all, the CEO needs to know that the CEO needs to know! MRP is not an extension of previous experience. It's a new set of tools for management. If management doesn't understand the tools, how to implement them, and how to use them, the company won't run differently even though the tools are available.

The CEO needs to recognize that MRP is not a data processing system. The responsibility for success cannot, under any circumstances, be delegated to the data processing and systems people. All they can do is provide the technical service to make the tools available. The results must come from management using the tools.

The following sections, then, summarize what the CEO needs to understand about:

1.   The problem.
2.   The solution.
3.   What the critical elements in MRP are.
4.   How MRP must be implemented.
5.   How to operate the business with the new tools.

Each of these subjects is covered in more depth within this book. The problem and the solution were discussed in Parts I and II of this book. The "critical elements," implementation, and operation are discussed in Part IV. This chapter is intended to put it all in one place in summary form to give the CEO the big picture and to provide a handy reference. The CEO's specific responsibilities are the subject of the opening chapter (#8) of Part III.

Section 2
Understanding the Problem

The CEO should understand that:

1. Scheduling is fundamental in managing a manufacturing company.

2. Before the computer came along, and even after the computer was available, most manufacturing companies did not do scheduling, they did "order launching and expediting."

3. Order launching and expediting creates a phoney backlog that generates false information about purchase commitments, machine loads, etc.

4. Lack of good scheduling information is at the root of the problems of inventories being too high, customer service not being high enough, and productivity being below what it should be throughout the typical manufacturing organization. The informal system results in finger-pointing instead of teamwork, "funny numbers" in the financial area, and the inability to establish real accountability in a manufacturing company.

5. The present system doesn't work. That's why people don't keep the numbers correct. And any advice that we "make the present system work before we put in a new system" is dangerously naive. Most inventory systems were designed to answer the question, "When to order?" when, in fact, in a manufacturing and distribution system the question, "When is the material really needed?" is crucial. When the formal system does not answer that question, the informal system - the shortage list - will. The challenge of MRP II is in teaching the people in the business to operate with a formal system rather than the informal systems they have used all their lives.

6. The CEO should expect that people do not diagnose the problem as a scheduling problem, nor do they typically understand the phoney backlog syndrome, and, consequently, they don't know how to address the problem.

Section 3
Understanding the Solution

The most important things for the CEO to know are:

1. MRP II is a simulation of a manufacturing busi-
    ness. The shortage list was made by asking,
    "What are we going to make, what does it take to
    make it, what do we have, what do we need to
    get?" That is exactly the logic of MRP. That's
    why MRP works. That why the question, "What
    are the other systems besides MRP?" is invalid.
    Any formal system that answers these questions is
    MRP. Any formal system that does not answer
    these questions will be supplemented by an infor-
    mal system that does. A manufacturing or distri-
    bution business cannot be run without answering
    the question, "What materials do we really need
    when?"

2. What the elements of closed loop MRP are. The
    CEO should understand the basic functions per-
    formed by the production plan, master schedule,
    material requirements plan, capacity requirements
    plan, the dispatch list, the vendor schedule, and
    the input/output report. These are all covered
    in Appendix 1. It isn't necessary for the CEO to
    understand all the details and mechanics behind
    these basic functions. It is necessary to know
    what reports generate what information.

3. MRP II is not just a production and inventory
    control system. In the past, because systems
    didn't work, there were many different systems.
    Today, we recognize that whether we express the
    universal manufacturing equation in units or in
    dollars, the system is the same. The production
    plan is in units, the business plan states the
    same thing in dollars. The material requirements
    plan is in units by item, but the format is the
    same as the controller uses for cash flow pro-
    jection. Once the operating system works and
    people can be taught to keep the numbers right -
    which they can if the system is useful to them
    and helps them do their job - then the financial
    numbers can be derived from the operating sys-

tem in a very straightforward manner. That - technically - is the foundation of Manufacturing Resource Planning: MRP II.

4.   The formal system for each company is not "unique" since the problems are not unique. The reasons many people think that systems have to be designed uniquely for each business is that the systems that they had in the past didn't work, and thus they all looked different. The systems that do work all look the same, since MRP II is a simulation of the universal manufacturing equation.

5.   MRP is not a computer system. Some people believe that if the lead times are correct, the economic order quantities are all right, the bills of material are correct, etc., we can push the button, have a computer print paper, and suddenly a manufacturing business will run differently. This, of course, is utter nonsense. If people in the factory, for example, don't work as hard using the new tools to prevent the shortages as they once worked to fix the shortages after they happened, MRP cannot possibly live up to its potential.

6.   Because MRP simply provides tools for people, there can be no accountability for the people to use the tools intelligently if they can't answer the question, "Why did the computer tell me to do that this time?" As a consequence, the basic principle for MRP systems, once they have met the fundamental criterion of being a valid simulation of reality, is:

MAKE THE LOGIC OBVIOUS TO THE USER.

Section 4
Understanding the Critical Elements in MRP II

The critical elements in MRP II can be broken into three fundamental categories:

1. Technical.
2. Basic data.
3. People.

The technical area is the computer program - the software - for doing MRP. The need for a standard system that is simple was discussed above and the CEO should be sure that the technical part of MRP doesn't become a technical "boondoggle," but is attacked like a business project, very methodically and expeditiously. Many companies get bogged down in this area and seem to suffer from "paralysis through analysis."

The material requirements plan determines what material is needed by taking the master schedule, and calculating requirements using a bill of material, and posting requirements against an inventory record. The capacity requirements plan takes the shop orders and planned order releases that come from the material requirements plan and uses this shop schedule with a routing file, to post requirements against a work center file to determine what capacity is needed.

The basic data elements of closed loop MRP are:

1. Master schedule.
2. Bills of material.
3. Inventory records.
4. Routings.
5. Work centers.

These are the elements of data that didn't have to be right in an informal system, and, consequently, are not correct in most companies. They must be correct to make a formal MRP system work properly.

The people, of course, will have to be educated to understand how to use a formal system. In a formal system, it's important to keep the numbers correct to generate valid schedules, and to develop an atmosphere of credibility and working together as a team.

The critical elements listed above, the technical, data and people elements, are what it takes to make MRP work. The CEO should know that this is a checklist he can use to diagnose MRP if there are ever problems with it. They have to be in the computer program itself, in the data area, or in the people area. These are the things that must be done to do MRP correctly; this is the complete list of things that people do wrong when MRP doesn't produce the results it should.

The CEO should also be constantly emphasizing the proper priorities. Most companies give the highest emphasis to the technical area because they think MRP is some kind of a computer system. The CEO should insist that the technical area and the data areas be done correctly, but that the bulk of the attention be put to the most critical area of all, the people area. The CEO should put a great deal of emphasis on education because that is particularly critical. Too often, education is looked upon as a "good thing." But that's not the case with MRP. It must be taken very seriously, and done very professionally because operating with a formal system is <u>not an extension of experience</u> for the people in the company.

The two most critical areas for the CEO to watch are top management and first line supervision. The top management has to provide the leadership in making this kind of system work so it can give them better information to plan and manage with. First line supervision is where the plans have to be executed. Not that other people don't have to be educated, but these are the most critical people of all, and it is the CEO's responsibility to be sure that they understand MRP in its elegant simplicity.

Section 5
Understanding How to Implement MRP II

There is a detailed implementation plan in Appendix 3, but here again, it is not essential that the CEO understand every step in implementation. It _is_ essential that the CEO understand:

1. The need to constantly re-emphasize the proper priorities for the critical elements. Most companies without proper direction will spend the bulk of their time trying to choose the best software and put the least effort into the most important area: the people.

2. Basic steps which include:

   a. First cut education for the key people - particularly the top managers in each functional area - who will be involved in the justification.

   b. Justification of MRP II based on specific results and committed to by the functional managers (discussed in Chapter 16).

   c. Appointment of a responsible project manager full time, a high level experienced person who knows the company, the products, and especially the people.

   d. Filling in the detailed implementation plan (mentioned above) for the specific company.

   e. A regular management review of the project to keep it on schedule, chaired by the CEO.

3. Project accountability. No implementation plan is valid without names on it, names of the people who are accountable for making things happen. If the stockroom, for example, reports to the plant manager, the accountability for achieving inventory record accuracy to support an MRP system rests with the plant manager.

   What if the MRP II effort doesn't produce results? What if it's just a waste of money?

There is no reason why it should be if it's done properly. The reason many fail to attain the potential results is that the CEO does not understand what has to be done. That's exactly the point: The <u>overall accountability</u> for success with MRP II <u>rests with the CEO</u>, and the <u>name of the CEO</u> should be at the <u>top of the project plan</u>.

4. The need for massive education. This is the key to success with MRP. There has never been a successful MRP user that said, "We educated too much," or an unsuccessful one that has not said, "We educated too little." (Education is discussed in detail in Chapter 18.)

5. That the system must be installed step by step and the conversion done using a "pilot" program (this is discussed in more detail in Chapter 17). While a tight time table is important to maintain enthusiasm, it's most important to do the job properly. The pilot program is the only responsible way to convert to an MRP program.

6. The key measures that must be watched even before a pilot program goes on the air. They are:

    a. Inventory record accuracy.
    b. Bill of material accuracy.
    c. Routing accuracy.

    If inventory records based on cycle counting are not at 95 percent, bills of material 98 percent, and routings at 95 percent plus, the implementation should be postponed until these records are right. There is <u>no way</u> that the <u>records will get better</u> after the system goes on the air. People simply won't use it if it doesn't give them the proper information. The informal system did not require accurate information. The formal system does, but the formal system will never be used by people if the numbers are not right at the very beginning.

7. The need to be sure that people understand <u>line accountability</u> for success. If the plant manager, for example, is sitting back waiting for someone in production control and systems to

make MRP work, MRP probably isn't going to work.

Section 6
Understanding How to Operate Using MRP II

Operating more professionally with MRP II involves:

1. Managing by objectives. Setting objectives, establishing accountability, educating people to understand what they need to do, giving them the tools to do the job, and measuring performance. This is the way inventory records will be made accurate, the way bills of material will be made correct, the way marketing will be made a part of the master scheduling function, the way production planning will be assigned the responsibility for making valid plans and measured for doing this. And the way manufacturing and purchasing will be measured for executing these plans.

2. Establishing and operating with new policies to execute the objectives. Policies that often didn't exist before. Policies on production planning, master scheduling, forecasting, and engineering change, for example. Chapter 19 discusses some of these policies in more detail.

3. Making effective plans. The CEO should get his top marketing, manufacturing, engineering, and financial managers together at least once a month to make the production plans. In this meeting, a course should be established for the company and conflicts resolved. The production plans drive the entire MRP II system. This is such a critical responsibility for the CEO that it will be the major subject for Chapter 8.

4. Making sure that the plans are <u>executed</u> vigorously. MRP doesn't solve problems, it simply tells people what the problems are far enough ahead so that they can solve them. The CEO should make sure that people aren't waiting for MRP to fix the problems that are <u>their</u> responsibility to fix.

5. Using the "handles" to manage. The primary handles are:

a. The production plan that sets the production rates for product families and thus controls overall inventory levels (or order backlog levels), production and purchasing rates, and, ultimately, cash flow.

b. The master schedule controls the mix within these overall rates.

c. The material requirements plan breaks that mix down into detailed schedules for components and raw materials.

d. The capacity requirements plan breaks that schedule down into capacity requirements in standard hours to meet the schedule.

e. The dispatch list is the shop schedule, specifying which items are to be worked on in each work center.

f. The vendor schedule does the same thing for the "outside factories."

g. The input/output report monitors output against the capacity plan.

6. Measuring performance. The critical performance measures are discussed in more detail in Chapter 19.

The CEO should know where to look to determine whether a problem is due to the wrong production rate, the wrong production mix, whether the shop is not generating the capacity to meet the plan, whether they're not working on the right items, etc.

The CEO should set a very high priority on using the formal system to manage. This means keeping numbers right, making valid plans, telling the system the truth so that it can portray the truth. The CEO should be constantly looking for signs of the informal system that are bound to appear if the formal system starts to deteriorate. The shortage list is a good indicator. If MRP is being managed properly, <u>there should not be a shortage list</u>.

The CEO has a stewardship, a responsibility for keeping the formal system operating properly. It would be tragic to have it deteriorate and require the work to install it to be done all over again.

The CEO should constantly emphasize what the system can do and what it cannot do. When the system presents information stating that the amount of capacity required is not available, that is not a fault of the system. That is simply a representation of a problem within the company. People are not used to working with a formal system for production planning, and they often tend to blame the system when everything doesn't go exactly the way they would like it to go. These same people wouldn't blame the accounting system if the system gave them bad news, and the CEO should set the example and develop a realistic understanding of these new tools. Part of the CEO's responsibility in keeping a formal system operating will be a continuing education program, not just to educate new people coming into the company, but to keep the experienced people operating at their best. A professional pilot regularly updates his education, not just to learn new things, but also to make sure that bad habits aren't developing. Keeping a company operating at a high level of professionalism with the tools made available by MRP II requires the same attitude toward education.

PART III
Managing all of the Resources of a Manufacturing Company More Productively

Chapter 8
The CEO's Role in MRP II

Section 1
"THE" Production Plan - We Had it and We Lost it

Alfred Sloan in his book, <u>My Years With General Motors</u>, (1) describes how General Motors' management learned many years ago about the significance of the production plan. The depression during the early 1920's found General Motors - a very young company then - with inventories out of control. Reading Sloan, a few important messages come through:

1. The reason finished goods inventories get too high is that a company makes more than it sells.

2. The reason component inventories get too high is that a company purchases and manufactures more components than it uses in production.

3. The production plan that establishes the product family production rate is the basic control on finished goods inventory (and, as a consequence, customer service), component inventory, and leveling manufacturing production rates. Since the production plan determines how much labor and material will be purchased, it is a major control on cash flow.

4. The top executive in a manufacturing company <u>must</u> sign off on the production plan since that is management's most basic control of a manufacturing business.

The production plan is such a basic tool, why didn't every executive in every manufacturing company recognize its importance? Perhaps the term "production planning" sounds like something that production control people should be doing; it obscures the fact that the production plan is management's primary handle on operating a manufacturing business. Then, too, the concept was easy, but implementation was difficult. Before MRP, for all practical purposes, there was no direct connection between the production plan and the more detailed - usually informal - plans used throughout the rest of the company. Perhaps the fact that it was so fundamental was part of the problem in gaining universal acceptance and application of the production plan - we seem to have a natural aversion for "blocking and tackling."

For a while, we got sidetracked into believing that inventories would be managed by the "scientific" calculation of economic order quantities and safety stocks. Somehow people got distracted from fundamentals. One company did a very professional job of reviewing their lot sizes. They compared the current lot size inventory with the inventory that would result from the proposed new manufacturing lot sizes. They compared the total set up hours for the current lot sizes with the set up hours that would result from the planned lot sizes (a far more effective approach than most people tend to use where they calculate each lot size with consummate faith that the resulting total will somehow be desirable). After the new lot sizes were implemented, the corporate auditors verified that this lot size calculation helped to reduce inventory. Later they learned that the factory had gone on a four-day week for several weeks. Their reaction was, "It was the production cut back that reduced inventory, not the lot size calculation after all!" Somehow they felt that there was some trickery involved! No one ever told them that new lot sizes will only indicate the new level of inventory that the company can operate with. In order to reduce inventory to that level - assuming that it is a lower level - less inventory will have to be made or purchased than is sold or consumed! No mathematical calculations by themselves will make this happen.

Perhaps Alfred Sloan also should have said, "The way work-in-process can be reduced is to put less in than is taken out." This simple fundamental concept was also lost in the naive sophistication of the early years of the computer age. Sophisticated priority schemes and load leveling techniques were claimed to reduce work-in-process and reduce lead time. In fact, this only happened when these techniques were used in conjunction with capacity planning approaches that helped to increase output. Increasing the output to a higher level than the input reduced work-in-process, and this reduced lead time.

Because so called "inventory management" techniques received so much attention, it was often assumed that the inventory management system should simply "trigger" orders into the factory, and that the factory could then be loaded to "infinite capacity." Many companies took the approach that the factory should be "treated like a vendor" and little attention was paid to real production planning.

Even MRP was originally discussed without much attention to the need for a master schedule. Many of the books and manuals on MRP today either ignore the need for a production plan or confuse the production plan with the master schedule.

Since management didn't have any real way to control inventories, they resorted to brute force methods in many instances. Inventory was reduced by edict - and, of course, customer service soon suffered. Some managers insisted on signing requisitions for all purchases over a few hundred dollars. Companies in desperate straits used the ultimate brute force method of cutting off all incoming receiving in a desperate effort to avoid a cash crisis!

That is not to say that some companies didn't do a good job of production planning. A number of them did. But their formal system couldn't translate management's plans into the detailed plans that the factory and purchasing would use in their day-to-day operation.

Today, because the tools <u>are</u> available, management in a manufacturing company has a way to keep from "making more than they sell." But now that these tools are available, it's important to emphasize Sloan's message: The <u>production plan</u> is the <u>responsibility</u> of the <u>chief executive officer</u> of the company.

Section 2
Managing the Production Plan

The production plan states a production rate, usually in terms of units, but sometimes in terms of dollars, pounds, or some other general measure. The purpose of the production plan is to give management a broad planning handle that is more relevant than simply planning in dollars, but that shows the big picture far better than planning by part number. Production plans are typically made by product families such as "all model 30 pumps." That product family might have many different sizes and configurations of pumps within it. The schedule for producing the different sizes and configurations is the master schedule itself.

The production plan is usually made over a one to two year horizon. It is typically broken down into monthly increments. In some companies, particularly where they have to control inventories to keep them very close to the target at the inventory low point (at the end of a peak selling season), they will break the production plans down into weekly increments during this period.

The plan is made by taking the current inventory for a make-to-stock product, or backlog for a make-to-order product; planning any desired change in the inventory or backlog at the end of the planning period; and establishing the production rate by adding or subtracting this from the sales rate. The production rate thus equals the sales rate, plus or minus the planned change in inventory or backlog.

Figure 8-1 shows the typical production plan for the month ending 3/31.

Month Ending		Sales (thousands)	Production (thousands)	Inventory (thousands)
3/31	Plan			
	Actual			60
4/30	Plan	30	35	65
	Actual	25	36	71
6/30	Plan	30	35	75
	Actual			

Figure 8 - 1.   The Production Plan

There are 60,000 units of this product in inventory. The plan calls for increasing that to 75,000 units ahead of the peak selling season. That increase of 15,000 units over a 3 month planning period will require monthly production to be 5,000 units higher than the planned sales rate.

The actual sales, production, and resulting inventory are monitored in the production plan. Many companies would also show cumulative sales and production to date, as well as a pre-established tolerance for inventory or backlog that indicated when the production rate would have to be changed.

The production plan is the "regulator." It regulates the amount of inventory or backlog that will exist by controlling the production rate. It regulates the amount of material that will be made and purchased because the master schedules, the material requirements plans, and the capacity plans are all derived from it. It regulates the level of work-in-process because it drives the master schedules and material requirements plans that release work into the factory, as well as the capacity plans that control the level of output from the factory. Because it is the regulator for all of these activities, it regulates cash flow and is the foundation for the business plan.

Since the master schedules are derived from the production plans, the totals in the master schedules must equal the totals in the production plans. In this way, the production plans act as a control on master scheduling.

One of the advantages of the production planning exercise is that it brings choices into sharp focus for management. One company made sophisticated, mechanical doors for commercial buildings. Their sales were quite seasonal because these doors would normally have to be put on before winter weather came. Inevitably, they would be concerned about the amount of inventory they had in the spring and cut back production, only to increase it by working overtime in the fall. Every year they had problems delivering their product during the peak season.

When they introduced production planning, management could see the amount of inventory that had to be built. It was more than they planned to budget for, but if they had any hope of hitting a level production rate and retaining their skilled workers, they had to get the funds to build this inventory.

Changing production levels was certainly one of the alternatives at this company, but it's important to remember that the amount of capacity that a company has available doesn't always permit this. A level production rate throughout the year requires the lowest level of capacity. If production is cut back below the sales rate during one part of the year, it will have to be increased so that it is greater than the sales rate at another part of the year. There's nothing wrong with doing this as long as the consequences are recognized in advance.

Sometimes the most obvious problems are lurking around the corner, but for lack of a formalized production planning function, management finds out about them too late. One company making a highly profitable line of valves was producing 90 units per month, and had about 45 units in inventory. Because it was a fairly limited product line with most of the activity in a few items, this inventory level was considered to be just satisfactory. The sales rate, however, was running at 120 units per month. When a production plan was made for the general manager showing 30 units less being produced each month than were being sold, it became obvious that there would be a negative inventory balance within two months and a serious customer service problem following that. The general manager wanted to know why production couldn't be increased above 90 units per month, and the answer was that purchased parts couldn't be obtained.

This is the classic kind of dilemma that the production plan poses. Production planning highlights the "other decision" inherent in decisions that are being made. When manufacturing decided that they could only make 90 valves a month, the "other decision" was that there would soon be a customer service problem. Since this product line represented a major contribution to profits, there would also be a profit problem if valves could not be shipped. Finding out about this ahead of time, the general manager can put some extra effort into trying to solve the purchased parts problem as quickly as possible. Given enough time, it undoubtedly can be solved, and the production plan helps to focus his attention on the problem in advance. But there are plenty of real world problems that can't be solved immediately. What if production cannot be increased above the 90 unit per month level for several months? Another option is to have a marketing program on another profitable product to make up for what will be lost when valves can't be shipped. The very least the general manager will be able to do is tell his superiors ahead of time that he will not be able to meet the profit plan if that is the ultimate outcome of his efforts. Telling them in advance, rather than making excuses afterwards, is certainly a better choice.

Another company had a very optimistic sales department. Even though current sales to date hadn't met the forecast, they were in the habit of telling management that some good luck was just around the corner and that they would meet the forecast with a sudden surge in sales. The production people who listened to this and saw management eager to accept the good news finally laid out some production plans to show the consequences of planning production to meet an over optimistic sales forecast. If the forecast didn't materialize, a large inventory build-up would result. Management certainly never sanctioned the large inventory consciously, but by accepting the sales forecast, they actually did. This is another classic example of the "other decision."

Production planning can provide a better control than people often get when they use backlogs as a measure of the business level, rather than monitoring demand against a production plan. In one highly integrated company where one division makes a product that is processed by a second division, and ultimately goes to a third division, they had this problem regularly. Somebody in the first division would quote a longer lead time. The second division would then place orders sooner and this forced the third division to do the same thing. When management heard that the backlog had increased from 6 months to 18 months, they thought that there were serious problems. When production plans were made to illustrate the production rates required at each division, it was obvious that the problems were paper problems caused by the lead time syndrome, not by a real increase in business.

A good example of a most critical application of the production plan is during the start-up period for MRP. One of the first results that should come from installing MRP is an inventory reduction because MRP does a better job of matching up needed components and helping people to get the right material at the right time. The only way inventory can be reduced is to make and purchase less than is being consumed. Production plans for supplying plants and major vendors should be made to show their planned rates of production during this initial start-up period. It could represent a dramatic drop in their production rates that could be disastrous. Looking at the problem this way, management can decide whether or not they want to prolong the time for the inventory reduction in order to keep the vendor or supplying plant from running out of work for a short period of time.

The important issue is that production planning gives management a highly visible control. A company shouldn't assume that MRP, left alone, will always give the most desirable results. ("Correct" individual decisions don't necessarily generate a desirable total effect!) When production plans are used properly, they can allow management to make sure that they are running MRP, rather than having MRP run them.

The monthly production meeting is the critical element in developing the production plans. This is where the CEO has to take an active role. The production plan should not simply be made and sent around for people to initial and "OK." At this meeting (chaired by the CEO), marketing, manufacturing, finance, and engineering should discuss the alternatives, discuss the problems, and often make tough, unpleasant choices. The objective of this meeting isn't necessarily harmony, but consensus in setting a course for operating the business.

The following quote discusses production planning at Wright Line: (2)

"The key to their success is a monthly production meeting which brings together top and middle management including the vice-president of marketing with his distribution and forecasting people, the vice-president of manufacturing with his production planning people, and the vice-president of finance with his key people.

"In our meetings (says the president), we receive inputs from all members of the team. All discussions take place in that one meeting so we all agree on one production plan and stick to it. Therefore, we avoid the many little meetings, and spend a lot less time hand-wringing and second guessing our plan.

"MRP is a whole new way to run the business. It helps us meet our primary goals of good customer service, minimum investment in inventory, few layoffs, and an efficient, low cost operation."

The CEO has to establish the policies for production planning (discussed in the next section of this chapter) and master scheduling (discussed in Chapter 9). These policies will cover such things as the "time fences" within which changes are very difficult and expensive to make. They should cover the interaction among marketing, engineering, manufacturing, and finance in resolving daily issues. Most of these issues, of course, should be resolved at lower levels and the CEO should only become involved when there are problems that can't be solved at those levels. These are the difficult ones - by definition - and this is where the CEO needs to be a "bullet biter." MRP II doesn't hide the difficult choices, it brings them to the surface. It allows the CEO to make decisions knowing their impact. And the CEO should recognize that if people want to make the master schedule a wish list, what the consequences will be. The master schedule will accept anything, even something that's unrealistic. And the result inevitably will be for the formal system to break down, the company to ship less and to have more mismatched components.

The CEO needs to understand the importance of trade offs and to understand that there are times when he simply must say "no." Above all, he must emphasize to his people that they are not to blame the system for the realities of running a manufacturing business, but to recognize that all the system does is portray the limitations of the company.

Section 3
Establishing Production Planning Policy

The production planning policy should state:

1. The objectives of production planning. To set rates of production to control inventories and sales order backlog while meeting customer service requirements, and operating the manufacturing facilities as efficiently and at as level a rate as possible.

2. Who is accountable for the inputs and the sign off on the production plan, and the frequency and detail of these inputs from marketing, manufacturing, engineering, and finance. Most companies would have a production planning meeting at least monthly involving the vice presidents of manufacturing, marketing, finance, and engineering.

3. How far out the planning horizon extends. A typical company would specify in their policy, for example, that the planning horizon was a rolling 12 to 24 months, with a new month added as the old month was dropped, and the intervening months reviewed.

4. Where the planning "time fences" are. There comes a time when the commitment to production has been made, and any dramatic changes will be extremely expensive. This time fence could be one month, two months, or three months into the future; and the policy should state what the impact of changes within these time fences will be in such terms as, "a change within the sixty-day time fence will mean that twenty percent of the material commitments have already been made. A dramatic increase in production rates will be difficult to establish unless there has previously been a layoff and there are employees waiting for recall. These items should be checked."

5. The frequency of the review period. Typically, the production plan would be reviewed monthly, or more frequently if sales were not materializing against the plan.

6.   The categories of product families for production planning. Production plans should be made in units, pounds, or even in standard hours (standard hours by work center would be the normal way to express the production plan for a screw machine shop, for example), not just in dollars, although the units will be converted to dollars for the business plan. The objective is to pick product families smaller than total dollars (although dollars for a product family could be a valid planning unit in many instances), and larger than individual units that fall into relevant groups that can be used by management to express policy.

7.   The responsibility for the forecast input. This must come from marketing.

8.   Inventory guidelines as to how much inventory or order backlog would normally be expected to be maintained.

Once a closed loop MRP or MRP II system is functional, the system operates "in lock step." All of the detailed plans result from the production plans because that's where everything starts. The production plan is top management's powerful handle on the MRP system.

Section 4
Teamwork with a New Dimension

A college professor posed the issue, "We hear about Toyota getting better than 25 inventory turns a year and striving for even more. Does American industry need to put more emphasis on inventory turnover?"

A good question. But the real issue is far larger. Why <u>do</u> the Japanese achieve phenomenal inventory turnover rates? Here are a few reasons:

1. Every Honda Accord comes equipped with a radio, and rear window wiper and defogger. Air conditioning is a dealer installed option. Product variety for Japanese cars is much more limited than in the United States. That makes a major contribution to inventory turnover.

2. A stamping line that takes 8 hours to change over in a U.S. company has an equivalent in a Japanese company. Their changeover time is <u>45 minutes</u>! The machines were designed not just for high production, but also for quick changeover.

3. Workers, in many Japanese companies, order their own replenishment parts from supplying departments and recognize the objective of "just in time" delivery to keep inventory turnover high. The attitude is that inventory on the factory floor hides problems and inefficiencies.

In most American companies, the marketing, production planners, machine designers, and factory workers assume inventory management is someone else's problem. Production control, accounting, and engineering believe that quality control is someone else's problem. Methods people, computer programmers, and telephone operators often think that customer service is primarily a club that the sales people use when their commission checks are not as high as they'd like them to be. The typical American company would probably address the problem of productivity by establishing a new staff function. The Japanese company makes it <u>everyone's concern</u> and that is one of the keys to their success.

If you listened to a real expert on inventory management he would say, "Start with top management, and then
get everybody involved." Someone who really understands
quality control would say you must, "Start with top management and then get everybody involved." So the Japanese
approach isn't entirely unknown in the United States, even
though it isn't applied as well as it should be.

But there is more to it. They don't just have a
project to control inventories at one time, another project to
focus attention on cost reduction, and another project to
highlight quality control. All of these go on simultaneously. All of these objectives of the business are the objectives of all of the employees of the business at all times.

We've heard "teamwork" so much that we get tired of
the word. But this is teamwork with a new dimension.
This is the kind of teamwork that isn't just sloganeering.
It is a better, more productive way to manage.

Americans have a real problem with teamwork - perhaps that's why we seem to need to use the term so much.
Americans are individuals, not team players. And there is
a specific reason for this, it isn't something the Japanese
have inherited, it is something they teach their children
from the time they first start school: the individual must
be subordinate to the group. The objectives of the group
are all important. Everyone must work together to achieve
these objectives. This is a conscious, studied, posture
that the Japanese adopted after World War II to help themselves to emerge from the depths of a catastrophic defeat.

We must understand this: the "state of equilibrium"
for Japanese people is to work together effectively as a
group. The state of equilibrium for Americans is to pull
apart into smaller, parochial groups that compete against
each other. Management must recognize this because breaking down the walls, getting rid of our attitude that quality,
for example, is the concern only of the "specialist" is
fundamental if we are to get the kind of results we can
from harnessing American energy, creativeness, and ingenuity to work together more effectively. And this requires a
constant, conscious effort in leadership. The minute the
pressure is off, Americans are bound to return to their own
little "compartments"; that is their state of equilibrium.

The American approach to building a wall around every
department and function has been counterproductive. When

looked at in perspective, it is illogical and indefensible. Some managers believe there is something stimulating about having departments compete against each other; this is true. But the competition must be for the same, not for different, objectives.

Today, because we are beginning to recognize the importance of manufacturing in our manufacturing economy, there is some discussion about the problems that have been generated by CEOs who were primarily marketing and financial people. The conclusion of some of these articles and talks is that a company would be far better off with someone from manufacturing running it. There is no question that the CEO of a manufacturing business needs to understand the fundamentals of running operations. But this doesn't necessarily require a manufacturing background. In fact, background isn't the issue. If we replace an executive suffering from marketing or financial myopia with another one who has manufacturing myopia, nothing will have been accomplished. If we are to attain our potential in our manufacturing companies, we must have CEOs that understand running a manufacturing business in all of its facets, and know how to provide the leadership to get everyone in the company working toward the best overall interests of the company.

The opportunities that MRP II present for the CEO are virtually limitless. But, undoubtedly, the greatest opportunity of all will come from using the tools that make it possible to have a better game plan as a keystone in an overall effort at developing a new American attitude toward working together. Because that, after all, is Japan's real secret weapon.

Footnotes

1. Alfred Sloan, <u>My Years with General Motors</u>, (Garden City, NY: Anchor Books, Doubleday and Company, Inc., 1972), Chapter 8.

2. "Productivity: Out of MRP a New Game Plan," <u>Modern Materials Handling</u>, January 6, 1981.

Chapter 9
MRP II in Marketing

Section 1
The Role of Marketing in MRP II

Tragically, in far too many companies, MRP has been installed as a production and inventory control technique, not as a whole company system. In companies that have taken this attitude, marketing thinks of MRP as "their system," not "our system."

In other companies, marketing steps up to their responsibility for making a forecast as input to MRP, but it all ends there. They do little to sit with the manufacturing people and actually work out production plans and some of the details of the master schedules. (1)

Now, there is a company game plan. Overall plans can be translated very precisely into detailed plans at the factory and vendor levels for both material and capacity. Now, marketing and manufacturing have an opportunity to work together like they never could before. As one executive in a company using MRP put it, "We no longer have an adversary relationship. It's no longer a question of where are we going and where are _they_ going. Now, we decide where we are going together." The same executive indicated that the _amount of contact_ between manufacturing and marketing had decreased since they installed MRP. But the _quality_ had improved dramatically over the irate kind of communication that used to be commonplace when there wasn't a game plan they both agreed to. At the lower levels, the communication between the product managers and the production control people had increased.

In one company that has used MRP to coordinate marketing and manufacturing's activities very well, they operate this way:

1. Twice a week there is a scheduled meeting between the product marketing people and the production planners. At that time, individual customer orders may have to be moved in or out. The master schedule may have to be revised.

2. There is a monthly meeting between area sales managers and the plant manager to review the master schedules and update the forecasts.

3.   There is a monthly production planning meeting which the CEO runs with his top marketing, manufacturing, financial, and engineering vice presidents. Changes in product mix, sales trends, competitive situations and the like are discussed, and issues are resolved by the CEO.   This is the overall planning by product families that updates the production plans. The master schedules are derived from these plans.

The key here is regularly scheduled communication to keep the master schedule up to date and in line with the latest field requirements. The master schedule is the primary tool that marketing and manufacturing will use to work together.

Companies that are really making MRP II work find that it can be a major marketing tool.   When people in marketing know what manufacturing is producing and are communicating with them regularly, more of the right items get made and shipped to the customer.

Section 2
The Master Schedule

The master scheduling policy for one company started with the statement, "The master schedule is the property of manufacturing because it specifies what will be produced." But wouldn't it be just as realistic to say, "The master schedule is the property of marketing because it specifies what will be made for the <u>customers</u>"? There is no reason why the marketing department could not do the actual master scheduling. They would then be accountable for the inventory investment; for providing plans that would enable manufacturing to run the factory efficiently, and at a level rate; and for keeping the master schedule "doable."

In practice, of course, master scheduling will most likely be a function within the manufacturing department. This is primarily because of tradition. But there is also a practical reason: the feedback in a closed loop system about what is actually going on with the vendors and the factory is more readily accessible to the manufacturing department as part of their normal routine operation. Nevertheless, the master schedule has been included in the marketing chapter in this book to emphasize its significance as a tool for marketing and their role in making it and using it effectively.

The master schedule is a statement of what will be produced. Understanding what a master schedule <u>is not</u> is a good first step in understanding what master scheduling really <u>is</u>. A master schedule <u>is not</u>:

1.   <u>A sales forecast</u>. A sales forecast doesn't take into account the objective of leveling plant pro-duction. Nor does it represent what is doable based on the availability of material and capacity, the desirability of sequencing jobs for manufac-turing efficiency, etc. The sales forecast is raw input to the production plan in terms of product families, and to the master schedule in terms of forecasts for finished goods items for a make-to-stock product or the master scheduling modules that would be used for most make-to-order products.

2   <u>A production plan</u>. The production plan establishes production rates for product families. The master schedule is derived from the production plan and is a specific statement of the end items or product modules that will be required. (The different types of master schedules for different types of products were discussed in Section 6 of Chapter 3.)

3   <u>An assembly schedule</u>. The master schedule and the assembly schedule could be the same for a make-to-stock product and for a few make-to-order products where the end item can be defined before the customer order is received. For an assembled-to-order product, the assembly schedule is different from the master schedule. The assembly schedule specifies the final configuration of the product rather than the modules that are in the master schedule.

4.   <u>An automatic creation of some computer decision rules</u>. Some theoreticians have suggested that the sales forecast, the actual sales, the cost of production, the cost of overtime, the cost of inventory, the cost of lost sales, etc., could be fed into a computer algorithm that would create an "optimized" master schedule automatically! In the real world, master scheduling involves too many decisions from people to make this practical. Decisions concerning things like: How important is that order? How will people in the factory feel about working overtime again this week? What other ways can we bring our ingenuity to bear to get the job done? The master schedule requires good management. And good management cannot be programmed into a computer. Those who try to do it "automatically" will automatically destroy the accountability for the master schedule. The computer can help by signaling when actual sales are not materializing according to forecast and give the master scheduler rescheduling messages. But at all times, the responsibility for the master schedule has to rest with the people. There is no way to delegate anything this important to a computer.

5.   <u>A wish list</u>. The master schedule cannot have "past due" items in it because this will generate

"past due" component schedules. It cannot have more in it that can actually be produced. It cannot show items in time periods when they cannot be produced for various reasons such as purchased material shortages, engineering problems, etc. Any of these abuses will result in distorted priorities and destroy the ability of the formal priority planning system to generate valid schedules.

Keeping the master schedule realistic is one of the real challenges in running MRP. One company installed MRP very quickly. Their major division had put it in successfully many years before and they sent some systems people to a smaller division to put in MRP. After it had been operating for a few months, the inventory was increasing, customer service was no better than before (if anything, it was somewhat worse), and expediting was still the real scheduling technique. Diagnosing the problem was quite straightforward. The foremen had a schedule generated by the computer which showed virtually every job in the factory "past due." It was clean and untouched. The foremen also had a shortage list in their back pockets. This was the real schedule.

A check of the stockroom showed that material was being accumulated for production in order to generate shortage lists. A check of the master schedule showed that there were 49,000 units past due and due in the current month, when the previous month's production had been 9,000 units and the month before that was 9,500! Inventory was going up because most of the parts for all of the products were being brought in. But the shortage list was still the scheduling technique because seldom did they have all of the parts for any of the products. The solution was to reduce the master schedule to the maximum number of units that they felt could actually be produced based on getting material in from vendors, producing components in manufacturing, etc. Then the master schedule was increased gradually to keep it ambitious, yet attainable. The theory in the past had been, "We have no capacity limitation in assembly. Our only limitation is component availability." But putting out a master schedule that requires all of the components to be brought in immediately is totally unrealistic. And in a manufacturing company, the day the formal system is mismanaged and cannot answer the question, "What material is really needed and when is it needed?", the informal system, the shortage list, will inevitably appear.

Some production control managers don't like to move an item to a later date in the master schedule even though it actually can't be built when it was supposed to be. Their thinking is, "If I don't keep the pressure on for the other components, one of them won't be available later when the missing component comes in." But that kind of thinking is wrong. In Figure 9-1, Job A was originally scheduled to be built in week 3. One of its components failed to pass receiving inspection and was sent back to the vendor who had some serious problems involving reworking tooling which meant that he couldn't possibly get more material back to the customer before week 7. In order to keep people working and ship the dollars required to meet the company budgets, Job B was moved from week 6 to week 4. But Job A was not moved to week 7. The people in purchasing were working hard to bring in the components for Job A even though one critical component, without which the job could not possibly be built, tested and shipped, couldn't be available until week 7. Because they worked on Job A, they didn't get the parts in for Job B. Priorities are relative. Components can't be brought in before they're needed because they will be brought in instead of other components that are really needed.

WEEK 1	WEEK 2	WEEK 3	WEEK 4	WEEK 5	WEEK 6	WEEK 7	WEEK 8
		JOB A			JOB B		

Figure 9 - 1. Revising the Master Schedule

Perhaps one of the most serious psychological hurdles to overcome is exactly that concept of "keeping the pressure on." Production control and marketing people don't want to "let the factory off the hook" when they haven't been able to produce at the planned rate. This is why they want to show a big backlog in the master schedule. They feel that rescheduling that backlog merely lets the factory "reschedule themselves out of trouble." But unfortunately, big "past due" backlogs confuse priorities just when it is most critical to make the right things.

The distinction must be made between having a plan to measure performance against versus having a plan to operate with. Fairly standard procedure in most MRP systems is to "take a snapshot" of the master schedule for a given month item by item, and then monitor actual performance against the plan. The plan that is being measured against <u>cannot be changed</u>; the plan that is being used to run operations <u>must be changed</u> to keep it realistic.

Nevertheless, it's important to emphasize that the objective is to make the master schedule happen. A great deal has been said about the rescheduling capability of MRP, and while that is truly one of its strong points, it has been overemphasized. Many Class A and B MRP users <u>hit their master schedule 100 percent</u> most of the time. They don't have to change it. They <u>change lower level schedules</u> to enable them to do this.

So the objective is to make the master schedule happen. But if this really can't be done, the master schedule must be revised to keep it realistic.

The master scheduling process includes the following functions:

1.   Making the master schedule.

2.   Updating the master schedule because of "top down" changes such as the sales not meeting the forecast for a given item.

3.   Order entry - when the customer's order consumes inventory in a make-to-stock situation or the master schedule in a make-to-order situation.

4.   Customer delivery promising.

5.   Doing simulations to answer the "what if" questions.

6.   Updating the master schedule because of bottom up changes like machine breakdowns, vendor delivery problems, etc.

7.   Relieving the master schedule by issuing assembly orders, for example.

<u>Making the master schedule</u> involves breaking the production plan down into specific units. For a make-to-order product such as pumps, the master schedule might indicate that one thousand model 30 pumps will be made each week. Using a planning bill of material that states the

percentage of each option that is normally expected to be ordered (the planning bill of material is discussed in Chapter 13, Section 3), the production rate in the production plan is broken down into the number of specific sets of components for the master schedule. Similarly, in a make-to-stock situation, the item forecasts that are used in the master schedule and the product family forecasts that are used in the production plan, must be reconciled. (This is discussed in the forecasting section of this chapter.)

The master schedule is made once when MRP is started, then each week or month, a new increment is added. If the planning horizon, for example, is twelve months, each month a new month will be added.

The production plan is usually stated in monthly periods. These must be converted into weeks or days in the master schedule since it generates priority plans which must be stated in weeks or days.

Updating the master schedule because of top down changes means changing it when forecasts change and monitoring it regularly to make sure that sales are materializing as forecast. If, for example, the planning bill of material called for ten percent of the electric motors for a product to be 230 volt motors, and the actual sales were less, the master schedule would have to be revised.

Order entry must be done in terms that are compatible with the master schedule. If a forklift truck is being manufactured and the master schedule modules are engines, transmission, masts, hydraulics, etc., the customer order must be entered in terms of the specific engine, transmission, mast, and hydraulics required. Each of these major modules of the product is then reviewed against the master schedule to make sure material is "available to promise."

The customer promise is made by matching up the modules in the customer order with availability in the master schedule. Figure 9-2 shows a simplified master schedule. It shows the actual master schedule (MPS), the actual demand - these are customer orders posted against the master schedule - and the amount left available for future orders, the "available to promise." Availability for one component could be several weeks earlier than availability for another. It is the latest component that will determine the week into which the actual customer order is promised, unless there is a way to get the other components at an earlier date. If necessary, because of the urgency of a particular customer's order, other orders could be moved out or additional capacity and material that were not in the original plan could be obtained by working overtime, expediting, etc. Any requests for reschedules by a customer can be reviewed in the master schedule to see if they are feasible. No longer is it just a case of moving one customer order up without looking at the consequences. No customer order can be made earlier than planned if the master schedule is full, and no additional material and capacity is available, unless something else is moved out.

Master Production Schedule
Engines

	Week							
	1	2	3	4	5	6	7	8
Master Schedule	80	0	100	0	0	120	0	120
Actual Demand	40	40	30	30	30	40	40	20
Available to Promise	0	0	10	0	0	40	0	100

Figure 9 - 2. The Master Schedule

Simulation is one of the very useful tools of a modern MRP system. "What if we wanted to make 20 extra model F forklift trucks per month?" The MRP system could be used to determine the additional material and capacity that would be required. People would then have to determine when this additional material and capacity could be made available. With MRP, they can answer the "what if" question rationally rather than by guessing.

Execution problems may require updating the master schedule from the bottom up. There are times when a component is scrapped and a replacement order has to be run in the factory. The dispatcher will relay this information to the material planner who will then contact the master scheduler if there's any question about the ability of the factory to replace this material and meet the original required date. The urgency of the requirement, how close it is to the current time period, and many other considerations will influence the decision made by the planner and master scheduler about the scrap replacement order. If it is urgent enough, the order will be expedited to try to get it through by the original required date, especially if it means meeting the current master schedule commitment. It must be remembered, however, that expediting one job means rescheduling another to a later date unless additional capacity and/or material is available.

The master schedule is normally relieved when the units in the master schedule move into the current time period. At that point, an assembly order will be issued, material will be picked from the stockroom, and sent to the assembly department. The units are now removed from the master schedule because the component requirements have been satisfied.

It's important to recognize that the material requirements plan is merely a simulation of the shortage list. It determines what material is needed at the stockroom door. One company, for example, put in an MRP system and had trouble immediately. They used the assembly schedule shown in Figure 9-3 as their master schedule indicating that they would be making two units in week 5, three in week 6, three in week 7, and two in week 8.

Assembly Schedule — Model 71-E

Week 5	Week 6	Week 7	Week 8
2	3	3	2

Stockroom Pulls

	Week 4	Week 5	Week 6	Week 7	Week 8
Batch Assembly	10				
Final Assembly		2	3	3	2

Figure 9 - 3. Simulating the Shortage List

When MRP works, it's a simulation of the shortage list, which can eliminate the shortage list. When it doesn't work, checking the shortage list and identifying the discrepancies can point to the problem. The shortage list in this company showed that 10 sets of parts were being pulled out of the stockroom in week 4 rather than as shown in the assembly schedule. This company makes labeling machines and they make 10 units in "batch assembly" and then final assemble them to the customer specifications.

Their mistake was to use the final assembly schedule as the master schedule. When the master schedule was changed to show 10 sets of common parts required in week 4 and unique parts to meet the customer specification required as shown in the assembly schedule (Figure 9-3), MRP worked properly.

One of the key people who will be a go-between for marketing and manufacturing is the master scheduler. The master scheduler usually reports directly to the materials manager, production control manager, manager of planning, or it could be the marketing manager. The job of the master scheduler is working with others in the organization to reconcile what we would like to do with what can be done.

A good master scheduler doesn't have to be Superman. Master scheduling policy, discussed in the next section of this chapter, will spell out the responsibilities of various people in creating, maintaining and making changes to the master schedule - it doesn't all fall on the master scheduler. Nevertheless, this person is in a key position and should have good knowledge of the factory and what can be done as well as knowledge of the problems sales people face in the field.

During the installation phase of MRP, it would be a good idea to give the master scheduler some additional training. If the master scheduler has come out of the factory, it would be advisable to have this person travel with some of the sales people making customer calls, learning about problems in the field. On the other hand, if the master scheduler is from sales or marketing, it would be a good idea to put this person in the factory working with foremen to find out what the real problems of the factory are. The "master scheduler" has been discussed here as if it would be one individual, and it may well be in many companies. There are other companies where master scheduling will require several people.

Whether marketing makes the master schedule, and whether the master scheduler reports to marketing, is not particularly important. The important issue is that marketing and manufacturing recognize that they must work together to do the best job for the customers and for their company.

Section 3
Master Scheduling Policy

One company that has been highly successful with MRP says, "Marketing buys the inventory once it is made." Many manufacturing people think that because this company's marketing people have to "buy the inventory" it is "just punishment" when they don't do a good job of forecasting! But that is simplistic. Yes, marketing does own the inventory. But marketing and manufacturing work together in this company to make a master schedule that will meet three of the primary objectives in operating a manufacturing business:

1. Customer service.
2. Maintaining control over the inventory investment.
3. Running the plant efficiently.

Obviously, one of the objectives in running the plant efficiently is to keep it running at a level rate. If marketing made a master schedule that did not recognize that objective, or if manufacturing didn't try to respond when sales were not exactly as forecast, this company would have a disaster on its hands. The secret to their success is that they establish ground rules for making up the game plan. And, in spite of the apparently conflicting objectives of marketing and manufacturing, they work together to make a practical game plan that meets the company's overall objectives.

Today, there is a way to translate management's objectives into production plans that can then be translated into even more detailed master schedules, which will then drive the rest of the planning system. Rather than have marketing, manufacturing, finance, and engineering constantly debating what the ground rules are as they operate from day to day, policy for meeting these objectives must be established. The "out of bounds" needs to be decided before the ball goes into play. This policy is the responsibility of top management. The policy for production planning - management's handle on the system - was discussed in Chapter 8. There must also be a set of ground rules for handling the master schedule. There is no such thing as a master schedule until such time as there is a master scheduling policy.

A master scheduling policy should include the following points:

I. What It Is:

    A. The three conflicting objectives: customer service, inventory turnover, plant efficiency.

    B. What we would like to do versus what we can do.

    C. No past due allowed, cannot produce in a past time period.

    D. Master schedule is not a sales forecast, it's a production forecast, and, above all, must always be doable.

II. Forecasts:

    A. Who will forecast what.

    B. Forecasting techniques to be used.

    C. Measuring accuracy.

    D. Who will review, the frequency of review, scheduled communications.

    E. Forecasts should always be revised even if the master schedule cannot be changed. The forecasts should be updated regularly.

    F. Final accountability for the forecasts rests with marketing.

III. Making the Master Schedule:

    A. Who must do it?

    B. Who must sign off on it - usually the vice presidents of manufacturing and marketing sign off monthly.

    C. Rescheduling is preferable to changing quantities in the master schedule since lower level quantities may already have been started to match the original master schedule. Moving the next lot to an earlier or later period is more practical than increasing the quantity of an existing lot.

D. What is the planning horizon? Some companies use a twelve month master schedule with a new month added as each old month is completed. Others extend it two to three years out depending on their material and capacity lead times.

E. What are the planning time increments? The master schedule should be made in no larger increments than weeks in order to give lower level material good relative priorities (knowing what is needed for an entire month is not of particular value). Some companies prefer to state the master schedule in days.

IV. Communication:

A. Manufacturing and purchasing have the responsibility for feedback. They should be providing information on anticipated delays to the planners and the master scheduler so that replanning can be done before the problems occur rather than after they have occurred. This also gives time to evaluate the impact of an anticipated delay. An export order with a penalty contract and a letter of credit that expires within the next 10 days, usually cannot be allowed to fall behind schedule at any cost.

B. The frequency of scheduled meetings - formalized communications. Product planners from marketing, and production planners from manufacturing should meet at least weekly; area sales managers and the plant manager at least monthly; vice president of marketing and vice president of manufacturing and their staffs at least monthly for production planning.

V. Promises and schedule changes:

A. How time fences will be used. Figure 9-4 illustrates the policy at a pharmaceutical company. Everything within the first four weeks in the master schedule is firm. Any changes will have to be signed off by the manufacturing vice president. These changes could include changes to accommodate requests from marketing or changes to accommodate requests from manufacturing because of scrap, rework, or other delays. The responsibility of the manufacturing vice president is to affirm that these changes <u>must</u> be made because of a manufacturing problem, or a marketing problem. In either case, the master schedule must still be doable. Any changes to the master schedule between week four and week eight have to be signed off by the manager of planning as doable. Any changes out beyond week eight can be made by the master scheduler unless that person sees some problems that need to be called to the attention of someone else in the company.

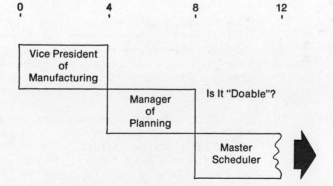

Figure 9 - 4. Master Schedule Approval

B. The master schedule is really a joint responsibility. In one company using MRP very successfully, manufacturing has to sign off any changes to the master schedule that move the schedule in. Marketing must sign off any changes that move the schedule out.

C.   There should be a spelled out response time for communication. If marketing asks for a promise or a schedule change, they should be able to expect an answer usually within 24 to 48 hours. If manufacturing requests an answer on why a forecast isn't materializing as planned, they should expect a response within a week or two since it takes marketing more time to get the information.

VI.   Controls on the master schedule:

A.   The production plan starts everything moving. It determines the amount of product that will be built, the amount of material that will be purchased and fabricated, and the amount of labor that will be used. It would typically be extended out twelve or more months into the future and signed off at least monthly by the chief executive officer of a manufacturing company.

B.   The master schedules should be totaled against the production plans to make sure that the amount in the master schedules equals the production plans.

C.   The production plans should be totaled against the business plan on a continuing basis to make sure that the production plans represent what management really expected the business to do from a financial point of view.

D.   The shortage list can be used as a control on master schedule quality. In a company where the master schedule is valid, there should be no need for a shortage list. Any executive who wishes to check on the operational effectiveness of MRP can check to see if the shortage list is being used rather than the dispatch list. This usually indicates that the master schedule is not being managed properly to predict the shortages effectively in the future.

E.   Who can change policy concerning the master schedule. This should be at the executive vice president level or higher.

F. Performance will be measured. Each month the master schedule should be measured to be sure that total dollars planned are being made. The percentage of the total items originally planned that are actually made should also be measured - a typical "bogey" is 95 percent. (Total dollars may still be produced 100% because some items are rescheduled into the current month while others are moved out.)

When a company finally has a company game plan, it's usually a new experience. And a lot of new problems show up. Problems that existed before, but problems that were buried in the confusion of shortage lists, expediting, and firefighting.

One company that operated this way installed an MRP system. In the past, the marketing people rarely told production when a customer wanted to reschedule and push his order back to a later date. When they were only able to achieve 50 percent of customer promises, this wasn't particularly important! No matter what the customer promise date was, there was a 50/50 chance the job wouldn't be shipped!

With MRP, the customer delivery promises were met 95 percent. Suddenly, the marketing people were very concerned that schedules be changed when customers wanted orders pushed to a later date. With MRP, the manufacturing people had a valid schedule that represented what they really intended to do to meet the shipping commitment. When marketing pushed an order out, manufacturing realized that this would jeopardize their ability to hit the shipping budget. The same was true in the past, but now it became far more apparent and important because the plans were being executed far more reliably. Manufacturing people refused to accept these reschedules. So marketing people went down to the shipping dock and made sure that these orders weren't shipped. The result was that the company did not hit their shipping budgets even with MRP. They were better than in the past, but not as good as they should have been.

The problem is basic. Now the company has a game plan that can be executed - something they never had before. Where it was not necessary to have policy expressed before, it must be expressed now. If it's necessary for marketing to move some customer orders out, then they should accept the responsibility for reducing the shipping budget by that amount - or moving some other "doable" orders in.   Customer reschedules are a normal part of a manufacturing business.   Marketing should be given a "bogey" and told that only so many dollars can be moved out in a given month   There will always be a small number of orders that represent the bulk of the dollars and a large number that don't really impact the shipping budget to any great extent.   But with this kind of policy, marketing can concentrate on trying to get the customers with the big dollars in the shipping budget to accept the shipments while not worrying about the many customers who don't have many dollars in the shipping budget.   Certainly, having marketing people go down to the shipping dock and stop shipments was not the answer to the problem.

An MRP system will bring information - and problems - to the surface.   It is up to management to face up to the real, immutable problems of running a manufacturing business and make policy that the system can help them execute.

Section 4
Forecasting

Realistic management recognizes that the forecast is input to the business plan, the production plans, and the master schedules. The master schedules determine what will be made, the amount of material that will be purchased and manufactured, and the amount of labor that is to be used. Without responsible forecasts, the rest of the planning in a manufacturing or distribution organization is going to suffer. And no one will suffer more than the marketing people who need the product to sell to meet their objectives. And the excuse, "We can't use MRP - our forecasts aren't good enough" simply doesn't hold water. MRP is a better planning, and particularly, replanning method. If forecasts were perfect, MRP wouldn't be needed. MRP's strength is that it can replan to cope with the real world where forecasts are not perfect.

Forecasting is the responsibility of marketing. That sounds like an onerous assignment to many marketing people. But the main concern of marketing should be what are usually called the "extrinsic forecasts." Those where there is an outside influence as opposed to "intrinsic forecasts" where the best information available is probably an average of past usage.

Extrinsic forecasts include forecasts for:

1. Product families.
2. New products.
3. Promotions.

Product family forecasts are the input to the production plan. Individual item forecasts will be the input to the master schedule. For a make-to-order product family, intrinsic forecasts will typically be used with any other information available from marketing to forecast the percentage of options to be used in the planning bill of material in order to convert the production plan to a master schedule.

While the responsibility for all forecasts rests with marketing, the data for intrinsic forecasts can often be supplied far more easily by production and inventory control people as a normal part of their routine activities. In a company making to stock, for example, there may be thousands of individual stockkeeping units in inventory. Those that are not new products or promotions can be forecast using past usage information.

A good approach is to take the information developed from these averages, total up the individual item averages by product family, compare these with the marketing forecast for the family, and allocate the sales forecast across the family based on the percentage that each product represented in the past. The "forecasts" are then given to the marketing department on a regular basis showing how they compare with past sales and how they total up by family group so that marketing can review and sign off on the forecasts. A typical approach would be to update the averages monthly and send them to marketing for a "sign-off" 10 days before they are used in the actual manufacturing scheduling systems.

One of the major pitfalls to forecasting that should be avoided is built-in bias. In some companies, the sales and marketing people making a forecast tend to be optimistic and make the forecast too high. One company gives a bonus to each business unit manager based on the percentage that the actual sales exceed the plan. These business unit managers consistently forecast too low. That way they can beat the plan! Unfortunately, they don't usually have the material available to meet actual sales because they didn't provide the correct forecast to do the planning to have that material available!

During the '60's, a great deal of interest was generated in forecasting techniques. Unfortunately, no matter how sophisticated these techniques look on paper, they all have one fatal flaw; they assume that the future will be like the past.

Forecasting based on leading indicators, for example, sounds sophisticated. But a forecast of brake lining sales based on gasoline consumption stopped working in the '60's when the original compact cars came in. These cars had very cheap brake linings. Even though they didn't consume much gas, they consumed brake lining at a very high rate. The historical relationship changed.

The "techniques" of forecasting read better in textbooks than they really work in business. One tractor manufacturer uses sophisticated econometric models, correlation analysis, predictions of disposable farm income, etc. to make their forecasts. When they are through, the only thing they have is a forecast of total dollar sales! This is probably one of the easiest forecasts for most companies to get. It's the product mix that's difficult. Econometric models (2) contribute little or nothing to forecasts of product mix. Overall dollar sales are usually heavily influenced by marketing, by management's sales objectives, etc., and the sophisticated techniques actually do more for window dressing than for reality.

The forecasting job often looks formidable in a company that makes a complex assembled product, to order, with many available options. Marketing always asks, "How can we ever forecast the combinations of options?" The answer is, they probably can't - nor do they need to. A company making generators, for example, has many different engines that can be used in combination with many different controls, starters, generators, stands, etc. The number of combinations is so high that many of the combinations will only sell one or two units in a quarter. But the fact of the matter is that the engine, the generator, and the stand don't have to be assembled until the customer order has been received. The important thing is to have the right generators, engines, and stands; not to be able to predict the combinations of these options - which is virtually impossible. From a master scheduling point of view, these combinations don't mean anything; they only become significant in the final assembly schedule. The forecast should be made for "generators" and a "planning bill of material" (discussed in Chapter 13) used to convert this to starters, controls, etc.

In some companies, there is a need to forecast thousands of finished goods items. Individual item forecasts are often best made using averages unless extrinsic information for promotions and new products or competitive situations is really known. One company serving the home decorator trade considered their product lines "very volatile." Their marketing product planners forecast each individual item of each product line every month and projected that forecast six months into the future month by month. It was found, much to everyone's surprise, that a six month moving average could do a much better forecasting job than the marketing people! They introduced too much subjectivity into the forecasts and constantly overreacted. A good forecast is one that uses intrinsic information like averages and overrides only when specific extrinsic information is known.

One of the techniques that was highly touted during the '60's was exponential smoothing. Exponential smoothing is a weighted moving average; nothing more, nothing less. Figure 9-5 shows an example of a moving average and exponential smoothing. Adding up the 10 weeks of sales shown in Figure 9-5, the average is 54 units. Using a moving average, the eleventh week of sales would be included next week, the first week would be dropped, and a new average would be generated.

Weekly Sales	Exponential Smoothing	
1 = 50	Old Forecast	= 54 × .82 = 44
2 = 60	Sales	= 69 × .18 = 12
3 = 73	New Forecast =	56
4 = 36		
5 = 40	Old Forecast	= 56 × .82 = 46
6 = 48	Sales	= 39 × .18 = 7
7 = 55	New Forecast =	53
8 = 70		
9 = 69		
10 = 39		
Total 540 ÷ 10 = 54		
Average = 54		

Figure 9 - 5.   The Moving Average versus Exponential Smoothing

Using exponential smoothing, an "alpha factor" is multiplied by the current sales and the old forecast is multiplied by one minus alpha (to make a weighted moving average work, the weight factors, or alpha factors, must always equal 1). Using an alpha factor of .18, which approximates a 10 period moving average, and multiplying that by the sales in week 9, the result is 12 units. One minus alpha (.82) is multiplied by 54 - the assumed "old" forecast. The result is 44 units. The new forecast then is 56 units. In the tenth period, the 56 units becomes the old forecast. The current sales are 39 and the new forecast becomes 53 - very close to the 54 that the 10 period average generated. Exponential smoothing and a simple moving average give almost identical answers in practice.

Why use exponential smoothing? It has only one advantage. It requires storing considerably less data than a moving average requires. This was an important consideration in the late '50's when the amount of data that could be stored in computer files economically was very, very limited. Today, that is no longer a problem. Exponential smoothing has one significant disadvantage. Because of its fancy name, people tend to think of it as a forecasting technique and forget the fact that techniques only help <u>people</u> to forecast. The responsibility for forecasting cannot be delegated to some computer techniques - no matter how fancy they are.

One of the most recent developments in forecasting systems is called "Focus Forecasting." (3) Focus forecasting applies particularly where there are many finished goods items to be forecast.

Focus forecasting was developed at American Hardware Supply Company, a cooperative that inventories the material for thousands of hardware stores around the country operating under the ServiStar brand names. American Hardware must forecast cooking utensils, snow shovels, garden hose, nuts and bolts, hammers, Christmas trees, etc. Bernie Smith, Vice President of Inventory Control/Long Range Planning for American Hardware, developed focus forecasting to meet this challenge.

Focus forecasting is not a technique. It's a <u>system</u> that can use any forecasting technique. The basic idea is to find out what techniques the people who do the forecasting - in this case, the buyers at American Hardware - actually use. Different buyers use different strategies like, "Compare this years' sales to date with last years' sales to date for the item and assume that the same percentage increase or decrease will exist for the next three months." Or, "Look at the total overall dollars sales to date and assume that this item will have the same percentage share of total dollars sales forecast for the next few months as it has for the last few months." These simple strategies - seven of them were actually used at American Hardware - are then tested by the computer each time a buyer needs a forecast. Whichever strategy works the best based on the last few months' sales is chosen by the computer to forecast the next few months' sales. The advantages of focus forecasting are:

1. It is easy for users to understand so people know when to override it and won't assign mystical qualities to the techniques being used.

2. It emphasizes simulation, not optimization (where the computer comes up with the "one right answer").

3. It can use <u>any</u> technique - including exponential smoothing if desired.

4. In practice, people have been able to use this system to do a very good job of forecasting.

Sophisticated forecasting techniques have been around for many years. In practice, they have had very little success. It can be demonstrated through simulation that a technique is technically superior. But it will not usually work better in practice if it fails to pass the test of transparency: "Why did the computer tell me to do that this time?" If the user cannot answer that question quickly and conveniently, he cannot be held accountable for using the system intelligently. The final responsibility for forecasting rests with the people. Techniques can only assist them.

A forecasting system for finished goods items, service parts, or options could operate this way:

1. Forecasting is done using simple techniques like moving averages and seasonal indices within a focus forecasting system.

2. These averages are summarized by family groups and given to marketing to use their judgment on what the family group total should be, and what impact price changes, promotions of new products, etc. will have. They can override any individual forecast where they think the average isn't a good forecast.

3. The revised forecast for the product group is then prorated across the family, and, if necessary, the family reorganized so it makes sense from a manufacturing point of view. Product groupings that make sense from a marketing point of view do not necessarily fall into logical production families.

4. Actual sales are then compared with the forecast regularly and forecasting performance is measured. (Methods of measuring forecast accuracy are discussed below.)

There are special kinds of forecasts for new products, for example, where it is well to state a high side of the forecast and a low side of the forecast for material and capacity planning purposes. New products are extremely difficult to forecast and one of the few techniques that seems to work well is the "consensus" approach. If a number of knowledgeable people who will not be swayed by others' opinions are asked to make a forecast on a new product, frequently this small sample can give a reasonable representation of customer reaction.

But whether the forecast is for family groups, individual items, or new products, the essence of forecasting can be distilled down to a few short quotes from Alfred Sloan's book, My Years With General Motors. (4) It's fascinating to watch Sloan address forecasting and watch the wheels turn in his mind as he writes and thinks about the subject:

P. l52. "Two things were involved: first the art of forecasting, and second, shortening the reaction time when a forecast proved wrong."

P. l54. "The essential elements are the forecast and the correction, each equally critical."

P. l58. "Thus, the more important thing in the end was not the correctness of the index (forecast) for the model year, but the sensitivity of actual market changes to prompt reports and adjustment."

That says it all! The basic principle of forecasting is to make the best possible forecast and then to keep it as up to date as possible. Good communication is the essence of good forecasting.

Sloan established the "Ten day sales reports" on automobiles. This enabled the manufacturers to find out what was actually being sold rather than what the dealers were buying. Prior to this, it was easy for a manufacturer to keep on producing and forcing dealers to take cars when the cars were actually not selling. The number of companies that have floundered financially because they did not gear their manufacturing schedules to their actual customer requirements would fill a large book.

Today, warranty cards are enclosed with many products from power tools to home appliances. Usually, these cards aren't really required by the manufacturer in order to guarantee the product. They are there to give good feedback on what is actually happening in the marketplace.

At one power tool manufacturer, warranty card return rates are followed very, very carefully and production rates are adjusted as actual retail sales go up or down.

One company making hardware products decided that a good way to sell these products would be to offer some new assortments to the hardware dealer and bring these assortments right to his door in a van to display them. The marketing department made forecasts for each of the new assortments, but everybody knew they couldn't possibly be right. Nevertheless, the company did a good job of supplying these products to the market because they emphasized communication and response. During the first four weeks of this promotion program, actual sales were phoned in from the field twice a week. During the second four weeks, they were phoned in once a week. By that time, patterns had developed and sales were reported through regular channels. Manufacturing was able to supply excellent support for this marketing program - not because the forecasting was that good, but because the feedback on what was actually happening was excellent.

Anything that gets measured tends to improve. Forecast accuracy should be measured regularly, and the reasons for major errors identified, so that they can be solved. Because the required forecasting horizon, due to manufacturing and purchasing lead times, is different from company to company, there are no universal "bogeys" for forecast accuracy. In a make-to-stock company, the forecast accuracy for product families, and by item, should be measured. In a make-to-order company, the forecast accuracy for product families and options should also be measured. A typical approach would be to take the actual sales for each two-month period and measure what the forecast was at the beginning of the two-month period versus the actual sales for the period. Then, the number of items within a predetermined forecast error would be counted and converted to a percentage of total items forecast in order to measure the forecasting performance. The existence of a consistent performance measure is far more significant than the actual measure itself.

It's important to remember, however, that the key to good forecasting is good feedback and communications. These are more important than all the forecasting techniques that have ever been devised.

Section 5
Strategic and Tactical Planning

MRP II can be the game plan for marketing, manufacturing, engineering, and finance to work together. When marketing uses MRP II to work very closely with the manufacturing people, facilities plans can be made two to three years in advance that will best handle the <u>anticipated</u> product mix. Once again, the major benefit from this will accrue to marketing because manufacturing will have the capability to produce the product they need to take care of the customer's requirements.

The plant manager of one company that had installed MRP commented, "Normally, I would be concerned at this time about whether or not we were going to hit the shipping budget by the end of the month. I'm not anymore. I know my people have the tools to make that happen. Right now, I'm working with marketing on the production plan nine months from now. What they would like to sell is beyond our production capabilities. We aren't going to be able to make the business plan happen if we can't get together on a more doable plan. To me that's one of the great advantages of a formal system like this. We can work together, and plan together better than we ever could before." This kind of strategic planning can be more effective using MRP, and so can the tactical planning.

A company making carpenter's tape rules introduced a new product in the mid '60's. The new rule had a locking blade that was mylar coated and a satin chrome finish. It was a sensation. The company had one mylar coating machine. It was running three shifts seven days a week making tape rule blades. The marketing department decided to have a promotion program for the new tape rule. Their thinking made sense to them. They felt that they could really knock the competition out of the market if they could launch a good advertising and promotion campaign. Unfortunately, the manufacturing people were only one week ahead of the back orders and couldn't possibly do anything to increase production. They had a new mylar coating machine coming in within three months, but until that time, a promotion by marketing people would simply have generated back orders rather than shipments and could easily have entirely disillusioned the customers with the product if they found they couldn't get deliveries.

In a simple situation like this, it was not difficult for manufacturing and marketing to realize that they weren't working well together. But most situations in a manufacturing business are not this simple. There are many product lines competing for the same facilities both within the plant and at the vendors.

Over the long term, manufacturing normally has to try to get the material, manpower, and facilities to make what marketing can sell. Short term, it's often very profitable for a company to have marketing put their efforts into selling what manufacturing can make. This not only means more profits, it means more commissions. It's simply a case of having - and using - the information MRP provides so that manufacturing and marketing can work together more effectively. There is no way that a profit plan will be accomplished if marketing is selling what manufacturing can't possibly deliver. MRP provides the tools to generate the information so that manufacturing and marketing people can work together developing short term marketing tactics. One of the very powerful tools for doing this is simulation that was discussed earlier in this chapter.

Here is an excerpt from an article talking about the use of simulation at the Tennant Company who make industrial floor maintenance equipment such as riding sweepers, scrubbers, etc.: (5)

The vice president of manufacturing points out, "We ask ourselves, what if we make certain changes in the master schedule? Then MRP simulations predict the impact of the proposed changes: on manpower requirements, equipment requirements, parts availability, product inventory, product delivery time, and order backlog.

"We can also predict the impact on the company's overall financial and production plan, and top management's goals for service and profitability.

"Most often, the need for simulations stems from product family changes, increased manufacturing activity, or close-in schedule changes: within the normal time it takes to produce a product.

"A typical question answered by MRP simulation is, 'How soon can we change the product mix?' For example, Tennant's marketing department recently wanted a quick change in the ratio of gasoline to diesel engines in a large engine-powered sweeper. Within a month, they'd have liked to start shipping a ratio of about 1.1 to 1 gasoline to diesel units, instead of the existing 2 to 1 ratio.

"This sounds like a simple matter of just swapping engines, but it's not. An engine change involves a large number of other part changes, including both manufactured and purchased parts.

"By using the 'what if' capability of MRP simulation, production quickly had the facts to say what could be done. What was found was that the existing ratio could be changed immediately, to 1.5 to 1, and 6 weeks later, another change could be made, to 1.1 to 1. In other words, marketing got their part of their requirements immediately, and the remainder within 6 weeks - without any loss in production efficiency.

"Tennant's materials manager points out that MRP simulation made it possible to give marketing a prompt and accurate answer, without waiting for the weekly MRP regeneration and full reporting of purchasing requirements. And Tennant's customers got reliable delivery dates."

In the compartmentalized environment that existed in many manufacturing companies in the past, marketing didn't really seem to care whether manufacturing could actually produce the product that they intended to sell. That was manufacturing's problem. But, of course, that's short sighted. If manufacturing can't produce the product that marketing needs, that is marketing's problem. MRP does not fix this problem, but it does provide the tools so that marketing, manufacturing, engineering, and finance can work far better as a team to satisfy the customer's needs. And that, after all, is everybody's job.

Section 6
MRP is a "Can Do" System

In the past, manufacturing people responded to marketing in direct proportion to the pressure that was put on them. When the marketing people finally said, "Make sure this one goes, we don't care about anything else," they could always do that. Today a manufacturing company has a system available than can give them the information to know what it will cost to push a "hot job" through, how long it will take to change production levels, when a customer order can be expected to be shipped. And the information can be factual because MRP II is a simulation of reality.

In the past, the factory had limitations on its ability to react quickly. But the system was even more limited. The factory could change plans quickly, but the system had no way to represent them. Today the system has potentially unlimited capability. It operates at the speed of light. The system now can be jiggled around far faster than the factory can respond. The challenge is to get the system synchronized with the factory so that it really represents reality.

To many people, MRP has become a good excuse for not performing: "We can't put that order into the schedule in less than normal lead time. We have an MRP system." Incredible that a machine which operates at the speed of light is being used as an excuse for being less flexible than we were with pencils, desk calculators, red tags, and sneakers!

One company was negotiating a contract with the General Services Administration. The negotiations went on for a long time and involved a very high volume of their product. Finally, when the contract was awarded, the GSA insisted that 2,000 units be delivered in 10 days. Normal lead time was six to eight weeks. This company used their MRP system to find out what materials would be needed, what other orders they would have to be taken from. They checked the vendors to find out how soon they could get more material and used their system to help them meet this unreasonable requirement. It meant a great deal of work for their factory during a slow period, and there was no way that the answer to the GSA could possibly be, "Sorry, we can't do it."

Just because MRP is a formal system doesn't mean that it is a rigid, inflexible system. The value of MRP isn't to show why it can't be done, but instead to show how it can be done. On occasion, marketing will have to live with the fact that some things can't be done, or that doing them will mean that some other things can't be done or that it simply costs too much. That is certainly better than making promises that can't be kept. It's better than expediting some jobs and pretending others won't suffer.

There is one overwhelming advantage when marketing recognizes what MRP is and works together with manufacturing to use it: Marketing is now far more the master of its own destiny.

Footnotes

1. The term Master Production Schedule is technically more precise. For brevity in the text, the term master schedule will be used in most instances.

2. It should be remembered that these are some of the prime tools of the economists who have a very dubious track record with forecasting.

3. Bernard T. Smith, Focus Forecasting: Computer Techniques For Inventory Control, (Boston, Mass: CBI Publishing Company, Inc., 1978).

4. Alfred Sloan, My Years With General Motors, (Garden City, New York: Anchor Books, 1972).

5. Modern Materials Handling, September, 1979.

Chapter 10
MRP II in Manufacturing

Section 1
Manufacturing's Thankless Task

In the past, manufacturing management simply didn't have the tools to do the job very professionally. Sales criticized manufacturing constantly for the inability to perform. Accounting criticized manufacturing for having too much inventory, too many cost variances, and little respect for the "numbers" that are needed to run the business. Engineering typically looked down on manufacturing as a disorganized, unprofessional activity. After all, what background does anyone need to become a plant manager? What do they even teach about that at the college level - isn't it mainly "time study" and "plant layout"?

Even the systems people held manufacturing in low regard. They could go to the accounting people and ask them what they wanted on the computer. The accountants would typically reply "accounts payable, accounts receivable, general ledger, budget reporting, etc." When they went to the manufacturing executive and said, "What would you like to do on the computer?", the manufacturing executive usually said, "I don't know. Got any ideas?" The accounting people were simply transferring an existing formal system that worked to the computer. The manufacturing people had never seen a formal system that really worked.

At the higher levels in the manufacturing organization, questions came up on a daily basis:

Can we ship this job in shorter than normal lead time?
Will we really meet the shipping budget this month?
Why isn't customer service better?
Why are we working so much overtime?
Will we be increasing or decreasing our manpower in the next few months?
Why is inventory so high?
Why is there so much scrap?
Can we introduce this new product on time?
Can we meet the customers' additional requirements and still meet our promises to other customers?
Why isn't our efficiency higher?
<u>Why is our order backlog increasing at the same time our inventory is increasing</u>?

These and other questions like them were very difficult for manufacturing management to answer without valid schedules.

And operating people didn't <u>believe</u> the schedules. They knew that the numbers were highly suspect. Instead of using the numbers to manage, they managed in spite of the numbers.

Some manufacturing managers did very well without the proper tools to do the job. But the informal system environment is insidious: it often makes good managers look bad, while those less competent, but more politically adroit, survive. The lack of a recognized set of professional tools, a defined body of knowledge, and a valid system made it difficult to really measure performance.

Management typically didn't understand the problem. Their peers simply thought it was the fact that the manufacturing people weren't particularly competent. In fact, the manufacturing people themselves typically didn't understand the problem or believe that there were solutions. The last place they looked for help in most companies was from the computer systems people. Early experiences with the computer confirmed their opinion that this wasn't going to help much. In fact, it would probably only make the problems worse.

Today, the tools are available to do a better job, and a body of knowledge is rapidly developing and being taught. Manufacturing management is becoming a highly respected profession in companies where MRP is functioning well.

Section 2
Using the Tools

Figure 10-1 shows the closed loop MRP system again. Many companies, as part of their production planning, do a "rough cut capacity plan" before they even generate a master schedule. This is done to see if they have a good chance of being able to achieve the production plan. The rough cut capacity plan is made for key work centers only and is usually made in monthly or quarterly time periods. The plan would say, for example, that to make 10,000 circular saws in the 6½ inch to 8½ inch product family (as stated in the production plan), a certain number of standard hours would be required in fabrication, in assembly, and on key equipment, like on the eight spindle screw machines, for example.

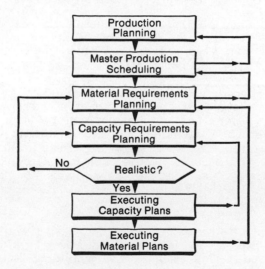

Figure 10 - 1. The Closed Loop Diagram

The master schedule is the statement of what is going to be produced and is a critical input to MRP. It takes management policy, as expressed in the production plan, and breaks it down to the detailed level.

The master schedule must be realistic, and doable, at all times. Properly managed, MRP can predict the shortages so that manufacturing people can prevent them.

But if the master schedule is overstated, has a lot of backlog in it, or in any other way is invalid, the first symptom will be the reappearance of the informal system: the shortage list. Managing the master schedule properly is one of the real challenges of MRP. The master schedule was discussed in detail in Chapter 9.

The material requirements plan is used by the planners in production control (or the "planning department") to:

1. Release orders to the factory and to vendors.

2. Reschedule open orders with the factory and with vendors. The planner must approve these reschedules and make sure they are desirable and doable. Once approved, these will be used to update the priorities on the shop dispatch list and the vendor schedule, and provide the input to capacity requirements planning.

Released shop orders and planned order releases from the material requirements planning system generate the "shop schedule." This schedule is run against the "routing" file, and then against the work center file to generate the capacity requirements plan. The routing shows the sequence of operations to be done in producing an item and also shows the standard hours required for each operation as well as the work center where it will be manufactured. A work center is a machine, a group of machines, a person, or a group of people with the same manufacturing capabilities. The product of the capacity planning function is a report that states - in standard hours by time period (usually weeks) - what capacity will be required at what work center to execute the plan.

As skilled manpower becomes increasingly difficult to find, capacity planning becomes even more significant as a management tool. One company, a machining division supporting a number of assembly divisions of the same corporation, is an excellent example of the kind of problem that exists today. Each of the assembly divisions orders whatever parts they need from the machining division with a "standard lead time." This standard lead time is based on production time only. This puts the machining division in a position where they have to guess at their material requirements, but even more significantly, they have to guess at their capacity requirements. As a consequence, the machining division virtually never makes a significant change in manpower levels until they are very far behind schedule and have enough backlog to justify the change.

Although many of the divisions ordering parts have material requirements planning systems, none bother to give their planned order releases to the machining division so that they can plan their capacity requirements! It takes several weeks to get a qualified worker. The typical company would like to plan to keep the worker working as long as possible. The capacity planning information made possible by an MRP system is an extremely significant management tool.

One company that makes bearings was used to reacting to the incoming order rate to change manpower levels. Shortly after they first put their MRP system on the air, the general manager was told that they would have to add people by August to several key operations. His reaction was, "But the incoming order rate hasn't really increased!" Checking with marketing, however, he found that they anticipated a higher demand in September and that this was reflected in the master schedule even though the incoming order rate had not yet picked up. Workers were added and the component production rate increased. As a consequence, the company was able to take a half million dollars in additional business away from their competition in September because they were prepared for it.

Another significant facet of capacity planning is facilities planning. The typical approach in years past was for someone to propose a capital budget request for a new machine. Frequently, however, that machine was justified based on current volumes or sometimes on anticipated future product volumes, but rarely based on the entire projected future product mix and capital requirements for all machines. The fact that a machine is a good investment doesn't necessarily mean that it is the best investment. Very few companies live in a world where capital is not limited. Consequently, the real question is how to use the limited capital to the best advantage of the company.

With an MRP system, the capacity planning programs can be used to project the standard hours of capacity required one, two, three, or even more years in advance. These projections can be made monthly, quarterly, or at any desired frequency. They should be based on the anticipated product mix as indicated by marketing. The company can then determine how best to invest its capital in new facilities. Facilities planning, in most companies, is often done from the "bottom up," machine by machine. With an MRP system, it can be done from the "top down," and a number of "what if" situations can be simulated to decide how much capital will be required for new facilities and how that capital can best be invested to support anticipated future product mix. The vast majority of companies today don't do as good a job as they should in "top down" facilities planning. Even those that do, however, could do a lot more simulations to test the impact of different plans with an MRP system.

Input/output reports are the commonly accepted capacity control device. They compare actual standard hours of output with the plan to make sure that each work center is producing at the planned rate. If a work center is not producing at the planned rate, something will have to be done to increase output, or the master schedule will not be met. These reports are called input/output reports because it is important to measure the number of standard hours going in as well as out. Thus, if a work center appears to be behind its projected output requirements, it is easy to see whether or not the cause was the lack of input from one of the feeding departments.

One of the most difficult areas to control in a manufacturing company is the work-in-process. The amount of work-in-process is, of course, a function of input versus output. See Figure 10-2. In a factory without an MRP system, work-in-process normally expands to fill the space available on the factory floor!

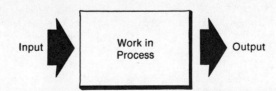

Input → Work in Process → Output

Figure 10 - 2. Handles on Work in Process

With MRP, output is controlled by the input/output reports while the input is controlled by the master schedule. The level of work-in-process required in a manufacturing company can be determined work center by work center. Work-in-process is in-process "safety stock." It is there to keep work centers from running out of work when there is a fluctuating input. By measuring the amount of work-in-process over a period of time at each key work center, the high level and the low level can be compared to determine the amount of variation and the amount of queue that is actually required. This can then be built right back in to the scheduling rules that are used in a closed loop MRP system.

With a formal capacity planning and control system, significantly lower levels of work-in-process can be attained. Nevertheless, it's important to educate workers so that they realize that the lower level of work-in-process is a planned and desirable objective rather than just an accident. In most companies, workers have learned to work to the informal capacity planning system; <u>the physical presence of backlogs</u>. When they see these backlogs diminish, they tend to slow down the work pace because they are afraid that they will soon be running out of work if they don't. They must be taught to work with the formal capacity planning and control system rather than the informal one they are used to.

The <u>dispatch list</u> is the factory's scheduling tool. It is issued daily to each work center, usually first thing in the morning. As the material requirements planning system changes required dates, the individual schedule dates for each operation are changed in relation to the required date. These dates are not kept on the shop paperwork, but instead are kept in the computer. As the dates change, individual operation schedule dates are changed accordingly. The dispatch list provides the information for the department foreman to use in determining which job to start next. The fact that dates change does not mean that a job currently being worked on should be taken off a machine in most cases. It merely means that the dispatch list tells the foreman which job to <u>start</u> next. It gives a list of the jobs in priority sequence by operation schedule date (derived from the shop order due date based on MRP). These priorities, of course, are driven through MRP. If, for example, the master schedule changes, the related shop orders will have their schedule dates changed accordingly.

One foreman asked the question, "We now have a schedule that comes to us every two weeks. Won't a new schedule every day be rather nervous?" A valid question, but the answer was very simple; the formal schedule now comes down to the shop every two weeks. The informal schedule is an expeditor walking into the foreman's department every few minutes. As one foreman who is using

MRP said, "I used to have many expeditors trying to tell me what to do when. Now I have only one thing to follow - the schedule."

The closed loop MRP system provides manufacturing management with the information they need for planning and controlling capacity and scheduling. But, of course, the results have to come from the people who use these reports.

One company started out with MRP and didn't do very well at first. They had not handled their master schedule well, maintained accurate inventory records, or educated their people properly. When they didn't get much in the way of results, they decided to take a fresh start; the vice president of operations called everyone into his office and told them that it was up to each of them to make MRP work. The manufacturing manager talked to his foreman. He said, 'That daily dispatch list, the schedule that you get generated by the computer, is based on the material requirements plan predicting the shortages, and re-predicting them as things change. If we work to that schedule, we will be working on the shortages for next month and the month after, rather than finding out about them after they happen. I want you to work to that schedule religiously." The foremen did. When expeditors came down to get "hot jobs" run, their reply was, "It's not at the top of the schedule!" The expeditors went back to the master scheduler to change things to make sure that the most needed jobs came to the top of the dispatch list. Because the foremen were doing their job well - they virtually forced the production control people to do their job well. In no time at all, this company achieved the benefits that they had expected from MRP - and considerably more besides. They also proved a very solid point: <u>Foremen like good schedules</u>, they <u>like</u> to work to schedules. The problem is that <u>they never had valid schedules in the past.</u>

Section 3
Allowing Foremen to Manage

It's been said that, "Everybody's mistakes end up in manufacturing." Perhaps that statement could be extended to say, "The foreman is the ultimate victim of every poor schedule." The average American foreman spends the bulk of his or her time firefighting because of material shortages and poor schedules.

The foreman's real job is to:

    I.   Supervise people.
    2.   Educate and train people.
    3.   Make sure the tooling is working properly.
    4.   Make sure that each operation is producing efficiently.
    5.   Solve process problems.
    6.   Install methods improvements.
    7.   Provide the required capacity.
    8.   Execute valid schedules.

These are the things that <u>don't get done</u> while foremen dissipate much of their time trying to compensate for poor schedules. These are the things that foremen <u>can have time to do</u> when an MRP system really works properly.

The basic tools that the foremen will use the most in an MRP system are:

1.   The dispatch list to provide the daily shop schedule by work center.

2.   The capacity plan to show where increases or decreases in capacity will be required well into the future for both manpower and facilities planning.

3.   The input/output reports to be sure that the capacity plan is being executed properly.

When an MRP system is managed properly, the foremen are among its most enthusiastic supporters. Getting the expediting "monkey off their backs" is one of the most significant things that has ever been done to improve the quality of life for foremen, and to give them the time to think, plan, and manage better than they ever could before.

Section 4
The Production and Inventory Control Function

The very name, production and inventory control, was a giveaway. The inventory control people were the order launchers. They were the people whose usual response was, "It's on order!" Production control was largely an expediting function. The name, materials management, came into vogue during the 1960's and 1970's. The materials manager, as mentioned earlier, was a person who had not only production and inventory control, but purchasing, traffic, stores, etc. reporting to him.

Today, it probably would make a lot more sense to call these people the "planning department." And the planning department should include planning in dollars as well as units. This is discussed more in Chapter 12.

A typical organization, then, would include the department head who would be the manager of planning, a master scheduler reporting to this person, or perhaps more than one master scheduler if the volume required it. Reporting to the planning manager would be a central planning unit that would handle material requirements planning and capacity requirements planning and a shop planning unit that would handle dispatching.

Purchasing might or might not be included in the planning department. The organization is not as important as setting the proper objectives, making valid plans, and measuring performance against these plans.

And this is an important point for the manufacturing executive to convey to everyone. The function of the planning department is:

MAKING VALID PLANS THAT OTHER PEOPLE WILL BE HELD ACCOUNTABLE FOR EXECUTING.

In the world of the informal system, there was always a great deal of confusion over who was responsible for meeting customer schedules, meeting the shipping budget, etc. The planning people should have been responsible for making "doable" plans, plans that the manufacturing and purchasing people could sign off and execute. In the past, when there was a problem with shipments or inventories that were too high, or a customer service problem, the production and inventory control people were often blamed. But they didn't have the tools to do their job. With MRP, the tools are available, and they should be held accountable for making the valid plans. Just as the people who are supposed to execute the plans should be held accountable.

Like every function in the organization, the professionalism of the production and inventory control function has been dramatically impacted by MRP. In those companies where MRP works well, the inventory clerks and expeditors are now <u>real</u> planners. Planners who are working with marketing and manufacturing to come up with detailed plans to execute the overall production plans that top management has signed off. Planners who are measuring actual activity against the plan, and reporting deviations from the plan to the responsible people. Planners who have the proper information to give marketing, and who have established a high level of credibility with the marketing people. Planners who often have the difficult task of showing management the real alternatives like, "Yes we can increase the production rate on this product line, but we have a capacity limitation that can't be fixed until some new machinery is received, so it will mean working more overtime, subcontracting more work, or reducing the production rate on other production lines that go across the same facilities." Now that they have the information, it is their task to help management see the real alternatives rather than having arbitrary rules imposed like, "We won't work any overtime ever." There are times when the alternatives are considerably worse than working the overtime, and it's the job of the planning people to point that out.

Their planning will be now expressed in dollars, as well as units. Because dollars are the common denominator of business, they can communicate better with management. In one company where MRP is working well, the general manager said, "The planning function has become a vital part of our organization. These people are no longer looked upon as clerks and expeditors, they are just down the hall from top management."

Section 5
Doing the "What Ifs"

One of the toughest problems that manufacturing people had to face was giving information to other people, particularly marketing people or their superiors.

With a modern MRP II system, the computer system can be used as a simulator to answer the "what if" question. Here are some examples:

The president of a company making labeling and marking machines asked the manufacturing manager if they could manufacture and ship some milk carton labelers by December 3l that had just come out of engineering on November 1. The answer had to be "yes." It was a new product - very important competitively. They ran a special MRP run between regular MRP runs which told them what additional purchased material they would need. It also told them what additional capacity they would need. They manually compared this with their capacity plan that had been generated during the regular MRP run. The manufacturing manager's answer was, "Yes, it can be done; but we'll have to take some of machine X out of the January shipping schedule to do it. The new machine is going to overload us at one of our numerically controlled machining centers; and while we can subcontract the work, our subcontractors have general purpose machines and take longer to make parts. Machine X will be back on schedule by February." That was planning with facts.

Three things are important to note here:

1. A MANUFACTURING EXECUTIVE WITHOUT FACTS MUST ALWAYS SAY "YES." If the right person asks, "Can it be done?", the answer has to be, "Yes." And, of course, it can be done by pushing everything aside.

2. THE DIFFERENCE BETWEEN EXCUSES AND PLANNING IS TIMING. If the manufacturing executive says, "Yes, we'll get these, but we won't have any shipments of machine X in January," that's planning. On the other hand, if the "hot job" is pushed through and the president then comes around in February and says, "Whatever happened to machine X in January? Why didn't we

ship any?", the answer will be regarded as an
excuse.

3. MRP HELPS TO ISOLATE THE CONSEQUENCES.
    The milk carton labelers could have been pushed
    through without MRP. Manufacturing people do
    that all the time. But it wouldn't have just been
    parts from machine X that would have been
    pushed aside to make room for the milk carton
    labeler. It would have been some parts for a
    great many machines. (This explains something
    that management had difficulty understanding:
    One job got pushed through and was blamed -
    rightfully - for the many other jobs that weren't
    completed on schedule.)

A company making hospital equipment was faced with
increasing sales throughout the year. On four separate
occasions, corporate management asked, "Can we put another $3 million into the next quarter's sales?" They ran
some MRP simulations to test various combinations of product mix and then came back with a plan that would enable
them to add the extra shipments while at the same time
advising marketing which products' output could be increased. Certain product lines were right up to capacity.
They told their marketing people, "Additional sales in these
product lines won't generate income now; they'll only generate backlog." Other examples of this type of "tactical"
planning with marketing were discussed in Chapter 9.

Several years ago, a company that makes torque con-
verters, marine reduction gears, and power shifting transmissions was oversold in all of their major product lines.
They had capital they wanted to invest for expansion, but
certainly not enough to take care of all of the possible
business that was available in the boom years of 1973-74.
They used MRP simulations to tell them what facilities they
would have to invest in to satisfy various combinations of
product mixes. This could then be compared with the
profitability by product mix so that they could see the
amount of capital investment that would support these
combinations of product mix, therefore allowing them to
invest their capital to get the biggest return on investment.

One company that makes capital goods uses their MRP
system regularly to do simulations. Ninety-nine percent of
the time, this simulation is the result of a request from
marketing to make some kind of a change in the master

schedule. This simulation shows what the impact of that change would be on material, on production rates, etc. This company also uses their MRP system for financial planning, converting production plans into purchased material and labor dollars to show the impact of various combinations of product mix in the production plan. They are truly a user of MRP II.

An MRP II system is just a simulation of reality. Because it is, it can be used as a superior planning tool. But beyond that, it can be used as a simulator to answer the "what if" questions that manufacturing executives have wrestled with for years.

Section 6
Inventory Record Integrity and Accountability

Inventory record accuracy was used as an example of the application of the principles of management in Chapter 6. The steps in achieving inventory record accuracy are repeated here:

1. Establish the objective.
2. Assign line accountability.
3. Create understanding.
4. Provide the tools to do the job.
5. Measure performance.

There's a business in almost every town where inventory records are kept properly. Everything that moves in and out of the stockroom is counted. A transaction takes place with every withdrawal and every receipt. They have a limited access stockroom and nobody goes home at night if the records are incorrect. Inventory record accuracy is at the 99.99 percent level. The business, of course, is a bank.

Most manufacturing people are inclined to chuckle at that example. We all know that banks keep their records properly.

Let's examine the logic. One bank in a small town in New Hampshire states that they rarely keep over $250,000.00 on hand in their "stockroom." It would have to be a very small manufacturing company to keep this little "inventory" in its stockrooms. In most manufacturing companies, the inventory would be more likely to be one million, five million, ten million, or more. In most manufacturing companies, the idea of a limited access stockroom, of counting all material that goes in and goes out, of making sure that a transaction takes place whenever material does go in and out, of staying late until any discrepancies have been reconciled, of having inventory records at the 99+ percentage level seems foreign. Why? There is far more reason for a manufacturing company to have accurate records than there is for a bank. But, in the world of the informal system, there wasn't! And until the CEO - the Chief Executive Officer - sets inventory record accuracy as a significant business objective, it isn't going to happen. And until it does happen, formal systems will largely be a waste of money and a cause of great frustration. Running a business with a formal system requires a very high level of data integrity and a much more professional attitude on the part of everyone.

Once the objective has been set, the next issue in establishing and maintaining inventory record accuracy is accountability for making sure the transactions are handled properly and that inventory records are correct as a consequence. Limited access stores is a prerequisite to accountability. No stores manager will accept the responsibility for making sure the transactions take place as material moves if he cannot control who goes in and out of the stockroom.

Limited access stores can be one of the most difficult challenges that a company faces. Some companies like pharmaceutical companies, for example, generally have limited access stores. It's just a case of establishing accountability, measuring performance with cycle counting, finding out what the problems are in keeping inventory records correct, and fixing these problems. Companies making electronic products typically have limited access stores. They have good stockroom control. But many other manufacturing companies don't. Aircraft and automotive companies typically have little physical stores control and must expedite relentlessly to outwit invalid schedules.

The phrase "locked stockroom" is used frequently, but in the real world of manufacturing, a locked stockroom is not always practical. The means to accomplishing limited access stores are many. Here are a few examples:

Company A put a floor to ceiling fence around their stockroom with an electrically controlled gate actuated by a pull cord. The pull cord is far enough off the floor that only an electric truck operator can reach it. Inside the gate is a stockroom man who makes sure that unauthorized people do not enter.

Company B has an open stockroom door, but sitting inside is one of the stockroom people, and the desk is always manned. No unauthorized people are allowed to come in. They must go to the main stockroom entrance, get a badge, sign in, and be accompanied by a guide if there is a genuine reason for being in the stockroom.

Company C makes electronic products. Most of their officers, who are also the owners, are engineers. They enjoyed "shopping" in the stockroom until the day the president posted a notice saying that no unauthorized people would be allowed in - including himself. The engineers were, however, given their own supply of commonly used parts, and they were supplied regularly with a list of the parts that were in the stockroom. The stockroom manager had a copy of the MRP output report, and could issue anything that was requisitioned which would not affect a production schedule. Any requisition that could potentially affect a production schedule was referred to the planner who was accountable for having the material available for the schedule. A good example of making it easy to do it the right way.

Company D has a stockroom in a building several blocks removed from their main manufacturing facility. They call it a "parts bank." The aisles are given street names and the locations are given addresses. Anyone visiting the parts bank must pick up a badge in exchange for their driver's license and must check-out at the main desk in the stockroom to get the driver's license back.

Company E makes a product that has very large components. Many of these are stored in a yard. The yard area is surrounded by a fence, and the only entrance is through an electric gate that is actuated by a plastic identification card.

Company F makes an extremely large product, and their outside storage area covers many acres. It would be completely impractical to store this material inside the factory because it includes such items as booms for cranes. They paved the entire outside area. (Much of it had been dirt before, making it very difficult to plow the snow in the winter time!) They put a fence around the entire area, and built a two-story stores office. Material coming from the factory is dropped at an "in station," and the truckers working in the outside area are assigned particular zones to work in. They are held accountable for inventory integrity.

Company G makes schoolbuses. They were in the habit of storing material on the line. In fact, their factory looked like an enormous stockroom with an assembly line running through the middle. They erected fences alongside the assembly line. They now issue material to the assembly line and, for one of their recent schedules, issued over 17,000 components with only three shortages!

So the issue is <u>limited access</u> stores. The costs for re-laying out a factory that was not designed to have limited access stores can sometimes be very high. Nevertheless, limited access stores is an absolute prerequisite to accountability for data integrity. And it pays for itself.

In one company with a large outside storage area, the plant manager balked at the notion of having to add a few indirect people to control the stores inventory. A survey showed that there were usually 30 or more people in the outside storage area looking for material, counting material, etc. The welding superintendent and one of his setup men were seen outside along with numerous foremen, expeditors, buyers, production control people, etc. Having four or five stores people - even though they fall into the category of "indirect labor" - is certainly far more economical than paying a welding superintendent to look for parts. In the meantime, the company should charge scrap at welding due to lack of supervision to the cost of <u>not having</u> good stores control.

One company makes forgings. They typically make a three months' supply for one of their customers because set-up costs are high. They machine one month's worth at a time and ship these. Obviously, they have forgings in inventory in their factory. They had no person responsible for stores and were concerned about adding an "indirect" person to handle this function. A check indicated that the superintendent, general foremen, foremen, production control people, etc. spent between 12 and 18 man days a week looking for material, counting material and requisitioning more material because they couldn't find what the records showed. (Not to mention writing off as obsolete the material that turned up unexpectedly at the year end inventory!) The point is simple: adding one storekeeper to free up 15 man days of time - primarily supervisory time - makes a great deal of economic sense.

THE COST OF A STOCKROOM IS NOT SOMETHING A COMPANY CAN AVOID. THEY WILL ALWAYS PAY FOR STORES CONTROL. THE ONLY OPTION IS WHETHER THEY GET THE CONTROL OR PAY FOR NOT HAVING IT.

One last observation concerning "making it easy to do it the right way." Many stockrooms are manned only on the first shift when the factory is working two, or even three, shifts. It doesn't make sense to have sixteen people in the stockroom on the first shift and none on the second and third. Assembly foremen, for example, will get their material when they need it. They will go over the fence, under the fence, or through the fence if required. It is far better to service them properly by manning the shifts when the factory is working.

Performance measurement will be discussed in more detail in Chapter 19, but deserves some brief attention here. Cycle counting is a method for sampling the inventory on a daily basis. Some items are counted each day and the count is compared with the inventory records shown in the computer. Those where the actual count and the book count are within "tolerance" (this is explained in more detail in Chapter 19) are correct. Those outside of tolerance are incorrect. If 100 items are counted in a day, and 97 are within counting tolerance, the accuracy is 97 percent. Companies implementing MRP shouldn't go on the air with the system until inventory accuracy has reached at least 95 percent. There is no magic to this number; nothing but experience. The experience of successful users who have found that if they get their inventory records that good before they start their MRP system, inventory record accuracy will not be a problem in making MRP work.

Not the least of the benefits of cycle counting is the fact that auditors will not require a physical inventory if the cycle counting proves that the records are accurate. The money to be saved - not to mention the aggravation and the lost production time - makes cycle counting a real "payoff" proposition.

Keeping the on-hand balance correct is important, and it's also important to keep the "on-order balance" correct. An MRP system is more tolerant of inaccuracies in the work-in-process inventory than in the on-hand balance. If, for example, a production lot is received into stores and there are only 900 pieces instead of 1,000 that were expected, the 900 will probably last quite a while anyway, and there is time to reschedule the next lot to an earlier date. The "on-order balance" error will be found when material goes into the stockroom, not when it goes out.

Nevertheless, it is important to keep work-in-process inventory records correct, and the issue once again is accountability. One company that does a good job with work-in-process inventory record accuracy handles it as follows:

1. Material is counted when it leaves the stockroom and is issued into the first department.

2. It goes into an "in station" in the first department and does not move until the foreman or someone he has delegated, signs off that they accept the count.

3. When it moves into the next department, it goes into the "in station" there. Once again, it must be signed off by the foreman or his representative.

4. If there is any question about count, the sending department is called in to do a recount, and any missing pieces are charged against the sending department as scrap.

The foreman, then, has fiscal accountability for work-in-process, and scrap charged against his budget can affect his performance and, inevitably, his pay.

Bills of material and routings must also be correct if MRP is to generate accurate output information. Since bills of material and routings are primarily generated by engineering, they will be discussed in Chapter 13

Section 7
Related MRP Functions in Manufacturing

The fact that manufacturing scheduling did not work before MRP affected many of the related functions. Scheduling is fundamental. And if scheduling is a problem, then MRP can be a very practical solution. These are some of the functions that are logical candidates for MRP:

1. The tool room in a typical manufacturing company always seems to operate in "expedite mode." There are some legitimate crises, of course, like tooling that breaks and has to be repaired immediately. But the fact of the matter is that most of the last minute rush in the tool room is caused by an inability to keep the tooling schedule synchronized with the manufacturing schedule as needs change, machines break down, proper material isn't available, or the steel doesn't run properly in the coil feed. (Or a key person was absent so that a different job had to be run than what was planned.) Some of these problems can't be helped. But as one manager put it so aptly, "We suffer most from self-inflicted wounds."

The capacity planning function can also be very useful. Getting skilled people like tool makers requires as much advance notice and good planning as possible. Few departments in a company without MRP tend to suffer so much from chronic overtime as the tool room.

2. Some companies that have big forging presses, for example, have extremely complex tooling. One setup could require twenty different components for the dies, and some of these components may well be common to other setups. With MRP, the tooling schedule can be tied in with the manufacturing schedule and kept up to date as it changes to show tooling priorities and schedule conflicts.

3. Operating supplies is another area where an MRP system can be very helpful, not only in controlling inventory, but in having the right material at the right time. One bearing manufacturer includes, in the bill of material, the proper grinding wheel and the quantity required to manufacture each lot of bearings.

4. Much of the material used by a <u>maintenance</u> department has a fairly "independent" type of demand that is very hard to predict. On the other hand, when machines are to be rebuilt, this is just like a company selling a product with options. There are certain components that will always be used, such as seals and gaskets. There are others, such as the piston rings in an air compressor which may or may not be replaced when the machine is overhauled. Even items with a fairly independent demand can be scheduled far better using MRP because of its emphasis on when material is <u>needed</u>.

Obviously, a good preventive maintenance program fits hand in glove with the material planning, capacity planning, and dispatching functions of MRP. With this type of program, material availability can be planned very effectively around the preventive maintenance schedules. The preventive maintenance schedule is a very good start on the master schedule for maintenance and repair that will generate their MRP.

5. One large manufacturing company has its own <u>construction</u> division to build its facilities or add to existing facilities. They do everything but the actual structural steel work. The application for MRP in construction is obvious. Construction is really a kind of manufacturing where the tools are moved to the work rather than having the work moved to the tools. This makes construction even more challenging to schedule properly. Virtually anyone who has watched construction taking place can see that there are serious scheduling problems in most construction operations.

6. A similar type of problem exists for people who do their <u>final assembly at the customer's site</u>. A typical example of this would be a company building elevators. The material is shipped to the site and the construction crew actually erects it. Once again, the problems of having the right material to the right place and the right manpower there at the right time are exactly the type of problems an MRP system addresses.

7. In some companies, the <u>"shop packet"</u> - the paperwork that industrial engineering prepared to go out with each shop order - can be very large and contain a great deal of information such as the routing itself,

the blueprint, labor tickets, and move tickets. The planned order releases can provide advance notice so that these shop packets can be prepared before the shop order is to be released. In the past, some companies made this shop packet preparation time, which can often run as long as two weeks, a part of the actual lead time. With the planned order releases available through MRP, there is no excuse for this any more.

8. Many companies have <u>service or repair parts</u> that they must stock and ship to their customers when needed. In most companies, these parts are a real problem. Many companies make the problem even more difficult by having two different departments competing against each other for parts needed in service versus parts needed in production. A good principle to observe here is:

> Don't split the responsibility for making the "least worst choice" about limited resources. It's better to give one person the objective of supplying material for production and for service, and measuring that person on accomplishing both objectives.

It is important to realize that a prerequisite to any attempt to manage service parts better is <u>valid priorities</u>. For most companies, service parts are a great example of the invalid schedule dates that result from order launching and expediting. MRP, with its time phasing and rescheduling, can be used to predict and repredict valid need dates for service parts. Properly used, this will result in better customer service for service parts (which are usually one of the most highly profitable parts of any company's business) along with lower inventory investment.

9. Another area where MRP can be used effectively is <u>combining setups</u> or sequencing jobs that can be run most economically if they are run together. A company making chucks for hand drills, for example, has four different chucks that run through the same major setup. One chuck is plain, one has a knurl, another has a groove cut around the chuck, and another is the plain chuck only 1/16 of an inch longer. Obviously, if these chucks can be run together, the major screw machine setup that typically takes from 8

to 12 hours only has to be made once and the minor changes take only a few minutes. This can save a lot of setup time and free up a great deal of capacity since machines don't make parts (or money!) while they are being set up.

In the past, it was difficult to sequence these jobs so that they all were ordered at the same time. Using MRP, this is very convenient indeed. The inventory record can be coded to show which of the jobs go through the common setups. Then, whenever one of these has to be ordered, all others can be reviewed and their time supplies equalized as much as possible. In other words, if the amount on hand and on order for the first part will satisfy requirements out through the twelfth week, the order for the second part should be adjusted to provide coverage through the twelfth week. In this way, these parts will need to be ordered at approximately the same time the next time they have to be ordered.

The same type of approach can be used in a company making paint, for example, where proper sequencing of the jobs can minimize the number of times the equipment needs to be cleaned up. Because of its time phasing capabilities, the MRP reports facilitate this sequencing.

Some have asked, "What's beyond MRP II? What is MRP III?" The day will come when we recognize that network planning addresses universal problems throughout manufacturing and distribution companies. But it extends even beyond the basic manufacturing into tooling, maintenance, construction, new product planning, and virtually every activity that involves a number of interrelated tasks and subtasks that must be planned and controlled.

Section 8
MRP and Quality Control

Quality control people obviously benefit greatly from an MRP system. Foremen have more time to solve quality problems because there is less of the "crisis mode" out on the factory floor. As a result, quality problems tend to be dramatically reduced. The fact that production levels are changed less frequently (less hiring and training of new people) can help quality very substantially.

Quality control people should be aware of some of the things that can be done with MRP to help them in their job:

1. MRP can generate a dispatch list for incoming inspection so that the quality control people know which jobs to work on first.

2. MRP has a long planning horizon and can be used by quality control people to see what jobs are scheduled in the future, especially when there are processing problems. Knowing how much product is being made, and when, will help quality control people to judge the magnitude and urgency of the problem.

3. MRP can be used to assign priorities to the material that is in the MRB (Material Review Board) category. Knowing which of the MRB decisions have to be made first helps quality control people to work on the most important problems.

4. Because management people are better able to meet schedules, there is less pressure to ship marginal product.

5. Because management people have more time to work on quality problems, they are more effective in directing good solutions to these problems.

6. The emphasis on accurate documentation in an MRP system is of great benefit to the quality control people in getting the product made right the first time.

7. Because overall morale improves in a company where teamwork really works, it is much easier to get people interested in doing the job right the first time.

Of course, quality control people can also make a substantial contribution to the success of MRP. They are frequently in a position where they can do check counts as a matter of normal inspection procedures. Any help on data accuracy will help MRP to provide better information.

Much of the thrust of this book is on how a manufacturing company can be run more effectively. How shipping "bogeys" can be met. It goes without saying that the only shipments that count are those where the product meets the quality standards.

Section 9
Making a Profession of Manufacturing Management

In the past, manufacturing and the finance people usually had different sets of numbers in talking to top management. But since the finance people work with numbers all the time, they were usually able to prove that they were "right," while manufacturing was "wrong." The fact of the matter is that both sets of numbers were highly suspect. With an MRP II system where the operating numbers generate the financial numbers, this type of adversary relationship is no longer the "normal" way of life for manufacturing executives.

In the past, manufacturing and marketing were highly critical of each other. But with a company game plan that they agree upon together, via the master schedule, that situation no longer needs to exist. Every A and B user of MRP comments on the increased respect that marketing has for manufacturing and vice versa.

In the past, manufacturing was always critical of engineering because they had to make up the time that engineering lost in introducing new products or designing highly engineered products. Today with MRP II, the schedules for engineering and manufacturing are clearly defined. The accountability is established and a far better working relationship can result.

And one of the great benefits from MRP is that manufacturing becomes far more professional. With the advent of MRP II, there is a defined body of knowledge and undoubtedly more and more will be taught at the college level. Education for manufacturing executives in the future will no longer be a case of graduating from college and then "on the job training."

George Bevis, when he was Senior Vice President of Tennant Company, expressed it very well, "It is my considered opinion that the greatest single value of this whole activity is a quantitative improvement in the quality of life for the organization throughout the company starting with the president or vice president. I used to go to management meetings 10 years ago. I was the guy that was pointed at because I was the guy who consistently made promises that we didn't meet, who talked about producing things which were late. Today when our manufacturing people go to a management committee meeting and they report on their performance, the management committee says 'great, great, just wonderful, you've done it again.' There are <u>very few companies</u> in which <u>the manufacturing executive is the hero of the executive suite.</u>   With the tools MRP provides, our people have become professionals; and as the record shows, when they promise, they produce. As a consequence, manufacturing is looked upon with respect and dignity."

Chapter 11
MRP II in Purchasing

Section 1
Fixing the Lead Time and Phoney Backlog Problem

Certainly, one of the most difficult problems for purchasing people to cope with was the lead time syndrome:

1. As vendor backlogs picked up, vendors quoted longer lead times. Customers, in turn, ordered more to cover themselves out over the longer lead time, thus increasing the backlogs - causing another increase in lead times.

2. To compound the problem, order launching and expediting created phoney backlogs.

One way to handle long lead time quotes from vendors is to give them schedules well in advance. If the vendors are quoting a six month lead time, giving them schedules a year ahead of time would keep any announcements that lead times "are now eight months" and "are now ten months" from being a problem for purchasing people.

But, in the world of order launching and expediting, this simply wasn't a practical solution. Manufacturing people are reluctant to give purchasing their requirements very far into the future because they know things are going to change. They know that the forecast is wrong. The production schedules will be changing. And if they make any long range future commitments, they'll get material they don't need and will have trouble getting the material they do need.

A company using MRP can readily give vendors a six month or one year schedule. There is no problem keeping these schedules up to date in an MRP environment.

A sample vendor schedule is illustrated in Figure 11-1.

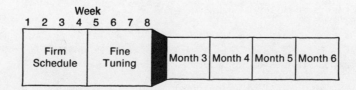

Figure 11 - 1.   The Vendor Schedule

1.   The first four weeks are shown in weekly time periods and are considered "firm." The company is committed to its vendor to try to hold quantities firm in each week and take these quantities. A real "crisis" could mean a change in schedule within the four week time period but only a crisis would justify it.

2.   The next four weeks are shown in weekly time periods. These will be fine tuned each week as the new schedule is sent to the vendor. The purchaser has agreed that if the vendor has committed to material, any dramatic schedule change that would cancel the need for that material would result in negotiations to keep the vendor from having to absorb the resulting losses.

3.   The next four periods are shown in monthly - actually four week - increments. In these time periods, the purchaser is merely asking the vendor to confirm that material and capacity will be available to meet the purchaser's requirements.

This schedule goes out on a weekly basis. It can be thought of as the release schedule for a given purchase order. The purchase order, as it was known in the past, was a contract with a schedule on it. Contracts don't need to be changed very frequently. Schedules should be reviewed at least weekly to keep them in line with current requirements. The idea of a "letter of agreement" and a weekly vendor schedule makes a lot more sense than the old purchase order concept for productive material.

Consider a company using this approach with their vendors. Assume that a given vendor announces that lead times have increased from six weeks to eight weeks:

1.   A company using MRP will not have to generate additional input to the vendor since they already have a schedule out six months or more into the future. This is a basic principle:

GETTING INTO THE VENDOR'S SCHEDULE OUT BEYOND THE QUOTED LEAD TIME ELIMINATES THE LEAD TIME PROBLEM.

2.   A company using MRP will not make any contribution to the phoney backlog if they manage the mas-

ter schedule properly. They will be rescheduling material <u>out</u> as well as <u>in</u> on a regular basis.

The impact that the phoney backlog has on our manufacturing economy was discussed in Chapter 2. An MRP system, properly managed, reschedules out as well as in and, thus, the phoney backlog doesn't develop. In our manufacturing economy as we learn to run our manufacturing businesses more professionally, the economy itself, as well as the individual companies, will benefit greatly.

Section 2
Scheduling the "Outside Factory"

Before an MRP program is instituted with the vendors, there <u>must</u> be an education program. The vendor who knows that his customers don't give him valid need dates, who knows that they will phone him to tell him what they <u>really</u> need, must be told that MRP <u>will</u> give valid dates or he'll still be waiting for the phone call.

The companies with the most successful MRP systems have brought their most important vendors in for a one day conference following an outline like this:

1. An introduction emphasizing that the subject matter will not be pricing, complaints about past deliveries, delivery failures, but instead, the new scheduling system: MRP.

2. A professional session on MRP using video-taped presentations to explain MRP and its application to purchasing.

3. A discussion by the company personnel concerning the validity of due dates and the fact that there will not be as many expediting phone calls except in the case of real emergencies. The theme will become "silence is approval." In other words, if the vendor does not notify the customer that he cannot deliver on the date specified, it is assumed that he can.

4. Discussion of the performance measurement methods to be used with MRP.

5. Questions and answers and summary.

Some smaller vendors may have to be educated at their own company, probably with a brief video-taped session. (Today video players are a common piece of equipment in virtually every company.)

The important issue, of course, is credibility. Time and again, it's been demonstrated that vendor delivery performance over 98 percent can be achieved when the customer is using an MRP system. When the supplier <u>believes</u> that the need dates are valid, when the supplier knows that he will hear from the customer _every_ time the schedule is not met, most suppliers will work very hard to meet the schedule. The poorer a customer schedules, the more the customer will blame the vendor for poor delivery. The better a customer schedules, the more likely he will praise the vendor for good delivery.

All of this assumes that there _is_ a valid schedule to work to. MRP must have accurate inventory records, accurate bills of material, and a valid master schedule or it will not generate valid schedules. Unfortunately, many purchasing people have been exposed to so-called MRP systems that are really not much better than what they had before. When MRP _is_ managed properly, however, it will generate and maintain proper need dates.

With the increased abilities that the computer gives us, there is more and more emphasis on treating the vendors as the "outside factory." Capacity planning information can be provided for vendors well in advance. MRP gives the vendor a long planning horizon that can be used for capacity planning purposes. One company actually converts the anticipated schedules for subcontractors into standard hours for _their_ work centers several months in advance. Obviously, this implies that the subcontractors' routings are on the customer's computer file. This is a particularly appropriate approach for a small subcontractor who may not have a computer himself.

Another company issues a daily dispatch list for its principal subcontractors who do heat treating and plating. The same dispatch lists that are generated for their own shop are also sent to the vendors to keep the vendors' schedules up to date. This implies that each subcontractor's work center would be listed on the routing, which is not a difficult problem.

The overwhelmingly important thing for the customer to supply to the vendor is valid schedule dates. This is what order launching and expediting could not do. This is what MRP _can_ do when it's properly managed.

It is ironic to think of the way this was handled in the past. The formal system was to give the purchasing department "due dates" that were almost inevitably incorrect because they did not represent the real need dates!

Consider the use of safety stock, for example. Assume that an item has an average demand of l00 per week and that the safety stock is established at 200. This means that the due date for the item has been moved up two weeks from the "drop dead date." Safety stocks always change need dates. If material is really needed in week l3, a safety stock of 200 units in the example above would change the due date to week 11 which is simply not true.

It's important to be able to have some cushion in a scheduling system so that everything doesn't have to be flown in and hand carried at the very last minute. But safety stock in its classical format did exactly the opposite of what was needed. It disguised the real need date rather than emphasizing it.

Companies using MRP very successfully in purchasing take exactly the opposite approach. They provide both the purchasing department and the vendors with the drop dead date (i.e. week l3 in the case above), but then have a common agreement that normal delivery should occur in week 11. Vendor performance will be measured on delivery by week 11. But purchasing and the vendor know at all times what the real drop dead date is. Valid need dates are shown in the formal scheduling system, rather than having the formal scheduling system generating wrong dates and the informal scheduling system trying to establish what the real need dates are.

Valid need dates are the cornerstone of an MRP system. This is what makes it a whole new approach for people in purchasing.

These valid need dates also become the basis for doing something that was extremely difficult to do before: measuring vendor performance. In the world of the informal system, it was out of the question to try to hold vendors accountable for delivering "on time" based on purchase order due dates. These dates were usually wrong to start with and became worse as time passed. When purchasing runs to the informal shortage list, they cannot measure vendor performance against schedule dates that are wrong. With an MRP system, vendor performance can definitely be measured against the scheduled date and definitely should be measured. MRP means that vendor performance measurement is no longer one of those nice things to talk about in the textbooks. It has become a practical reality in a number of companies. And vendor delivery performance is like anything else. When it is measured - equitably against a valid schedule - performance usually improves dramatically.

Section 3
Formalizing the Informal System

The purchasing director asked what MRP would do to help him with his most difficult vendor. The vendor was a sole source and never seemed to be able to supply all of his customer's requirements. When told that the main advantage of MRP would be to know real "need dates" - a must when a company cannot get everything they would "like to get" - the purchasing director responded, "I do know the need dates now, even without MRP!" The purchasing director was actually looking at the schedule six weeks ahead, week by week, for everything that used material supplied by this vendor. He manually broke these schedules down into material requirements, took into account the material on hand, and the material the vendor had in transit, and then each week gave the vendor a new schedule for requirements for the next six weeks! In fact, he had managed to invent a manual approach to MRP!

Anybody who has worked in purchasing has done manual MRP on a few items. When specific commodities were in real trouble, they had to know the answer to the question, "What material is really needed when?" Without a computer, however, MRP could only be done on a few trouble items.

When the "chips were down," purchasing people had to do things the right way, even though it was often the more difficult way, in the manual environment. Consider the following approaches that purchasing people have always used when they were in trouble:

1. Asking, "When do you really need it?" The formal system put dates on orders that were wrong. The informal system had to answer this question.

2. Allocating capacity when there wasn't enough to satisfy all the demands. This is what the steel mills did when people inundated them with orders. With MRP, a customer provides a vendor schedule and asks him to acknowledge that he has capacity to meet the schedule. In effect, capacity is allocated before there is a serious backlog situation, not afterwards.

3. Rescheduling in order to expedite. Virtually every person who has worked in purchasing has had to move one job <u>out</u> to a later date in order to get another one <u>in</u> earlier. But this usually happened after the problem occurred. An MRP system puts the emphasis on rescheduling <u>out</u> as well as <u>in</u> to get the jobs moved back that aren't needed, so that the jobs that are needed can be moved ahead.

4. Rescheduling to reduce inventory. With order launching and expediting, this is only done when the financial people insist upon it because they anticipate a downturn in the economy and are afraid of a big buildup in inventory. Without MRP, it's just too difficult to do rescheduling as a matter of routine. With MRP, it <u>is</u> routine.

5. Blanket orders and releases. Purchasing people have used this approach for years as a way to get more reliable sources and lower prices. One purchasing veteran recently said, "MRP sounds too much like blanket orders to me!" He was thinking of the problems of blanket orders and releases. Without MRP, getting the annual requirements for the blanket order was a research project. But it was nothing compared to the challenge of keeping release rates coordinated with changing requirements rates. Once again, both are natural by-products of a <u>well managed</u> MRP system.

This point must be emphasized most strongly - the MRP system has to be well managed. Today, the benefits of MRP are well recognized and well known, but most companies using it fall far short of its potential.

Surely the ability of the computer to handle masses of data has made MRP possible. But the computer's ability to generate paper doesn't mean that anything is going to happen as a result. All the paper does is give people - people in purchasing, for example - information so that they can do their jobs better. The information going in must be correct. This means that bills of material, inventory records, the open purchase order records, and the master schedule must be correct. Inventory records, for example, simply were not very good in companies in the past because the shortage list did not demand it. On the other hand, purchasing people knew that dates on orders didn't mean much because they would soon get a phone call about what was really needed.

MRP is nothing new for purchasing people any more than it is for manufacturing people. It is really just a <u>formalization of the informal systems</u> that have been used for years. The challenge of making MRP work is a challenge in teaching an organization to live in a world of formal systems rather than the informal systems of the past. But it's worth it. As one purchasing professional said recently, "Everyone benefited from our successful MRP system. But nobody got the kind of benefits we did in purchasing!"

Section 4
Making Money in Purchasing

When a salesman sells a dollar's worth of product, the company is fortunate if 15 to 20 cents comes back as pretax profit. Every dollar saved in purchasing returns 100 cents on the dollar to pretax profit. That doesn't mean that the salesman shouldn't be out there selling. Without him there would be no need for purchasing or anybody else. But it does mean that the purchasing person has a great deal of leverage.

How is money saved in purchasing? Many ways.

Some companies have worked out stocking or consignment programs with their vendors. The vendors supply the material on request by maintaining an inventory on hand either in their location or often having it available on consignment at the customer's location. At first, this may sound like it's just transferring the burden of carrying the inventory to the vendor, but, in many cases, it works out to be far more advantageous than that.

One company had a product line with approximately 80 items in it. Three different products in twelve packaging configurations made up approximately 90 percent of all of the dollar activity in the product line. The vendor and the customer worked out a program where the vendor maintained the three items in bulk and packaged to order with a very short lead time. In return, the customer ordered the less popular items in larger lot sizes. This gave the vendor less set-up cost, longer runs, and more profit in return for a slightly higher inventory investment. The increased inventory investment that the customer had on the very slow-moving items was insignificant compared to the dramatically reduced inventory investment and better response on the fast moving items. Since the vendor carried the fast moving items in bulk, it was a simple matter for him to respond quickly to any sudden increase in demand for a particular packaging configuration. This would have been extremely difficult for the customer to do. It would have meant repackaging the product, a very expensive process indeed.

The moral is very simple; when the customer and the vendor can work together, they can often work out programs that are beneficial to both. Many years ago, a comment was made that is still a fundamental truth in purchasing: There is more to be gained from <u>intelligent customer - vendor negotiations</u> than from <u>all the economic lot size formulas in the world</u>.

Another company had a product line that required a steel backing in typical lot sizes of 15 to 25 units. These lot sizes of steel were normally purchased cut to size from a steel warehouse. The price was quite high because of the small quantity. During a period when steel was in tight supply, they had great difficulty getting this steel. One of the foremen suggested that they try to buy steel in mill runs and shear it to size in their own plant. Unfortunately, there were 97 different steel specifications - all quite close, but none identical. The sales engineering department contacted the customers and told them that they could give very good delivery if the customers would order steel out of one of two sheet sizes. <u>All but one customer</u> agreed to go along with the suggested specification. For this particular application, the steel specification was not critical. Engineers specified different kinds of steel only because they had no other information to tell them what they <u>should</u> specify. The result of this program was to reduce the cost of the product, improve customer service, and, in fact, even improve quality. The steel sheet sizes were picked on the basis of taking care of the most stringent requirement of any customer that would use steel from that sheet, therefore upgrading the type of steel used for all other customers. There was a dramatic reduction in cost by buying mill runs of sheets rather than small lots from warehouses.

Today, this type of approach makes a great deal of sense. In fact, like so many things that we have done in the past, our approach to purchased cost reduction has <u>not</u> made real sense. Consider a company that spends one dollar on direct labor for every three dollars spent on purchased material. They will typically have many manufacturing or industrial engineers working to improve methods in the factory. How many, however, have any engineers working in the purchasing department <u>where there is usually much more potential return on the time invested?</u> This is certainly not to say that methods improvements in the plant should be stopped. Just because the outside factory is out of sight, however, it should not blind management to the fact that there is a great deal of cream to be skimmed in making more profit from more professional purchasing management.

But this takes time. And time is what purchasing people don't have, partly because of paperwork, requisitions, purchase orders, and schedule changes. These are all handled by an MRP system. The MRP system requires no requisitions or purchase orders for regular production material. (Obviously, purchase orders can be used for items that are ordered intermittently.) Since it issues a new schedule every week, there is no need for a lot of rescheduling paperwork. John Schorr, who was the Director of Purchasing at Steelcase when they installed their MRP system, said in "Modern Materials Handling", December, 1979 (1), "The weekly schedule goes out to the vendors with an agreed upon time frame within which the schedule becomes firm. The paperwork for the buyer is reduced by 90 percent."

But there should be no misunderstanding about MRP. While it takes the drudgery and paperwork out of purchasing, it is not an "automatic" system. The purchasing person is still accountable for making sure that schedule changes are valid, making sure that the schedules that are being sent to the vendor can be executed. The responsibility for getting the needed material has not been taken away. The only thing that has been taken away is the drudgery and the paperwork so that purchasing people can spend more time using their intelligence.

An article about Tennant Company states that, "Before MRP, of four thousand 'order launched' purchasing due dates audited in 1973, three thousand-two hundred were invalid and had no relevance to the production schedule. Now MRP updates purchase orders weekly, keeps priorities correct and dates valid. Vendors know that a due date at Tennant is indeed a true need date."(2) And that makes a world of difference in the amount of time purchasing people have to spend on paperwork and firefighting versus buying.

Section 5
The Impact on the Purchasing Organization

The classical relationship between purchasing, sales, and production control is shown in Figure 11-2. Assume that the production control person in the customer company wants to have an order for 200 pieces of material brought in by week three instead of week four. This information is conveyed to purchasing who, in turn, contacts sales people at the vendor company who, in turn, contact - production control!

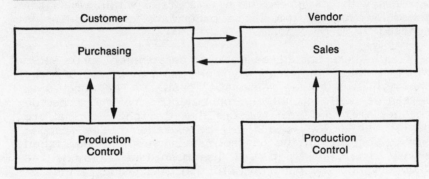

Figure 11 - 2.   Customer/Vendor Communications

The vendor production control person says, "We couldn't possibly give them 200 a week early. How many do they really need?" The purchasing person conveys this back to production control in the customer company. Production control then tells purchasing, "We could get along with 50." Purchasing conveys this information to the vendor sales department who convey it to their own production control people who acknowledge that they can do it. And this acknowledgement is then conveyed via sales back to purchasing back to production control.

It would be hard to devise a more cumbersome arrangement! Why is it necessary for people in purchasing and people in the customer's production control department to have a "one on one" relationship?

The answer is very straightforward. When the purchasing people are given invalid dates, production control people must tell them what they <u>really need</u>. Looking at it rationally - rather than from the experience born of the chronic poor schedules - this just doesn't make sense. Why not have customer production control people talking to vendor production control people? Why not have purchasing people freed up to do buying? It's being done today in industry and the real instrument for communication between the production control people is the vendor schedule discussed above.

There are some purchasing people who would object to this because there would likely be more than one production control person competing for service at the vendor's company. This attitude, however, is based on continuous expediting, and learning too late from the shortage list what the real priorities are. With less expediting, this is not as big a problem.

Another approach used with MRP, however, is to have a "planner/buyer" in the purchasing department. Then the role of production control is to generate valid schedules, and the role of purchasing is to execute them. Purchasing is accountable for having material in from the vendor on schedule through receiving inspection and into stores by the required date. Either of these approaches can be made to work with a formal system.

So the actual scheduling responsibility can stay with production control, in which case they "own the inventory"; or it can be given to purchasing, in which case they "own the inventory." Whoever does the vendor scheduling must, of course, be accountable for the inventory that results. One of the most satisfying things about seeing formal systems in practice is that success seems to become organization-independent. Companies with formal systems can organize in any manner and achieve results by establishing objectives and measuring performance against the formal system. When there is a valid schedule, purchasing can be measured and the vendor can be measured against delivery on the due date.

One concept that has been applied in recent years that does make a great deal of sense in practice is to separate the planner/buyer - perhaps a better term would be "vendor scheduler" - function from the actual buying function. Long ago, it was learned in systems work that if a user is told to head up the project team and continue to do his or her own job at the same time, the project will never get installed. Day-to-day problems always take priority. Making progress can always be postponed. Having certain people responsible for performing the buying function while others are primarily responsible for the vendor scheduling function means that buyers will have more time to do professional buying. They will not be distracted by the day-to-day details of scheduling and follow-up.

The buyer now is elevated to a position where the bulk of this person's time will be spent negotiating contracts, doing value analysis, working with engineering on standardization, working with vendors, and getting vendors to bid competitively. The consequence is that when the buyer does get involved in expediting, because the buyer is not doing it on a regular basis, the vendor will listen much more attentively.

One point that needs to be made very clear: MRP will not eliminate expediting. MRP gives better schedules, better priorities, lets the purchasing people know sooner where the problems are going to be. There will always be the vendor who has trouble delivering on time, the vendor who has quality problems. There will always be the need to have somebody get on an airplane to get the material in to make the schedule happen in a manufacturing company. The difference with MRP is that this is not the routine. It is the exception. And the result is 98-99 percent on time delivery to manufacturing.

Just as manufacturing needs to learn a "new set of values," so does purchasing. The open purchase order file is their responsibility. Keeping it up to date so that it is correct, so that the scheduled receipts in the MRP output report represent what is really on order, is their job. Like any other measure of performance, there needs to be a tolerance. If, for example, 10,000 of a particular purchased component are ordered and 9,990 come in, the open purchase order should probably be closed out. On the other hand, if a small number of specialized components are being ordered for a special customer order, each item would have to be received before the purchase order could be closed out.

As in any computer based purchasing system, there are many other reports that can be made available beyond the vendor schedule itself. A computer system can be used to show how many dollars are being spent with each vendor, to show how many dollars are being spent by commodity, or by any other logical grouping or timing.

The most important result of a well managed MRP system is that purchasing people have more time to do their jobs. They can spend less time firefighting and more time buying. An MRP system can help elevate purchasing to a higher level of professionalism than was ever possible before.

Footnotes

1. <u>Materials Management in Focus</u>, p. 17.

2. <u>Purchasing World</u>, April, 1978, p. 16.

Chapter 12
MRP II in Finance

Section 1
It Was Just "Accounting"

Accounting, in the past, was primarily historical. It was a "score-keeping" function. "Keeping the books" to show management where the company had been. Surely cost accounting did set standard costs for control and there was some overall gross financial planning. But the detailed planning and control in most companies left much to be desired. The problem was fundamental: the numbers in the operating system that manufacturing used were not valid and, consequently, the numbers that accounting had to use were, to a great extent, invalid.

Inventory shrinkage is one of the greatest fears of the financial executive. Taking the annual physical and finding that a few million dollars that were supposed to be there aren't, can often get a company on the front page of the Wall Street Journal as they re-project their earnings. Inventory shrinkage comes right out of profits.

Why does inventory shrinkage occur? Ignoring cases of outright theft which are really not the primary cause of inventory shrinkage in most companies, the real cause can be pinned down to one thing; bad reporting of information. Bad reporting is a natural by-product of maintaining two different systems. The accounting system is driven from a set of transactions that may or may not be the same as those that drive the operating system. Even that doesn't matter because:

1. The formal operating system isn't the one that's being used anyway.

2. The operating people rarely see the impact on the financial reporting before a disaster like an inventory shrinkage occurs because they simply don't use these numbers themselves.

Numbers are essential to running a business. But in a manufacturing business, if the numbers in the formal system that manufacturing uses are wrong (only the formal system generates numbers!) then accounting must maintain a separate system and that's a difficult and challenging job.

In the past, financial people often had to "reconstruct" numbers or "back into" financial figures, like work-in-process, because they didn't have the actual numbers to work with. For example, the most effective way the financial executive could defend himself against inventory shrinkage was to "set up a reserve." Reserves to protect against inventory shrinkage were just a form of "institutionalized error."

Today, there is a better way.

Section 2
Making the Numbers Right

It's been well said that:

> "It's difficult to drive an operating system off a system designed for accounting, but it's easy to drive an accounting system off an operating system that really works."

The annual physical inventory is a good case in point. The individual items may be very inaccurate, but as long as the pluses and the minuses cancel each other, the financial people are satisfied. Unfortunately, in a manufacturing company where they lost electric motors but found gear boxes, the gear boxes are not of great value to production people as a substitute for electric motors even though the dollars balance out perfectly.

On the other hand, a company that maintains its inventories accurately enough to run an MRP system will have 95 percent or better accuracy by item (the methods for doing this and the cycle counting for measuring it were discussed in Chapter 10). Obviously, if the records are kept this accurate item by item, they will be far more accurate in total - typically 99+% in practice. When the operating inventory records are accurate, costing them out to provide an accurate inventory valuation is very straightforward indeed.

A good cycle count inventory can make it unnecessary to take a physical inventory. Cycle counting is especially useful because it means inventory discrepancies tend to be identified as they are occurring rather than having the one big "moment of suspense" while the annual physical is being taken.

A good MRP system requires good physical control of material. And that is a plus for the financial people. One company had turret lathes out on the factory with bar stock located alongside the turret lathes. A material handling engineer felt that this was the "most efficient" approach. His theory was to move the material first and handle the paperwork later. The controller admitted that his standard cost system wasn't terribly good, partly because of poor scrap reporting. This also caused inventory shrinkages at the end of the year that had a serious impact on profit pro-

jections. And this should not surprise anyone: certainly no
turret lathe operator is going to report scrap religiously
when it's easier to just take another bar out of the rack!
The only proper way to control scrap reporting, inventory
records, and to have accurate standard costs is to have the
material in stores and to issue it in the proper quantity for
each job. Then, if there is scrap, more will have to be
requisitioned and scrap will have to be reported. Control
of the physical movement of material is essential to data integrity, not only in the operating system, but also in the
financial system.

When the operating system does work - and it can with
MRP - then accounting can use it as a foundation for a
better financial system. One company's controller reported
that more progress had been made with inventory accuracy
since the installation of MRP than in all the years before
when he had been pushing to get something done.

Section 3
Converting MRP to Dollars

Manufacturing people were usually at odds with the financial people because they didn't understand where the numbers were coming from and why the numbers didn't agree with what they were doing. The financial people were usually frustrated because the numbers that they were expected to show to management concerning the performance measures (that management gets measured and paid on) were in conflict with manufacturing's numbers. But underneath, they were dealing with the same basic logic. Any financial person who has done a cash flow projection is familiar with the basic format and terminology of MRP: "on hand," "gross requirements," "scheduled receipts," and "projected available balance." The fundamental logic of running a manufacturing business is the same whether it's expressed in units or dollars.

Seven Basic MRP Reports **From Closed Loop MRP**	1. Production Plans 2. Master Schedules 3. Material Requirements Plans 4. Capacity Requirements Plans 5. Input/Output (Output Control) 6. Dispatch Lists 7. Vendor Schedules

Figure 12 - 1. Seven Basic Reports from MRP

Figure 12-1 shows a list of standard reports that are used in a closed loop MRP system. (The mechanics for closed loop MRP are discussed in Appendix 1.) Figure 12-2 shows the financial reports that can be a by-product of these operating reports in an MRP system.

Operations	Finance
Production Plans	Business Plan
Master Schedules	Shipping budget, (make to order companies) transfers to inventory (make to stock companies)
Material Requirements Plans	Current inventories, projected consumption, purchase commitments, manufacturing schedules, and projected future inventory balances
Capacity Requirements Plans	Labor requirements by labor grade
Input/Output Reports	Standard hours of output by work center in units and dollars
Dispatch Lists	Work in process, labor reporting, efficiency reports
Vendor Schedules	Commitments by vendor

Figure 12 - 2. MRP II Reports

Figure 12-3 shows the production plan. The production plan is expressed in units. Figure 12-4 shows a business plan. Note that it is exactly the same format. The business plan is expressed in dollars rather than units. In most companies today, one group makes the business plan, another group makes and maintains the production plan, and the two drift very far apart during the fiscal year's activities.

Production Plan
(In Units)

Month Ending		Sales (thousands)	Production (thousands)	Inventory (thousands)
3/31	Plan			
	Actual			60
4/30	Plan	30	35	65
	Actual	25	36	71
6/30	Plan	30	35	75
	Actual			

Figure 12 - 3. The Production Plan

Business Plan
(In $)

Month Ending		Sales (thousands)	Production (thousands)	Inventory (thousands)
3/31	Plan			
	Actual			6,000
4/30	Plan	3,000	3,500	6,500
	Actual	2,500	3,600	7,100
5/31	Plan	3,000	3,500	7,000
	Actual	3,800	3,200	6,500
6/30	Plan	3,000	3,500	7,500
	Actual			

Figure 12 - 4. The Business Plan

In a company where the production plans are kept current and costed out properly, they should be the basis for the business plan. Actual sales, production, and inventory can be recorded against the production plans and they can be used as <u>control reports</u>. The business plan can be kept up to date as production plans are changed. Management can see the financial impact of changes in the production plans on the business plan.

The master schedule, costed out, is the basis for "transfers to inventory" in a make-to-stock company or the shipping budget in a make-to-order company. This is, of course, the same as "production" in the production plan. Management can review the projected shipping budgets to make sure that the objectives of shipping to budget and shipping the right orders to the right customers are being properly reconciled.

Figure 12-5 shows the inventory of components for a company making pumps. The inventory file is coded to show which components go into the pumps. The first column in the projected available balance shows the on-hand inventory in units extended by the cost. This is the current number of dollars of pump components in inventory. Projected gross requirements from the MRP system are costed out, as are scheduled receipts. The projected available balance shows the projected future stockroom inventory month by month based on the projected gross requirements derived from the master schedule which, in turn, is derived from the production plan and, in an MRP II system, represents the detailed execution of the business plan.

Pump Component Inventory — in $(000)

		Month			
		1	2	3	4
Projected Gross Requirements		250	250	300	300
Scheduled Receipts		250	250	270	290
Proj. Avail. Bal.	540	540	540	510	500

Figure 12 - 5. Pump Component Inventory

Costing out the material requirements plan and summarizing it by product group categories results in:

I. On-hand inventory (in dollars) by product group.

2. How much material will be consumed (in dollars) to support the current production plans ("requirements").

3. What will have to be purchased to support the current production plans (in dollars).

4. What the projected stockroom inventory balances by product group in dollars should be for months into the future.

5. What will have to be made - this is the shop schedule that will become input to capacity planning and can be converted into labor dollars.

Comparing the actual withdrawals from stock against "requirements," the actual purchases against the plan, and the actual inventory dollars against the projected balances, tells management if the plans are really being executed - and if the business plan is actually being executed at the detail level.

From a manufacturing point of view, the output of material requirements planning is released shop orders and planned order releases - the shop schedule. When this is run through the capacity requirements planning section of a closed loop MRP system, the result is the standard hours by work center, by time period, required to satisfy the master schedule and the production plans. This can be converted to labor dollars by labor grade, by time period, and by product group. From this information, management can see how many dollars of material and labor will have to be purchased by time period to support any given production plan with its particular product mix. Some companies, in order to project cash flow with greater accuracy, actually offset the due dates by the payable dates.

Costing out the open shop order file that is used to make the dispatch list yields current work in process in dollars. Labor reporting is usually tied in with dispatching and is the basis for labor efficiency reports. The vendor schedules costed out tell how much of the purchased material is due to be shipped by vendor by time period to support the plan.

Perhaps, the most important result of an operating system that can work is inventory valuation. When the inventory records are correct - as they have to be for an MRP system to operate - having accounting cost these records out to get the value of the inventory is a very straightforward matter.

When the operating system works, using it to drive the accounting system means that accounting has better numbers to work with than ever before. It also means that the operating system makes more sense to management than ever before because dollars is the language of business. And when the operating system and the financial system are saying the same things, the financial people and the operating people can talk the same language to management rather than presenting conflicting information.

Section 4
Financial Planning and Control and the "What Ifs?"

With MRP II, the elements of a control system do exist. The purchase commitment report, for example, can become an instrument of financial planning and control because:

1.   There is no false backlog (assuming it's properly managed, particularly at the master schedule level).

2.   It states what future purchases should be to support current production plans rather than relying on historical comparisons.

3.   It is stated in product groups that make sense rather than strictly by commodity (although it can be sorted by commodity if purchasing wishes this information).

4.   Actual purchases and inventory can be compared against the plan.

5.   It is a real control system with a plan, feedback to compare against the plan, etc.

Standard cost was one of the techniques that was developed in the early 1900's in order to better measure manufacturing performance and, thus, control it better. One financial consultant made the following observations about standard costs:

The only fundamental change in standard costs since it was developed in the early 1900's has been to put it in the computer. It's been very difficult to calculate the impact of changes in volume on standard cost in the past. The standard cost system was a static system trying to operate in a dynamic world. In order to make it usable, financial people tended to add more sophistication and complication to it trying to cope with change. MRP is fundamentally a simulator. When the financial figures are tied into MRP, the impact of changes can be calculated readily. And finally, approaches to standard cost can be greatly simplified to make them more understandable and usable by management. (1)

One company that has a highly successful MRP system has integrated it with their financial system and calculates their standard cost as follows:

1. They develop a master schedule based on a sales plan and produce a material requirements plan and a capacity requirements plan.

2. They get the purchased cost and run it against the plan to get material dollars by item, by product group, and in total.

3. They run the labor cost by the capacity plan which shows standard hours of capacity required by work centers to get their labor dollars by item, by work center, by family groups, and in total.

4. They spread the overhead over the planned production rates and divide this by units in order to develop their total product cost.

5. They may do this several times to test the effect that swings in volume would have on product cost.

This company is able to develop standard costs during the annual budgeting process and can review them regularly as production plans change.

Using MRP II as a simulator, management can now get factual answers to questions like:

1. Does the product mix in the projected shipping plan give us the desired shipping dollars?

2. Will the product mix in that shipping plan meet the projected _profit_ plan?

3. What is the profitability by product line at the projected volumes (spreading overhead across different volumes has a significant effect on profitability).

4. With the anticipated product mix, what will the purchase commitments have to be and what will the labor purchases have to be?

5. Can we <u>afford</u> next year's business plan?

These are just a few of the questions that can be answered with this type of system.

Section 5
How Much Inventory is Enough?

Perhaps one of the most important questions that can be answered is the old classic, "how much inventory is enough?" Reams and reams of paper have been filled on this subject, and most of what has been written is "mumbo jumbo." There are books that tell how the manager can go to statistical tables to determine the levels of safety stock required and calculate the economic order quantities and, with this information, determine the optimum level of inventory. Unfortunately, this is all based on theory that has not held up well in the real world (see Appendix 4, The Order Point Inventory Model). According to this theory, inventories would be managed by adjusting lot sizes and safety stocks. In the real world, inventories are not managed directly. In fact, there is no such thing as "inventory management" per se. Inventory management is a by-product of scheduling. When material can be brought in just when it is needed, inventories will be managed effectively. At Toyota, the Japanese get phenomenal inventory turnover, and they describe their system as the "just in time" system.

Some managers read publications where they can get industry averages for inventories to see if they are doing well. Unfortunately, these industry averages assume that all companies in the "metal forming industry" should have the same turnover rate (whether they own their own cold rolling mill or purchase steel on the outside; whether they sell through distributors or have 17 branch warehouses of their own!). Industry averages also assume that the average is right! There is no reason to believe that these averages are right for the companies in the survey - much less for the company trying to answer the question, "How much inventory is enough for us?"

MRP can be used to very easily answer the question, "How much inventory is enough?" Figure 12-5, shown earlier in Section 3 of this chapter, illustrates the method. Costing out the on-hand balances for a product group can show the amount of material on hand to support sales or production requirements in the case of components. Costing out the requirements line can show how much material will be consumed period by period. Costing out the scheduled receipts line and the planned order release line can show how much material will be coming in. The projected available balance shows the projected inventory balances by time period that will be required. This, for example, is the amount of stockroom inventory that is "enough." And only three things could possibly change that:

1. Increasing the lot sizes would leave more "residue" inventory above immediate requirements thus resulting in higher inventory levels. Decreasing lot sizes would have the opposite effect.

2. Increasing safety time (whether it is expressed in "time" or "quantity") would bring material in earlier than needed thus resulting in increased safety stocks. Decreasing safety time would reduce safety stocks.

3. Changing the master schedule.

But the important things, in practice, are not the lot sizing or the safety stocks, but the company's ability to make the schedule happen as planned. Obviously, MRP could be used to simulate the effects of different lot sizing rules and safety stocks without using theoretical probability tables. But that's not the real issue. The real issues are these:

I. Is the master schedule doable?

2. Did purchasing bring in the material on schedule?

3. Did manufacturing make the material on schedule?

4. Did the shipments go out as planned?

If these plans are met - and this is the other half of the challenge in running a manufacturing business with MRP, executing the plans - projected inventory balances will turn out as planned. And these plans can take into effect new product introduction, anticipated changes in mix, changes in the marketplace, etc.

The stockroom inventory has been used in the discussion above. The "scheduled receipts" in MRP could be costed out and totaled for manufactured items to develop work-in-process inventory in dollars. Since shop order progress is monitored by work center for shop dispatching, the amount of labor that has actually been applied to a job is readily available.

How much work-in-process inventory is enough? The big variable that affects how much work-in-process is needed is queue-in process safety stock. The amount really required can be determined by sampling the actual queue at each significant work center. The <u>difference</u> between the high and the low is the amount needed to keep the work center from running out of work. This can be built back into the scheduling rules used by production control and, consequently, into the lead times in MRP. As lead times are shortened, MRP will release orders <u>later</u>, thus reducing work-in-process. And MRP II can be used to plan and monitor what this level of work-in-process will be.

MRP can be used to plan inventory budgets by product group. The important point is that <u>inventory level</u> is now an obsolete concept - with the proper tools, we have learned to think in terms of <u>inventory flow</u>. Now the monitoring of the actual inventory dollars can be based on a rational plan giving managers a true <u>control</u> over inventory investment.

Section 6
Using Standard Cost for Decision Making

Some form of standard cost system is used by most manufacturing businesses. It represents the "plan" against which costs are to be "controlled."

Unfortunately, standard cost can be very misleading when used for decision making by people who do not understand the implications of a standard cost calculation. The basic standard cost is broken down into three elements:

1. Labor.
2. Material.
3. Overhead.

Here are a few examples of the kind of silly conclusions that can be drawn by people looking at standard costs without knowing what the cost figures represent:

In a company with a very heavy press department, it was suggested that the presses be moved into an adjacent department so that there would be a lower overhead rate, thus resulting in reduced manufacturing costs for a product. This suggestion was made by a graduate industrial engineer!

In another company, several people proposed that overtime was really more economical than regular time because the product cost would be lower! And they cited the following example:

Straight Time		Overtime	
Labor	$1.00	Labor	$1.50
Material	$3.00	Material	$3.00
Overhead	$4.00	Overhead	$ .50
Product Cost	$8.00	Product Cost	$5.00

Obviously, with overtime, the labor cost at time and a half will be $1.50 per unit of product rather than $1.00. The material cost will stay the same, but the overhead will drop dramatically. Working overtime will not increase the plant manager's pay, the pay of the industrial engineering department, production control, etc. Consequently, only the variable portion of the overhead - die maintenance in a press shop, for example - should be included in the product cost since it is assumed that all other fixed overhead was absorbed at the planned production rate.

A third company made some make or buy decisions in what appeared to be a very straightforward manner. They had a product that they could produce in their own factories or have produced by a subcontractor. The first year they started, their costs were as follows:

<u>Factory cost per unit</u>	.25
<u>Outside purchased cost</u>	.22

So they decided to buy more outside and produce less inside. The following year the costs were as follows:

<u>Factory cost per unit</u>	.32
<u>Outside purchased cost</u>	.23

They decided that this made it even more profitable to buy material outside. By the third year, the costs were as follows:

<u>Factory cost per unit</u>	.45
<u>Outside purchased cost</u>	.25

And as the company apparently "saved more and more money," their profits on the product line plunged dramatically.

The problem in each of the cases cited above is the failure to understand what standard costs are really all about.

In the first example, no reduction in actual overhead could be attained by moving the presses across the line into another department. The big overhead cost in the press department was the die maintenance shop and its tool makers and expensive equipment. Moving the presses into another department would have meant that die maintenance costs would have had to be included in the overhead in the new department, thus distorting the true cost of products that were not made on these presses. And <u>defeating the purpose</u> of the move!

The overtime example rests on one fundamental assumption: that all fixed overhead will be absorbed on the regular production rate. If the overhead has been applied properly, this is the case. But why not add more people and make the additional product on straight time rather than overtime, thus reducing the cost to $4.50 rather than $5.00? The point here is not that overtime is less expensive than straight time, but that added volume will reduce product cost because it gives the overhead a broader base to be spread across.

In the third example, it's easy to see what's happening. The standard cost included a great deal of overhead that the subcontractor simply doesn't have - inventory carrying costs, industrial engineering cost, etc. When more product is purchased and less made, this overhead - which is a real cost - will be spread across a smaller base. This will increase the cost to manufacture the product inside and, ultimately, reduce profit.

These are all examples of ways that have actually been used in practice to make bad decisions with standard cost. The problem is very straightforward:

EVERY STANDARD COST FIGURE ASSUMES
A GIVEN PRODUCTION RATE.

One classic mistake that a number of companies have made in make or buy decisions is using the overhead rate by labor or machine hour. This does not solve the basic problem because the overhead rate was based on a given volume, and if that volume is going to change, the overhead rate is no longer valid.

Using standard cost for make or buy decisions, for example, can best be done using MRP. Here, alternate plans can be tested to determine:

1. If we purchase these outside, what effect will it have on our costs inside?

2. If we purchase this material outside, what effect will the change in volume have on overall profitability?

Overhead represents a very large portion of the standard cost. Decisions using standard cost should always recognize that the standard cost is established for a given volume. Any decision that will change that volume should be made only after simulation to determine the impact of that change on overall company profitability.

Section 7
The Planning Department

The terms "production and inventory control" today are obsolescent because they really are just labels for the order launching and expediting functions. The term "accounting" is one that may also disappear during the next decade. As one financial executive said, "We have done a great job of telling management where they've been, but a very poor job of showing them where they are going."

"Financial planning and control" will be the task of the financial people, and they and the operating people will be very closely tied together. As mentioned earlier, there will someday be a "planning department," planning in units and planning in dollars, working together to provide management information to plan and control with.

There will undoubtedly be a lot more emphasis on fiscal accountability. Planners will have the accountability for inventory levels for each of their product lines and they will be accountable for being sure that the numbers represent what is really going on. Foremen will be held accountable fiscally for the amount of material - and, consequently, the dollars - that they are handling in their departments.

And the financial people, instead of being an isolated score-keeping group, constantly battling with operating people about what the numbers really mean, will become far more a part of the team.

MRP II will integrate - as it has in a number of companies already - the operating systems and the financial systems. Key financial subsystems will be integrated into the operating system such as:

1. Accounts payable.
2. Payroll.
3. Inventory transactions and stock status.
4. Cost systems.
5. Billing systems.

When this is accomplished, management has something that has never been practical before because a workable operating system was never practical before. Today, management can have <u>one reliable set of numbers</u> to use to run the business.

Footnotes
_____

1.   Andre Martin (MRP II financial consultant, and edu-
cator, Montreal, Canada), correspondence July 15, 1981.

Chapter 13
MRP II in Engineering

Section 1
Engineering in the Mainstream

We have done our best to compartmentalize the major functions in a manufacturing enterprise. But, there is no need for marketing unless production is making a product. There is no need for production unless engineering has developed that product. There is no need for engineering unless finance has obtained and maintained the funds to keep the business operating, and there is no need for finance if marketing isn't there to sell the product. The major functions in a manufacturing business are indispensable to each other.

In the past, however, engineering was seen like virtually every other function: in a vacuum. They didn't see themselves as members of a team. In fact, in many companies, the various functions saw themselves as <u>competitors</u>!

Engineering's feelings were summed up very well by one professional engineer who said, "In my first few years in engineering, I thought that producing the bill of material was the last official act in the engineering cycle." The idea that providing and maintaining proper data to run the business was a function of engineering simply didn't come through in a company where the informal system was the real system. Accurate data was not important.

As one plant manager said, "Two things that would slow us down faster than anything else would be to work to the dates on the shop orders and work to the blueprint."

It's not unusual to see a company where the tolerances on the prints cannot reasonably be expected to be met by the factory. The reaction of the people in the factory is to feel that the tolerances are just a "target." The reaction of the engineering people is to tighten up the tolerances. No one works to the tolerances that they've established so they make them tighter!

This is the climate of the informal system. A climate where information could not possibly be used for control and, consequently, accuracy was not given a high priority in day-to-day operations.

The problems of the informal system show up in the way bills of material are traditionally handled. The typical company has several bills of material; one for finance, one for manufacturing, one for production control, one for engineering, one for the service department, etc. And they seldom agree with each other! The lack of a common game plan meant each function in the company played their own game with their own tools.

Once a company starts operating with a formal system, engineering's role in preparing and maintaining basic data changes. Engineering data is no longer reference information, it becomes control information. Engineering data is the information that is really used to run a manufacturing business with MRP II. This means that bills of material have to be correct and be in a format that is useful for planning. It means that there has to be one consistent, simple part numbering system. It means that routings need to be correct in specifying the actual operations that a job goes through. Engineering change needs to be handled in a methodical fashion, as does new product introduction.

A company with a highly engineered product can use MRP II to tie in the activities of engineering, purchasing, finance, and manufacturing far more closely. No longer should the engineering people be working hard to develop a particular set of product specifications when, in fact, purchasing needs other information first for the long lead time items.

With a formal system like MRP II, the role of the major functions in a manufacturing company changes. In the world of the informal system, it was very much like the members of a golf team, all of whom are playing their individual games to help the team win. With MRP II, each player is more like a member of a football team whose activities need to be coordinated to dovetail with the activities of every other function so that the team can win. Engineering's contribution was important before. In the world of the formal system, it is absolutely vital. Without their active participation, MRP II can't possibly work well.

One company in Michigan provided a good example of the way engineering, manufacturing, marketing, and finance can head off in different directions on an engineering change. The general manager asked why a new product had been introduced obsoleting $50,000 worth of material that could have been used. The answer from production control was, "Engineering told us we had to do it." The answer from engineering was, "Marketing told us we had to do it." The answer from marketing was, "Nobody told us it was going to cost $50,000." MRP II provides some tools so that marketing, manufacturing, finance, and engineering can really plan and control engineering change.

One of the most frustrating problems in a manufacturing company is scheduling engineering. Engineering people don't put a lot of credence in schedules because they realize that schedules, in general, aren't valid. They see no reason why their creativity should be harnessed to a schedule when the manufacturing people pay little attention to these same schedules.

Scheduling engineering is just as important as scheduling manufacturing. And it isn't necessary to use complex techniques like PERT (Project Evaluation and Review Technique) or CPM (Critical Path Method). The same simple techniques that are used to schedule manufacturing can be used in engineering. The basic material requirements planning, and capacity requirements planning programs can be used to plan activities as well as materials in an engineering department. Once manufacturing schedules are valid, there is no reason why engineering schedules can't be tied into them and also be valid.

Section 2
A Common, Accurate, Bill of Material

Bills of material describe what material is required and how the product is put together (or "taken apart" in a company where semi-finished material can be finished many different ways to become the end item). Consequently, the bills of material in a manufacturing company affect many functions including:

1. Design engineering.
2. Manufacturing engineering.
3. Order entry.
4. Production planning and inventory control.
5. Manufacturing.
6. Finance.
7. Quality Assurance.
8. Product service.

When a company uses several bills of material, the one that engineering creates usually shows things from a design engineering point of view. This bill of material may show all electrical components in a group. A second bill of material, used by the planning department, will show the electrical components broken down into groups that are feature dependent. Components associated with a feature to electronically locate a table on a machine tool would be grouped together for planning purposes.

The manufacturing people would certainly want to know that a die casting (which engineering identifies with only one part number) can actually be finished by painting it orange, painting it black, or giving it a tumbled finish. The planning group will want to know this for scheduling purposes and so will the financial people for labor accounting purposes, even though engineering may see this as one die casting in the bill of material.

There may still be another bill of material, an informal manufacturing bill of material, that has information written on it like "shim to fit," or "when order calls for .062 cold rolled 1010, use 1020 trim in warehouse."

The problems with multiple bills of material are obvious. They seldom agree, yet they are used for engineering, planning, manufacturing, finance, product service, and product configuration control.

Configuration control means having a history showing that the product at a particular time had a particular set of materials going into it. Consider the task of a producer of electronic copying machines. The product is in a constant state of change. How do service people know which products contained what components? This same problem exists in the aircraft industry and many others. Configuration control is essential in these industries, but configuration control in a company with many different bills of material is certainly a challenge!

A common bill of material for all functions in the company is essential for MRP II. Coding can be used to add nonengineering part numbers to the bill of material or to print the bill of material in the format required by a particular function. A common bill of material data base means one uniform set of product structure information used by all functions and, consequently, drawing upon one set of correct information.

And that's the issue. Keeping bills of material correct. In the informal system, people didn't use the bills of material for planning very effectively so they didn't need to be correct. When they weren't, the people responded on the assembly floor, for example, by writing in the correct component and deleting the incorrect one that was on their bill of material. MRP II is a planning system. It's a system to prevent the shortages and other problems that lack of planning made routine in the past. But if planning is to be correct, bills of material must be correct.

Section 3
Making the Bill of Material a Planning Tool

Before MRP II, accurate bills of material which rep- resented the way the product was really made were not a requirement. One company that makes machine tools had a manual order point system in the inventory control depart- ment. They also had an inventory control manager who had been with the company for 25 years. He had a monthly meeting with the marketing and manufacturing people, and they decided on their assembly schedules for the next few months. He had many of the bills of material committed to memory. A few had to be looked up. But in this meeting - incidentally, it was called the "bill of materials meeting" - he did the real material requirements planning. While bills of material were not always accurate, the in- ventory manager knew how the product was being built, and had many manual corrections written into his version of the engineering bills.

With MRP II, bills of material are one of the founda- tions of a formal planning system. This means that bills of material sometimes need to be restructured for the following reasons:

1. To facilitate forecasting.
2. To facilitate planning. To make it possible for MRP to simulate stockroom pulls and, thus, gen- erate predicted shortage lists. (1)

When a lot of the planning was done working around the formal bill of material, its structure wasn't critical. In a formal system, it is critical that the bill of material be a useful planning tool. Several "nonengineering" bill of material structuring approaches are discussed in the balance of this section.

In a make-to-stock business, the product is defined. Thus, bills of material usually do not have to be restruc- tured for forecasting. In a make-to-order business, par- ticularly one making a modular product, bills of material may very well have to be restructured to facilitate fore- casting - or indeed to make it practical to forecast at all.

Figure 13-1 shows a common situation in a make-to- order business where there are any number of combinations of options that can be used together. In this example, the company is making generator sets that include a gasoline engine, a generator, a base, and a control unit.

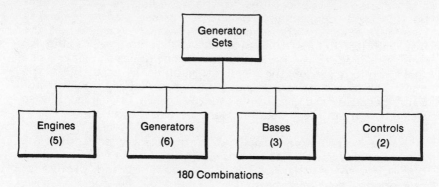

180 Combinations

Figure 13 - 1.   The Combinations of Options

Any of the engines, generators, bases, and control units in this example can be used in combination. Consequently, there are 180 different possible combinations. Forecasting sales for each of these possible combinations is virtually impossible. And, if it isn't now, it ultimately will be. If the engineering department develops one more control unit, the number of possible combinations jumps to 270.

MASTER SCHEDULE CONTAINS:

Quantity	Engine	Generator	Base	Control
5	#1	#1	#1	#1
10	#2	#1	#1	#1
5	#1	#3	#2	#2
5	#3	#2	#3	#2

Order For: Engine   #3
             Generator   #3
             Base   #1
             Control   #1

Figure 13 - 2.   Master Scheduling in a Final Product Configuration

Figure 13-2 shows the kind of problems that can happen if a company tries to master schedule in terms of final product configuration. An order was received for a product consisting of engine number 3, generator number

3, base number 1, and control number 1. There is no such product included in the master schedule, even though there are number 3 type engines in the schedule as well as number 3 type generators, number 1 bases, and number 1 controls. Each of these modules is really assembled at the last minute before the product is shipped. Trying to master schedule a final product configuration may mean that, while each of the product modules is actually in the plan, the customer order must be scheduled at a much later date because the master schedule made it impossible to recognize that these modules were actually available.

The point is very simple: in the master schedule, the final configuration of the product is irrelevant. The important concern is the individual components and groups of components that are needed. Instead of 180 possible combinations, the master schedule should include 5 engines, 6 generators, 3 bases, and 2 controls for a total of 16 items to be forecast rather than 180. As orders come in, order entry breaks them down into engines, generators, bases and controls, and matches them with what was planned in the master schedule. Figure 13-3 shows the master schedule for engine number 1 and generator number 3.

Engine #3	Week 1	2	3	4	5
Master Schedule	10	10	10	10	10
Actual Demand	10	10	7	5	2
Available to Promise	0	0	3	5	8

Generator #3	Week 1	2	3	4	5
Master Schedule	5	5	5	5	5
Actual Demand	5	4	3	3	2
Available to Promise	0	1	2	2	3

Figure 13 - 3. Master Scheduling by Module

The master schedule line represents the amount to be actually made, "actual demand" is really the number of engines or generators that have been "committed" against customer orders. "Available to promise" indicates the number of units in the master schedule that have not been committed to customer orders. An order requiring engine number 3 and generator number 3 would be matched against the master schedule. The example in Figure 13-3 would indicate that engines are available in week 3 and a generator is available in week 2. Therefore, the customer order would be scheduled to go into assembly in week 3, and the available to promise for engines and for generators would be reduced by one in week 3 as the customer order was posted against the master schedule.

When a product - like the one described above - is modular and the bills of material aren't, people have to develop stopgap approaches. The "add/delete" bill of material is an excellent example of a bill of material that can be used for reacting, but not for planning. Using the add/delete bill of material with a product - assume it is generator sets - the bill of material is made up to show engine number 5, generator number 5, base number 2, and control number 2. When an order is received for the same configuration of engine, base, and control, but with generator number 6 instead of generator number 5, generator number 5 can be deleted and replaced by generator number 6 for order entry and product configuration purposes. This approach starts from the wrong premise. Better to have the bills of material developed in product modules and add to them rather than subtract from them. If generator number 6 was never included in the planning function, it is not likely to be there when the orders are actually received. Add/delete bills of material are a stopgap for translating customer orders into bills of material that can be used in manufacturing. They do not in any way facilitate the planning to make sure that the material and the capacity will be there when the customer order is received.

One of the techniques that can facilitate planning in the master schedule is called a "planning bill of material." Figure 13-4 shows an example using a planning bill of material. It breaks the generator sets down into engines, generators, bases, and controls, and it indicates a percentage based on history or forecast for each option. Engine number 1, for example, normally constitutes 20 percent of total customer demand. Therefore, if there are

200 generator sets being made per month, 40 units of engine number 1 should be planned. The planning bill of material is an excellent example of a nonengineering bill of material. It is used for planning purposes only and has no significance for the engineers. Yet, it can draw upon a common data base and greatly facilitate the planning function.

For 200 Generator Sets Per Month

	#1	2	3	4	5	6
Engines	20%/40	30%/60	10%/20	25%/50	15%/30	
Generators	30%/60	10%/20	10%/20	15%/30	5%/10	30%/60
Bases	40%/80	30%/60	30%/60			
Controls	60%/120	40%/80				

Figure 13 - 4. The Planning Bill of Material

Planning bills of material may include more than specific items or subassemblies. They may include groups of items that need to be scheduled together. An electric motor manufacturer, for example, may supply the motor with a ball bearing or a plain bearing. The forecast will be broken down into the number of ball bearings and plain bearings, or the percentage of these, in the planning bill of material. But the end bell for the ball bearing and the end bell for the plain bearing obviously have to fit the type of bearing to be used. The planning bill of material would identify that the ball bearing and the end bell that is machined to take a ball bearing should always be planned together in matching quantities.

There are other nonengineering bills of material called "kit numbers." These consist, typically, of groups of low value parts like fasteners, etc., that always go with a particular option or are common to a product. Rather than identify each of the components individually, they are grouped together under a "nonengineering part number" called a "kit." Thus, with one number in the master schedule, an entire group of components that goes with a particular feature can be properly scheduled.

The problem of adding nonengineering part numbers has been covered, but there are many times when there are engineering numbers in the bill of material that need to be eliminated or worked around for planning purposes. Consider, for example, a subassembly that engineering has defined on their bill of material. In practice, this subassembly is built on the assembly line and put right into the product. It does not go in and out of stores because it is built on a lot-for-lot or "as required" basis. In other words, if 100 assemblies are to be made, 100 subassemblies will also be made.

This would be a simple matter to deal with if the item never went into stores, then it could be ignored in MRP. But there are circumstances where it well might go into stores. They include:

1. A production overrun.
2. Not enough of a matching component to use up all of the units manufactured.
3. Service part requirement.
4. Customer return.

In other words, there are times when items that are "built on the line" (often called "phantoms") need to be identified in the scheduling system in order to recognize that they are available. Companies not recognizing that MRP is a simulation of the real world often got themselves into serious paperwork complications trying to handle this situation.

One company developed a paperwork system for putting material into the stockroom and taking it out wherever "phantom" subassemblies appeared on the bill of material. These subassemblies didn't actually go into stock. This company went through the paperwork steps because they showed the phantom subassembly in their inventory file and felt they, therefore, had to treat it like any other subassembly. Of course, they had great difficulties keeping the paperwork straight. To simulate the way things really happen is difficult enough without trying to do extra paperwork that doesn't mean anything.

Another company making medical equipment decided to move material in and out of the stockroom whenever an engineering subassembly appeared on the bill of material. They would, for example, take a base, put a bearing support box in it, and because this showed as a separate part number on the bill of material, move this material back into the stockroom. Later the material was moved back out to have the bearing inserted into the support. The assembly procedure that used to take a few days now became several weeks because they tried to make the real world conform to an engineering bill of material that really didn't represent the way the product was built. The first company tried to handle the paperwork to simulate material going in and out of the stockroom whenever a subassembly appeared on the bill of material. The second company actually physically moved the material in and out of the stockroom. Neither of these approaches was a good solution to the problem.

Users have developed a technique for handling this condition called the "phantom" (or "transient") bill of material. Using this approach, an overrun of sub-assemblies, for example, could be put into stock. The computer logic would notice that the overrun was available and would do all the planning at lower levels taking this into account. But because "phantom" subassemblies are assigned zero lead time and use no lot sizing techniques other than "lot-for-lot," requirements would fall right through to the lower level components because these "built on the line" subassemblies would normally not be ordered, nor put into inventory.

It's important to recognize that the master schedule translates production plans into specific components and groups of components. The bill of material is the instrument for doing this. It's obvious that every item to be scheduled must be identified uniquely. The example of a die casting that could later be painted one of two colors or given a tumbled finish was used above. From an engineering point of view, that may look like one die casting; from a scheduling point of view, there must be four part numbers, one for the unfinished die casting and one for each of the three possible finishes.

In other words, part numbering and bill of material structures must represent the way the product is actually scheduled. Consider the example of a pharmaceutical company where the bill of material shows the drugs that will be used and the packaging material on the same bill of material. Scheduling couldn't possibly be done without some modification to this bill of material. The drugs will be pulled out of the stockroom at the very beginning of the production cycle. The packaging material will be pulled out at the very end.

Since MRP is a simulation of the shortage list, it works the same way. It is a simulation of the "stockroom pulls" of material.   When this is kept in mind, the logic of bill of material structuring is easy to understand.

Section 4
Part Numbering

Undoubtedly, one of the most interesting intellectual exercises involved in developing manufacturing systems has been the creation of significant part numbers. With this scheme, the first two numbers represent the product, for example. The second three numbers represent the size. The next four represent the material, etc. Unfortunately, significant part numbering schemes generally fail for two reasons:

1. No matter how much foresight the originator has, there will always be something that requires more numbers than the originator had planned on. The second characteristic assumed to be described by two numbers, for example, needs to be described by three. Significant part numbering systems fall apart rapidly in the real world for this reason.

2. Significant part numbering systems generate extremely long and awkward part numbers. Since a digit must be allowed for any possible contingency in describing the product, significant part numbering systems often have 12 or 15 different digits when a nonsignificant part numbering system could have used 7 or 8.

The whole idea of a significant part numbering system loses validity with the availability of modern computer systems. There is no reason why the computer system can't store a description of the product and its material, etc. without putting this into the part number. With manual systems, it seemed to make sense to have the part number represent the way the product was made, the material it was made from, etc. With computer systems, there is no longer any need to do this, and part numbers now can assume their rightful function of being "unique identifiers" rather than "descriptors."

Perhaps, the ultimate example of using part numbers poorly was a company in the aerospace business which decided to use part numbers supplied by the Department of Defense, their vendors, or their customer to describe their components. Computers are high speed idiots. They would have difficulty coping with the filing problems of parts numbered:

HO-14325-64
17458911A
QQRHH51-433

In this particular company, material would come into stock against a back order, but the chances were great that no one would know that the material arrived since the filing system became totally incomprehensible - even to human beings. A filing system that human beings couldn't possibly understand would, obviously, be a disaster for computers.

The principles involved in part numbering are:

1. Each item to be scheduled needs a part number.
2. A part numbering system should be simple.
3. Part numbers should be short.
4. A part number must be a unique identifier - not a descriptor.

Section 5
Fixing the Bills of Material

MRP is far less tolerant of bill of material errors than it is of inventory record errors. Bill of material accuracy must be at 98+ percent before MRP can work, according to experienced MRP users. An inventory record error might be on the plus side or there might still be enough material for immediate requirements even though there wasn't as much material as the records showed. But a bill of material error is usually significant in that it either calls out the wrong component or omits a component. The best way to get the bills of material fixed is to take someone from engineering and someone from manufacturing and have them go over the bills of material and correct them. In many companies, this is a major project that will take three or four people a year or more to complete.

Bill of material accuracy can be checked at the stock-room door. The inventory transaction form for an un-planned withdrawal should have a place to note whether this was because of a bill of material error or some other reason. The number of bills of material that are pulled during the week should be counted, and the number that had errors should be counted, with 98 percent considered a minimum objective. Obviously, bill of material errors should be reported immediately and fixed. But, that is a by-product of the performance measure being used to make sure that the "process" of making and maintaining bills of material correctly is working at an acceptable level of performance. The prime objective is to find out why the errors are occurring and fix the cause of the errors.

Section 6
Routings

Figure 13-5 shows a typical routing. The routing shows the operation sequence, the standard hours per operation, etc. Capacity is planned in standard hours and credited in standard hours. Thus, if the capacity requirements plan calls for 15 hours of work, when that work is completed, 15 hours will be credited on the output report against the plan. Even if the standard is off and the job really took 18 hours, 15 hours were planned and 15 hours were credited. Thus, there is considerable tolerance in the accuracy of the standards required in an MRP system. Obviously, if the standards are biased in any given direction, output will tend to be higher or lower than planned over a period of time. Nevertheless, the MRP system itself does not require precision in the standards. And that's a good thing, because there are a number of companies that would have an awful lot of work to do to get their standards corrected if that were a necessity in an MRP system!

Part No. 80021 — Locater Pin

Oper.	Dept.	Work Center	Desc.	Setup	Per Piece
10	08	1322	Cut Off	.5	.010
20	32	1600	Rough Turn	1.5	.030
30	32	1204	Finish Turn	3.3	.048
40	11		Inspect		

Figure 13 - 5.   Routing

It is essential, however, that the routing represent the way the job actually moves through the shop. It should accurately depict which work centers the job must go through. If it doesn't, the capacity planning will be against the wrong work centers, and most importantly, the dispatch list - the daily schedule that goes down to the shop - will not show the job going to the correct work center.

This doesn't mean that alternate routings can't be used in MRP. Because MRP is a simulation of the real world, anything that can be done can be depicted by MRP. It does mean that when an alternate routing is used, the capacity planner who decided to use it must show that this shop order is using the alternate routing. That will keep the dispatching correct.

Fixing routings usually requires a fairly substantial effort before MRP goes on the air. After it is on the air, the routings can be maintained by having the foremen report back based on the dispatch list any time there is an error in the routing. Whenever a job shows on the dispatch list and isn't really in the department, the routing could be the cause of the error. Whenever a job is in the department and doesn't show on the dispatch list, the routing could be the cause of the error. Routing accuracy can be measured by counting the number of routings that are issued to the shop each week and the number of routing errors that are reported back from the shop each week. Routing accuracy should be at 95 to 98 percent to have MRP work properly.

One of the stumbling blocks for many companies in getting MRP on the air is getting the routings corrected. Most routing files are a great example of the 80/20 rule. Eighty percent of the activity takes place in twenty percent of the routings. If all of the routings in the file are to be corrected before MRP is installed, this could be an almost insurmountable task for many companies. But there is a practical approach to it facilitated by MRP:

1.   Have the routings checked and corrected for the 20 percent of the items that have 80 percent of the activity before the MRP pilot is started. (See Chapter 17 for more information about the "pilot.")

2.   As MRP goes on the air progressively, use the planned order releases for several weeks ahead to indicate which routings will have to be reviewed and corrected.

3.   This can be continued through the early stages of capacity planning and dispatching to make sure that the routings that are going to be used in the near future are correct.

When the routing file is not completely correct, capacity planning won't be done properly. Nevertheless, this is usually a practical way to get an MRP system up and operating without having to wait for all of the routing file to be corrected. The number of significant errors due to erroneous capacity planning is most likely going to be quite low.

Section 7
Engineering Change

An example of the cost of an unplanned and uncontrolled engineering change was given earlier in this chapter. Two things are required to plan and control engineering change properly:

1. A system that shows the proper timing for phasing in engineering changes and the material obsolescence that will be involved with these changes.

2. A group of people who will use this information to make responsible decisions that are best for the company

Engineering changes fall into three basic categories:

1. At once (usually required because of a problem with the product in the field).

2. A "time fence" - or "effectivity date" - beyond which old material cannot be used for a variety of reasons such as a law that forbids its use after a given date.

3. Use up all available material and phase in the new material.

The "at-once" engineering change, while often very expensive and sometimes disastrous, is the easiest one to schedule. All of the old material must be found and scrapped, and replaced with new material.

The second type of engineering change (must be done by a given date) is also fairly straightforward, and MRP facilitates planning to have this new material available on that given date. It becomes more complicated where inventory is maintained in many locations such as distribution centers, and distribution resource planning can help considerably in this kind of planning. Engineering change to an established date can also involve matching components. Then it becomes as complex as the "phase-in" engineering change.

The most difficult type of engineering change to plan is the "phase-in" change. Unfortunately, plans made once are likely to change as inventory changes, schedules change, etc. One of the big problems is keeping engineering change information up to date to minimize the scrap of matching components, and also to minimize production shortages, because material is supposed to be available but isn't yet.

Even without MRP, it would be possible to plan how a phase-in should take place. But keeping that up to date in the real world was the challenge. Coping with change is MRP's strong suit.

There are a variety of techniques that can be used with MRP to plan and control "phase-in" engineering change. Three of the most commonly used techniques are:

1. Engineering change effectivity dates. Using this approach, the computer system changes the planning from the old component to the new component on a given date. This date is planned in advance using MRP, but it must be reviewed regularly to make sure that the date is still valid. If, for example, there are matching components that have to be changed at the same time, and one of them has some scrap or a particularly large service requirement, that could change the effectivity date.

2. The phantom bill of material routine for phase-in. Using this approach, the component to be replaced is treated like a phantom and the new component is put in the bill of material at the lower level. This allows the requirements to net against the old component, but to plan for the new component when the old component will be used up. This approach gets more difficult to handle when there are several components that are being replaced simultaneously, and users should be aware of the potential for misrepresenting costs on a product cost buildup, since both the new and old components are contained in the bills of material.

3. Lot number control. Using this approach, an engineering change is planned for a particular time and tied to a particular lot number. While

more complex from a computer program point of view, this is probably the most satisfactory method because it requires less review to make sure that requirements haven't changed substantially. As requirements change, the timing of the lot can be changed, and all related components can respond to this.

There are a number of objectives in establishing an engineering change system. An MRP II system can be used to simulate the effect of the engineering change in balancing inventory, minimizing obsolescence, predicting the cost of the change, and evaluating alternative plans.

MRP can provide the technical tools to plan and monitor engineering change and the cost of engineering change. But a committee composed of people from production planning, purchasing, marketing, manufacturing, engineering, and finance should be accountable for implementing engineering changes. Any engineering change is a compromise between marketing, engineering, manufacturing, and financial objectives. It should be planned using MRP II and monitored closely to see that the change achieves the desired result.

Section 8
New Product Introduction and the Highly Engineered Product

The problems of introducing a new product are very similar to the problems involved in making a highly engineered product which is, in fact, a new product each time it's made. Many people don't think MRP can work in this environment. In fact, this is exactly the environment where MRP is needed most.

Perhaps the notion that MRP does not apply stems from the fact that complete bills of material are usually not available early in the design or manufacturing cycle for new products or highly engineered products. Engineering is working on these constantly during the development of the product. Nevertheless, long lead time material needs to be specified, even though the bill of material is not complete.

Even a partial bill of material can be very helpful. As the schedule changes, priorities for components or activities in engineering can be moved around so that efforts are being spent in the right area. Engineering, for example, should not be spending a lot of time getting customer approval on a blueprint when the contract has been moved out into the future. Their efforts should be spent on getting customer approval on some blueprints that are in the "critical path."

The informal system was dependent upon communication between engineering, purchasing, and manufacturing. They communicated with a partial bill of material until such time as the bill of material was fully developed. To some extent - hopefully - engineering's activity was directed at developing specifications for the longest lead time components in the product first. Without MRP, this wasn't always true. Using MRP, it can be true. Once again, MRP provides the game plan for people to work together more effectively. But they must use it.

Section 9
Scheduling Engineering

Many techniques have been proposed for scheduling engineering. MRP is a simple form of network planning that can be used in any situation where there are a series of interdependent events to be planned and controlled. There are great advantages to using the same planning system (MRP II) in engineering as is used in every other aspect of the business, as opposed to using systems that tend to look different to the user like PERT or CPM.

The material requirements plan can be used to schedule activities in engineering as well as required material, if there is any. The capacity requirements plan can be used with estimates of time requirements to plan engineering capacity.

MRP, of course, was originally designed for material requirements planning. But building a product involves the same concepts as PERT and CPM. There are "events" or "tasks", and these are equivalent to the part numbers in a bill of material. There is "precedence," and this, of course, is exactly the way MRP works. Certain material has to be available before it can be machined, parts have to be available for assembly, etc. And there are "subtasks." This is a breakdown of a major task into its basic elements. Once again, a closed loop MRP system has routings that show the subtasks (like turn, inspect) to complete a task. MRP can be used to schedule engineering because an MRP program doesn't know the difference between a number that represents a task and a number that represents a part.

In a company making a highly engineered product, one of the most onerous, yet constant, tasks in the business is making bids. These bids need to include material, manpower, timing, and cost projections. MRP II can be a great aid in making these bids, because MRP is basically a simulator of a manufacturing business.

One of the requirements in many contracts is that the scheduling system be specified as part of the bid. Today, PMS ("Project Management System"), and other techniques are recognized as planning and control methods for government contracts. MRP II isn't yet. It soon will be.

With MRP II, the company game plan requires that everybody works to a schedule. The MRP technique can be used to schedule engineering as discussed above, and indeed should be wherever there are a significant number of new product introductions or engineering changes, as is normal in the typical manufacturing company. In a company with a highly engineered product, engineering becomes a normal part of the production cycle.

One manufacturing company that has been particularly successful with MRP says, "The customer is the customer of manufacturing. Manufacturing is the customer of engineering." And now that valid schedules are available, engineering is measured on meeting their schedules, just like manufacturing is measured on hitting theirs.

Section 10
What's in it for Engineering

The very fact that a company operates with one bill of material rather than multiple bills of material makes many engineering tasks much more manageable. When maintaining inventory records, for example, a transaction history is a standard part of traceability. The transaction history merely indicates what has gone out, what has gone in, and what the transactions were that caused material to go in and out of inventory. This same type of transaction history can be used for configuration control. With this kind of traceability, configuration control can be maintained for government contracts, on projects involving nuclear production, etc. Today, in the automobile industry where product recalls are not uncommon, configuration control is required. When the manufacturer finds a problem, it's important to be able to trace back to the serial number of each car that might contain the component that caused the problem. (Nothing gets easier in manufacturing!) Traceability for customer service so that the service people can know exactly what was in each product produced at a given time with a given serial number can also be maintained.

One of the great advantages of MRP from an engineering point of view is convenient information retrieval. Engineering can get bills of material in standard format, where-used format, manufacturing format, etc., all drawing upon a common data base.

Probably one of the most important things that MRP II can help generate is a team effort, because it does supply the company game plan. And when engineering can work more closely with purchasing and manufacturing, even at the product design stage, it can add dramatically to company profitability. One company making computer disc drives, for example, had a product that was designed so that virtually any required configuration of the machine could be made by changing some printed circuit boards that slid easily into the machine through a readily accessible back panel. Engineering can do a great deal to work with purchasing and manufacturing on product standardization. And this can mean fewer items to schedule, less safety stocks to be concerned with, easier field service, etc.

MRP II then has become a "three-edged sword" for engineering:

1. It involves new responsibilities, particularly in providing <u>and maintaining</u> the control information, that will be used to manage the formal system.

2. It provides new opportunities for engineering to have better data available themselves for maintaining product configuration, making bids, etc.

3. It provides the vehicle for making engineering far more a part of the management team in running a manufacturing business.

In reality, the question, "what's in it for engineering," is about as valid as asking why one of the blockers on the football team should play his position. Engineering people have been trained to be rational. The fact that there is a need for better planning is obvious to them in the typical manufacturing company. Without engineering playing its very important role on the team, the better planning simply won't happen. The question really is not what's in it for engineering, but what's in it for the entire company - "What can each of us do so we as a company can win?"

Footnotes

1. For more on the Production Plan, the Master Schedule
    and the Assembly Schedule, see Appendix 1.

Chapter 14
DRP: Distribution Resource Planning

Section 1
The Traditional Approach

When MRP was first developed, it was thought of as a way to handle the "special case" of manufacturing inventories. But, as MRP became more widely used and people saw how much better it worked than the traditional approach in manufacturing, it became apparent that the principles had application in distribution as well. In fact, the MRP principles could be used to address the problems in managing distribution inventories that were caused by the traditional approach. The basic tenets of conventional distribution inventory management were:

1. The problem of distributing inventory would start after inventory mysteriously appeared from some unidentified source. In the real world, most inventory is manufactured somewhere. The notion that distribution inventories could be treated as a separate entity totally unconnected with manufacturing caused a number of inefficiencies in manufacturing. These inefficiencies resulted in excess inventories and inadequate customer service at the distribution centers.

2. Distribution center people could order whatever they wanted, whenever they wanted to. This "pull" replenishment system not only tended to jerk the manufacturing facility around, it also caused inefficiencies in distribution. Whenever an item was in short supply - and some items will be - the pull system tended to aggravate, rather than cope with, the problem. A few distribution centers wound up with plenty of inventory while many others were out of stock.

3. The order point technique would be used for replenishing distribution center inventories. In practice, the order point system worked almost as poorly in distribution as it did in manufacturing. It failed to address the issue of "when is the material really needed?" and only addressed "when to order?" Great emphasis was placed on calculating "precise" safety stocks using statistical methods. In practice, the control of distribution replenishment lead time turned out to be far more significant than the "precision" in the safety stock calculations.

4. Lot sizing would be done using the economic order quantity for each item (SKU - Stock Keeping Unit) at each distribution center. In practice, the numbers going into the economic order quantity (EOQ) formula are very crude, and imagined economies at the distribution centers didn't really come as a result of EOQ calculations. All the economic order quantities did was build an amplifier into the system - since distribution centers ordered more than they needed because of lot sizes.

5. Allocation algorithms would make it possible for the computer to automatically distribute "fair shares" of stock in low supply. Experience taught that having the computer "automatically" make this decision turned out to be a serious misdirection.

Some of these approaches, like having distribution centers order whatever they wanted whenever they wanted it, existed before the computer came along. Computer systems technicians tended to ignore the serious management problems of failing to integrate distribution inventory planning with manufacturing production planning. Instead, they concentrated on techniques like exponential smoothing, calculation of the mean absolute deviation to determine statistically precise safety stocks and allocation algorithms. The fact that little is heard about companies where these approaches have produced any outstanding, lasting results has not deterred the proponents in any way. A student who fell asleep in a distribution inventory management class in the 1950's and woke up in the 1980's would hear very little that was new.

But, today there is a great deal that is new. Manufacturing resource planning involves planning and monitoring all of the resources of a manufacturing company - including the distribution resource.

Section 2
Integrating Manufacturing and Distribution

One company with 80 percent of their sales going through their distribution centers, and 20 percent being shipped from their main plant location, rapidly learned the folly of assuming that inventory appears from nowhere. Their product had a seasonal sales activity. During the slow season when the factory had to build inventory, the distribution centers ordered nothing. They were measured on inventory turns, and took pride in the fact that they carried a low level of inventory. Meanwhile, the factory couldn't find enough storage space in public warehouses for the inventory they knew would be ordered by the distribution centers as soon as the peak season hit. The distribution centers assumed that inventory would always be available when they required it. It wasn't <u>always</u> available. When it wasn't, the distribution people blamed the factory. As is usually the case when the system doesn't function properly, people tend to blame other people!

Another company got their material from a number of subcontractors who ran their own small manufacturing facilities rebuilding automotive parts. The subcontractors were, of course, highly motivated to maintain a fairly level operating rate. The distribution centers reported to a marketing division and had no motivation at all to try to make manufacturing more efficient. The net result was that the subcontractors always ran behind schedule during the peak season, causing a great many back orders and poor customer service. They did this in order to have a backlog going into the slow season. Some of this got canceled, but much of it they manufactured before it was canceled. Each year, the same cycle took place. Each year, the marketing department suffered from their own misconception that inventory was an unlimited resource that could be turned on or off at will.

It's important for any distribution organization to realize that their product comes from their own or another manufacturing organization. If the distribution planning doesn't tie in with the manufacturing planning, there can be finger pointing and excuses, but ultimately, it will be customer service that suffers. The need to level production is very significant in a manufacturing operation. If this objective is not tied in with the objectives of good inventory turnover, and especially, good customer service, the distribution inventory investment will not generate the customer service results that it should.

Production plans in a manufacturing organization that supply a distribution organization should be made by taking the distribution requirements into account as well as the need to build or deplete inventories in the distribution system. MRP II is a game plan for integrating the activities of the entire manufacturing and distribution organization. MRP in distribution is called Distribution Resource Planning (DRP). (1)

Section 3
"Push" Versus "Pull" Inventory Replenishment Systems

If material is in short supply - and <u>something</u> will be virtually all the time - using the pull system will prevent the company from getting the best overall use out of the limited inventory. It's easy to demonstrate, in a company with a few distribution centers, that items on back order in one distribution center are available in other distribution centers. Some companies, as a consequence, develop complex computer systems for identifying this inventory and having it shipped from one distribution center to another. Paying to ship something twice is a sure way to eliminate any profit on the product. The important thing is to distribute the material properly with each distribution center replenishment order.

It is well to review the principles of management before trying to set up a workable system for controlling distribution inventories, especially where these are supplied by a manufacturing division and the distribution centers report to marketing. This makes the management problems that much more difficult to handle. The principles of management (discussed in detail in Chapter 6) are:

1. Defining proper objectives.
2. Assigning accountability.
3. Developing understanding.
4. Providing the tools.
5. Measuring performance.
6. Providing incentives.

The problem of establishing accountability gets quite complicated in a distribution center type situation. In one company, the distribution center ordered whatever they wanted whenever they wanted to. At the main plant, orders were shipped directly to customers or to the distribution centers. The planners' attitude was that distribution center replenishment orders were not as important as customer orders since they were "just to replenish inventory." This wasn't always true, but the production planners generally followed the principle, "Ship to the customers first and the distribution centers afterwards."

Looking again at the management principles, it's important to define accountability. Once again, it's important to observe the principle:

DON'T SPLIT THE RESPONSIBILITY FOR MAKING THE "LEAST WORST CHOICE" ABOUT LIMITED RESOURCES.

If, for example, the distribution center people report to the sales department (most of them do, in fact, whether the organization chart shows it or not), each distribution center manager will be competing with the main plant to get inventory. And, for that matter, competing against the other distribution center managers. This cannot possibly result in using the limited resource of inventory well. In one company, the production planners were assigned these responsibilities:

1. Customer service out of all locations - distribution centers as well as the main plant warehouse - for their product lines.

2. They were given a stock status report so that they knew what the actual customer needs were at each distribution center as well as at the main plant warehouse.

3. No longer were they measured on shipping performance to customers and distribution centers. Instead, they were measured on customer service out of every location. Whether or not they shipped material to the distribution centers at a given time was not the issue. The issue was whether the distribution centers had the material to ship to the customers.

The distribution centers were made responsible for:

1. Inventory record accuracy (on the stock status report). This certainly could not be controlled at the main plant location when the transactions were taking place at the distribution centers.

2. Forecasting (not for ordering). The main plant provided them with simple forecasts (based on averages) 10 days before they were put into the system. It was then the distribution center manager's prerogative to override these forecasts with any local knowledge about specific customer requirements.

In a very short period of time, the production planners at the main plant location who had been saying, "Ship to the customers first and the distribution centers later," were saying, "get the material on the truck to San Francisco. We only ship every two weeks and I'll have more material here at the main plant by Wednesday."

The principle of not splitting the responsibility for a limited resource is worth thinking about a little more. If the distribution centers are competing against the main plant for limited inventory, who in the company makes the "least worst choice"? Production planners report to the materials manager. The materials manager reports to the plant manager. The distribution center managers report to the district sales manager. The district sales manager reports to the sales manager. By splitting the responsibility for that decision, it is actually moved up several levels in the organization where it simply won't be made as a matter of daily routine.

Another important principle involved in distribution center inventory management is to concentrate inventory reserves at the main plant, especially when an item is in short supply or when the inventory is low, as it is at the end of a peak selling season. One company violated this principle and had continuous problems as a result. They would normally make a six to eight week lot size of each finished goods item and ship it directly out to each of their five distribution centers. An eight week supply will not last eight weeks at all distribution centers. One might last four weeks, another twelve weeks, etc. The one that lasts four weeks is going to require material right away. As a result of using this approach, this company had open distribution center orders for virtually every product all the time.

A far better approach is to concentrate the inventory reserves at the main plant location and to replenish the distribution centers in fairly small lot sizes. The inventory reserves can be deployed when there are extraordinary demands without having to cross ship from one distribution center to another.

Using the "push" approach means that a central location actually plans the distribution inventory levels, and replenishes distribution inventories, rather than letting the distribution centers just "order whatever they want when-ever they want it." The "push" approach is very compat-ible with MRP because it ties together the distribution and manufacturing planning rather than having it done indepen-

dently.   It also provides for the best use of the inventory
resource to give better customer service.

Section 4
ROP Versus DRP

For years, the conventional wisdom was that indepen-dent demand items, such as the finished goods SKUs in a distribution system, should be ordered based on order point while dependent demand items, such as the components going into an assembly, should be ordered based on mater-ial requirements planning. The fact of the matter is that the order point approach doesn't work very well for either type of item. As time phasing became more practical with the advent of cheaper computer storage capabilities, people began to put requirements for independent demand items into time periods. This was called the "time phased order point." (2) There were many advantages to this. The time phased order point, of course, generated planned order releases, and some companies made the tragic mistake of assuming that these planned order releases could be a master schedule by themselves without any management by people. This, of course, didn't work. Technically, distri-bution requirements planning is the same as the time phased order point, but the DRP approach recognizes that the planned order releases will be considered only as input to a master schedule in order to level planned loads and make the master schedule realistic.

The main problem with the traditional approach to the order point was that it didn't really do a good job of an-swering the question, "When is the material needed?" Consider the example in Figure 14-1. In this example, there is one distribution center that orders from the main plant. The distribution center usage averages 100 per week. Its replenishment lot size is 600.

In Case 1, the on-hand inventory at the main plant location is 1450 units. When the order quantity of 600 from the distribution center plus the direct customer demand of 100 reduces the inventory to 750 units, it is below the order point of 1200 units and more material must be or-dered. In Case 2, there are 1850 units on hand when the demand for 600 from the distribution center and the demand for 100 from customers is received. The inventory equals 1150 units which is 50 units below the order point. In Case 3, there are 1250 units on hand when the demand from the distribution center and normal customer demand is received and the balance is 550 units. In the order point system, it's assumed that each delivery should take place at the end of the four-week lead time in week five.

Main Plant   Demand = 200 per week (100 = average branch requirements plus
              100 direct to customer)
              Safety stock = 400 (2 weeks)
              Lead time = 4 weeks
              Order point = 1200

Using Order Point

Case 1: Main Plant	Case 2: Main Plant	Case 3: Main Plant
On hand = 1450	1850	1250
−700	−700	−700
750	1150	550

Order now, delivery week 5.

Figure 14 - 1.   Order Point

There are two major problems with using the order point in this example:

1.   Order point assumes that the replenishment due date is equal to the lead time - no matter how much inventory is on hand when the order point is tripped.

2.   Order point assumes 100 average weekly demand from the distribution center. The actual demand will average 100 per week from the customers, and 600 every six weeks from the distribution center - not an average of 200 per week.

In Case 1 - with 750 on hand, safety stock of 400, and demand of 100 per week (until week 6), the real need date is four weeks in the future - week 5. Coincidentally, the same date the order point would have generated.

But, in Case 2, the real need date is week 7 - not week 5. In Case 3, the real need date is week 3 - not week 5. If the data in the example were shown in a standard MRP/DRP format, the real need dates would have been apparent.

This example, of course, assumes that there is one distribution center. Imagine what would happen if there were three! If two distribution centers went below the order point one week, and a third distribution center ordered the following week, the chance of having the material coming in at the right time at the main plant would be nil. On the other hand, it would be possible for one distribution center order to trip the order point at the main plant when the other distribution centers had plenty of material on hand, thus bringing material back into the main plant inventory far sooner than it was actually required.

Some companies have regional distribution centers as well as local distribution centers. This adds another level to inventory, giving the order point one more opportunity to confuse the scheduling issue.

The point is very simple; the order point inventory technique tries to answer the question, "When to order" only, and does not address the question, "When is material really needed?" DRP does address the question of when material is really needed, and DRP constantly re-examines the need dates on the scheduled receipts to see if they need to be scheduled to an earlier or later date based on changing requirements. These schedule changes can be implemented right up until the time material is actually shipped.

The order point approach put a lot of emphasis on so-called "scientific computation of safety stocks"; the DRP approach puts the emphasis on proper scheduling of orders that are to be released as well as orders that have already been released. Good customer service is much more affected by good scheduling of replenishment shipments than it is by "precision" in the safety stock computation. Safety stocks at distribution centers don't have to be very large. They are needed only to cover demand variations during the distribution center replenishment lead time.

The subject of safety stocks was covered in Chapter 11, and the same approach can be used with branch warehouses. Safety stocks should be simple and transparent; and, under no circumstances, should they obscure the real need date.

One of the most important aspects of distribution inventory replenishment is to have a shipping schedule for the distribution centers that is adhered to religiously. Where distribution centers are replenished periodically, the shipping schedule is the control over lead time. If the Philadelphia distribution center is supposed to be replenished every other week, a schedule should be set up so that this shipment goes every other Wednesday, for example. And there should be a similar shipping schedule for each distribution center.

Shipping to a distribution center a few days late can do more to impair customer service than all the scientific safety stock computations could possibly do to make up for it.

The order point type system was designed to answer the question, "When to order." DRP is designed to:

1. Determine the proper need date for material both at the distribution centers and at the main plant.

2. Keep that need date up to date by indicating any time when material is needed sooner or later.

3. Integrate the planning of distribution center replenishment inventories with manufacturing inventories. DRP is simply MRP used in distribution and can easily be integrated with the manufacturing master schedule at the main plant.

4. Put the emphasis on controlling lead times rather than building large safety stocks to protect against lead time variations.

Section 5
Lot Sizing

Countless companies have had lot sizes calculated for their distribution centers with assumed "costs of ordering" and "costs of carrying inventory." They soon discovered that these lot sizes built amplification into the ordering cycle and placed more erratic demands upon the supplying facility than would have occurred if they had used simpler techniques. Economic order quantity (EOQ) calculations have rarely worked well in practice because they concentrate on calculating the correct order quantity for each item. If the correct order quantity is calculated for each item, that doesn't necessarily mean that the total result will be desirable - something anyone who has used these techniques in practice already knows. The notion that costs are linear - an assumption of the EOQ formula - is also not realistic. Increasing inventory levels ten percent will not increase the cost of storage, for example, by ten percent. Reducing the number of manufacturing orders, purchase orders, or distribution center replenishment orders by ten percent will not reduce costs proportionately. Beyond that, numbers like the "cost of carrying inventory" are simply not available. It costs money to carry inventory just as it costs money to be out of stock. No one really knows the "costs of carrying inventory" any more than they know the cost of being out of stock. The fact that it costs money does not support the assumption that this cost can, therefore, be translated into a neat, two-digit number to fit into a mathematical formula.

Concepts like the "cost of ordering" are difficult enough to pin down in a manufacturing environment, but they have little, if any, validity in the distribution environment. Some companies with a penchant for being "scientific" have simply assumed that the cost of ordering for distribution centers was $10 or $20 or $30, etc. Rather gross approximations for a "scientific" computation!

The best bet is to take the high value items and assume that the lot size will be equal to the usage during the replenishment cycle. If the distribution centers are replenished once a week, the lot size would be the quantity that is used in a week, or it could be a carton or pallet quantity or multiples thereof. Lower activity items would be replenished every other replenishment cycle. The lowest activity items would be replenished once every four weeks, etc. To take a practical approach to lot sizing, different replenishment lot sizes should be tested to determine the number of picks and putaways that would result versus the amount of inventory that would result. If each item were to be replenished monthly, for example, the inventory would be higher, but the picks and putaways would be lower.

It would certainly be a good idea to keep the lot sizes flexible in any distribution replenishment system. Items in short supply should be replenished every week (assuming that shipment is being made to the distribution center every week). During the peak selling season, it might be well to increase the frequency of shipping and, by doing so, decrease the lot sizes to get more mileage out of the inventory that will be at a minimum at the end of the peak selling season. During the inventory build-up period, shipments to the distribution centers could be reduced in frequency and the lot sizes increased.

Looking at distribution center lot sizes in aggregate, and using common sense, is a lot more profitable than trying to force the real world to fit into a mathematical formula. The formula has little validity in <u>any</u> applications. And practically <u>none</u> in distribution centers.

Section 6
Allocation

The notion that computers would "automatically" allocate scarce material was one of the worst blind alleys of all during the 1960's - "the age of naive sophistication." There is no way that a computer can be programmed to know all of the priorities at a particular time for a particular product in a particular location. They are going to be changing frequently. Even if the computer could keep up with all of these priorities, the issue is still one of accountability.

One company developed a series of sophisticated allocation algorithms for distributing material in short supply to their distribution centers. They went to a great deal of trouble to educate the distribution planners to understand how the allocation algorithms worked. Unfortunately, there is a significant difference between understanding how a formula works and knowing why it generated a particular answer at a particular time.

The distribution supervisor, when asked whether he thought the system would be a good one, said, "Yes, the decisions will now be objective instead of subjective, and marketing won't be able to complain anymore!" The distribution planners had a similar attitude. One said, "Nobody will be able to blame me anymore when material isn't in the right place!" Both of these people felt that the computer would somehow be accountable in the future.

A district sales manager is sure to ask, "Why, when I've just gotten three new accounts in my district, are you sending material in short supply to Atlanta?" The answer, "Don't ask me, the computer did it," will not be acceptable. Computers cannot be held accountable for allocating material in short supply. They should process information so that people can use their judgment in making that kind of allocation. Judgment is not a characteristic of a computer.

A good distribution allocation system would identify those items where there is not enough material to cover the normal requirements at each of the distribution centers. The next step would be to see if sending a one-week supply - assuming that the distribution centers were replenished weekly - to each distribution center could be done with the available inventory. The computer could then suggest that to the planner, and the planner would decide whether that was the best course of action or not. When there was not enough material to handle even one week's requirements, it would be up to the distribution planner to make the "least worst choice."

The idea that material would be allocated by computer "decisions" was a lot of sophisticated nonsense and still is. This type of thing simply doesn't work well in practice. Computer systems work best when they supply information to help people make decisions.

Section 7
Distribution Resource Planning

Once the DRP concepts have been used in distribution inventory replenishment, the system can be extended into distribution resource planning. This would include:

1. Planning the best traffic arrangements for moving material to the distribution centers at the required shipping frequency in the most economical way. Shipping less frequently will require larger lot sizes and more safety stock, but fewer shipments in larger quantities, resulting in lower freight rates.

2. Making sure that the individual shipments take best advantage of the cube available in the trucks or freight cars being used. The system can easily convert the planned order quantities in DRP into cubage and tonnage.

3. Breaking the sales forecast down into the number of orders and line items per order based on analysis of past activity. This can be used to determine the number of "picks" out of inventory that will be required to handle the forecasted sales activity by distribution center. The system can also be used to forecast how many "putaways" of incoming material there will be. DRP can be used not only to project inventory levels at the distribution centers but also manpower requirements.

4. Projecting space requirements at the distribution centers based on activity levels both in shipping and receiving.

5. Using DRP to help make better budgets based on activity levels. Budgets at distribution centers are comprised of:

    a. Labor (both direct and indirect).
    b. Traffic costs.
    c. Other fixed costs like leasing the building, insurance costs, etc.

Like MRP, DRP is a simulation of the way the business really operates. Therefore, it can be used to simulate in units, tonnage, cubage, dollars, man hours, etc.

Section 8
Making Distribution Work

Using DRP:

1.   The planning of distribution inventories will be tied in with the planning of main plant inventories and manufacturing and purchasing planning.

2.   Forecasting will be done using simple techniques like focus forecasting or averages (see Chapter 9) rather than sophisticated techniques that users don't understand.

3.   Timing and scheduling will be emphasized rather than "safety stocks" and "economic order quantities."

4.   The push system of centralized inventory distribution will be used rather than the pull system. The central inventory function will be responsible for distributing inventory to get the best results from the available inventory. The distribution centers will be accountable for inventory accuracy and forecasting. Customer service at the distribution centers will be measured, and inventory record accuracy and forecast accuracy will also be measured, because without measurement, there is no real accountability.

5.   Allocation will be done by people using data prepared by the computer. But people will be accountable for the allocation making the best use of available resources.

6.   Since DRP is a valid simulation of reality, it can be tied in with traffic, financial planning, manpower planning, etc.

For many years, very little happened in the field of distribution inventory management. Today, the knowledge that was gained in applying MRP II in manufacturing has been applied in distribution with outstanding results. Reduced inventory, reduced traffic costs, improved customer service - these can all be achieved when distribution inventories are managed properly.

Distribution centers exist for one purpose - better customer service. In practice, the way many companies organize and manage their distribution inventories results in higher costs, higher inventories, and very little improvement in customer service. And a great deal of internal competition and bickering. DRP is a proven way that can change distribution centers from an expensive and frustrating burden to a highly profitable resource.

Footnotes

1. A definitive book on the subject is <u>Distribution Resource Planning</u> by Andre Martin, to be released by Oliver Wight Limited Publications, Inc. in 1982.

2. It is discussed in Section 4 of Appendix 4.

Chapter 15
MRP II in Data Processing Systems

Section 1
Correcting Systems Misconceptions

Twenty five years into the computer age isn't really very far. Computers will be with us as long as there is civilization, and historians will some day look back in amusement at the way we "romanced" computers and some of the misdirections that resulted.

One of the responsibilities of data processing and systems people is to get rid of the misconceptions. The most serious of these can be condensed into five widely held notions that hamper progress:

Misconception No. 1.

The present system works.

Here is a quote from an article with one author's thoughts on that subject: "I start from the premise that there is currently a system in place -- My first goal would be to get the present system up to snuff, making such improvements as are to benefit any future refinements." (1) Making the present system work in the typical company is an exercise in futility. Most logistics systems weren't even designed so that they could work. They were designed primarily as order launchers, not as scheduling systems, because order launching was seen as the prime objective of inventory management; answering the question, "When to order?" Putting the efforts into making the present system work would be far more productive if they were spent on making the present informal system work. By using more aggressive people in the expediting function and trying not to let the experienced people move out of production and inventory control. The informal system depends very heavily on the experience of these people. Fixing inventory records, for example, in a company that operates with a shortage list will not have much impact on their ability to ship on schedule. In most manufacturing and distribution companies, there are usually at least two systems: one, the formal system described in the book of procedures, and the other, the "informal system" - the real system.

The notion that the present system works also leads people into other blind alleys. One lesson came through long ago:

SYSTEMS PEOPLE CANNOT DESIGN A SYSTEM FOR
THE USERS WITHOUT THE USERS BEING INVOLVED
OR THE SYSTEM WILL NOT WORK.

Consequently, the other approach is assumed to be,
"Ask the users what they want." (2) Asking the users
what they want in the accounting department is probably
quite reasonable. They will answer, "payroll, accounts
payable, accounts receivable, general ledger, budgeting,
etc." These are things that worked before. These are
things they will now put on the computer. But, in manufacturing, the system never did work. To go to the user
and ask him what he wants will not generate useful
answers, unless the user has been educated to know what
the tools are that have been made possible by the computer. Without that background, he would probably be
more interested in a motor scooter (to get him around the
factory floor faster!) than he would an MRP system.

Before wasting time, as so many companies have in
trying to make the present system work, two questions
must be answered realistically:

1.   Which present system? The formal or the informal
      system?

2.   Can the formal system really answer the question,
      "What material is really needed when?"

Misconception No. 2.

Each company must have a system "designed" for its individual application.

The fundamental manufacturing equation was discussed
in Chapter 3. Systems looked different in the past because
they didn't work. Consequently, many users felt that they
needed a "unique" system; and many systems people, especially consultants, were anxious to express their creativity by "designing" a system for the users.

The fact of the matter is that the logic of manufacturing is universal. Since the logic is standard, the
system must be standard, or it will not represent the way
the business really runs.

Misconception No. 3.

MRP is a production control system.

MRP started out as a production and inventory control system. As MRP evolved, it extended through the entire company replacing the many fragments of systems that attempted to deal with the universal manufacturing equation.

The more we learned about MRP, the simpler it became. When a company has one system in manufacturing that really works, it can be extended to generate the numbers used by the other systems. MRP is not just a production and inventory control system - it is a way to get the numbers - correct numbers - to run the business.

Misconception No. 4.

MRP is a complex system.

One author, who has never seen a Class A MRP system in practice, calls MRP "a currently popular complex control system." Certainly, sophisticated frivolity like "part period balancing with a look-ahead, look-back feature" can be added to MRP to make it complex. But, the logic of MRP is as simple as the logic of the shortage list or a cash flow projection.

As systems started working, because of the ability of the computer to manipulate massive amounts of data, we came to realize that the universal manufacturing equation was not complex in any way. The problem in the age of pencils and desk calculators was not the complexity of the logic, but rather the inability to manipulate massive amounts of data fast enough to have it be meaningful.

It's important not to confuse the technical complexity of the computer part of the system with the logical complexity of the system that the user perceives. From a data processing point of view, a system may be a highly complex sophisticated system involving duplexed computers, on-line real-time processing, multiprogramming, virtual storage, etc. But as long as the user can understand the logic and be able to answer the question, "Why did the computer tell me to do that this time?" there can be understanding, and consequently, accountability no matter how technically complex the system's internal workings are.

<u>Misconception No. 5.</u>

MRP is a computer system.

    For years, systems designers toiled diligently in conference rooms trying to decide which of the nine different lot sizing algorithms they would use in their MRP system. They labored with the confidence that if somehow "the system" could just be designed "right," all good things would follow. Unfortunately, we learned the hard way that the computer just prints paper or puts an image on a tube. Nothing happens until <u>people</u> do something.

    The school of experience is unforgiving. There can be all kinds of theories, but experience will displace the theories with facts. Before we went to the moon, some theorized that the astronauts would be over their heads in dust accumulated through the centuries. It didn't happen that way. And computers in manufacturing didn't happen the way the theorists predicted in the early years of the computer. One of the tasks of the data processing professionals is to educate people formally and informally - even in day-to-day conversation - to get rid of the misconceptions from the early "gee whiz" years of the computer age.

Section 2
The Standard System

Today, there is a great deal of commercially available software for closed loop MRP. And there is a great deal to be said for using commercially available software. Material requirements planning itself is a fairly complex program involving "exploding" bills of material (extending the bills of material into the total of each of the components required to manufacture the product), accumulating total requirements from all products for each component, posting these requirements against the individual component, accumulating all requirements, netting, calculating planned order releases, going through the explosion process again, etc. Today, very few companies write their own MRP programs. It is usually far more practical to use programs that are available. Some of this software is quite expensive costing between $250,000 to $300,000. Other software, particularly that available from the computer manufacturers, is considerably lower in price costing as little as $30,000 to $40,000.

There are two reasons often given for not using commercially available software:

1. There are too many existing programs for the commercially available software to interface with, and it would take longer to modify it than to develop the company's own software.

2. Software programs for MRP do not exist for the computer that the company owns.

Today, there are software programs that will interface with virtually anything. The use of standard software is the best approach because the cost of the development of proprietary software can be spread over a large number of customers rather than having to be absorbed by one company.

Whether or not commercially available software is used is a choice of the individual company. Whether or not a standard approach to the logic of MRP II is used is not a choice.

One company actually used the block diagrams from the program description manual from a large computer manufacturer that offered MRP software. The software had been proven and worked before. As a result, although this company had to write it to fit a different data base management program, the fact that they used standard logic made the system very usable. In fact, their system today is rated as one of the best MRP systems going.

The frustration that every corporate data processing/systems person has known - where each division wants their own "unique system to address their unique problems" - is a thing of the past. Today, there is a standard system and it should be the starting point for anyone installing MRP II whether they use commercially available software or develop their own. (3)

Software for closed loop MRP (material requirements planning, capacity requirements planning, shop dispatching, and vendor scheduling) is widely available. As this is written, there is little commercially available software that was designed to do MRP II, Manufacturing Resource Planning. An MRP II system would include:

1. The integration of the financial system with the operating system so that the financial system actually uses the numbers generated by the operating system.

2. A simulation capability to answer the "what if" questions like, "What if we added an extra 20 units into the master schedule in week 4. Would we have the material and the capacity to cover this requirement, or would we have to move something else out of the schedule?"

While very little software is available that includes these functions today, some is. And more will be available very rapidly as people recognize that simulation is a very powerful tool for management, and that having separate systems dealing with the same fundamental information leads to conflicting, inaccurate information. Once the operating system works correctly and the numbers represent what's actually happening, using it as a basis for the financial system is the only approach that really makes sense.

With MRP II, there is one basic set of numbers being used to run the business. The numbers are generated by the operating people and extended into dollars for the financial people. It eliminates a lot of system redundancy and constant patchwork, and of course, fewer systems are simpler to maintain. When one system doesn't work, companies will normally develop several other systems to try to do the same job. In a manufacturing company, for example, the question, "What material is really needed when," must be answered if the company is to ship product. Most companies have some kind of inventory ordering system, some kind of semiformal expediting system, and several informal expediting systems, including the shortage list, because none of them do the job properly.

The bottom line for data processing people is fewer systems, less duplication in systems, a lot less debating about the conflicting information that comes from the present systems. And, most important of all, the satisfaction of knowing that the systems are not just generating paper that will sit on someone's desk. MRP II is a system that can be used by the operating people, financial people, and all other members of the management team in a manufacturing company.

Section 3
The Mechanics of MRP II

Even with a simple regenerative system (4), simulation can be done. Of course, with a regenerative system, it's going to take more time and be more awkward from a data processing point of view.

If the question is, for example, "Can we add 20 units in week 4?", a separate material requirements planning/capacity requirements planning run using a work file (so as not to change the data base in actual use) could be made. It would be up to the user, then, to compare the additional material and capacity requirements with the regular MRP/CRP runs to answer the questions:

1.   What additional material will be required?

2.   What additional capacity will be required?

3.   What are the other items in the master schedule that are currently planned to use this material and capacity?

4.   Can these 20 units be added without sacrificing anything else from the master schedule by expediting purchased parts, working overtime to add capacity, for example, etc.? What items would have to be moved out of the schedule if there is no other alternative?

A net change system lends itself very readily to simulation even though few of them were designed with that in mind. Once again, a separate work file would have to be set up and the net change computer system logic would do the simulation. A few net change programs today do have this simulation capability designed into the system.

Among the financial reports that can be derived from operating information are:

1.   Inventory valuation.
2.   Projected inventory investment.
3.   Realistic purchase commitments.
4.   Realistic labor requirements in dollars.
5.   Work-in-process costing.

6. Overhead allocations both fixed and variable.
7. Cash flow projections.
8. Projected shipping budgets.
9. The business plan.
10. The profit plan.
11. Simulations: "What if sales for product "x" are 30 percent above forecast."
12. Make or buy decisions.

With MRP II, rather than maintaining a separate dollar inventory balance - affected by separate inventory trans- actions - the inventory records from MRP are used to cost out the inventory. The on-hand balance in finished goods can be costed out as can the on-hand balance in each of the component stores areas as represented in the material requirements plan. The work-in-process inventory can be costed out using the open shop orders.

Projected inventory balances can be made for finished goods and component stores by costing out the requirements in the material requirements plan and adding in the sched- uled receipts and planned order receipts. These, of course, are time phased in the material requirements plan and can be used to generate a projected inventory balance by product, the components that go into a product, by commodity, etc.

Purchase commitments are represented in the material requirements plan by scheduled receipts and planned order releases. Once again, these can be summarized by prod- uct, commodity, or vendor. A product family code, a vendor code, and a commodity code would typically be stored in the item master record.

The capacity requirements planning program takes the released shop orders and planned order releases from MRP and calculates standard hours by work center. Given the average rate for the labor grade in each work center - and making any adjustments for performance against incentives in an incentive system - total labor dollars by work center, and/or by product family, can be extended. If overtime is planned in some work centers where there is not sufficient capacity available to meet the capacity requirements during the normal work week, this, too, can be projected in dol- lars. Remembering, of course, that the variable portion of overhead such as the cost of gas to run a heat treating furnace should be included in this projection.

Work-in-process can be costed out by adding the labor cost that has been accumulated through the current operation to the material cost (job location by work center is shown in the open shop order file). Fixed and variable portions of overhead can be prorated or applied as accounting practice dictates in the company.

Overhead allocations are, of course, one of the most difficult - and nebulous - parts of costing. With MRP, however, it is possible, practical, and very important to project overhead allocations frequently to show the impact different plans will have on costs. The simulation capability of MRP II makes it possible to project - and re-project - overhead allocations far more accurately than was practical in the past in most companies.

The major elements in cash flow are:

1. Anticipated receipts of cash from customers.
2. Anticipated expenditures on labor, materials, and overhead.
3. Anticipated expenditures on fixed costs not included in manufacturing overhead such as marketing, research and development, and costs that are usually included under "General and Administrative."

The information in a closed loop MRP system combined with the information that is already available through accounting like general and administrative costs, for example, can provide very accurate cash flow projections.

The projected shipping dollars are available quite readily in a make-to-order product line by pricing out the master schedule. This pricing will have to take into account any discount schedules, interplant shipment prices, etc. But the basic information on what is going to be made and what will be shipped is available through the master schedule. For a make-to-stock product line, the master schedule costed out represents transfers to inventory. In this case, the projected shipping dollars is the forecast.

One of the greatest values of integrating the operating and the financial systems is the ability to keep the business plan and the profit plan up to date based on current production plans. Most of the dollar changes in the business plan are due to changes in production plans. These can be priced and costed out regularly to be sure that the business plans and the profit plans are synchronized with the current operating plans.

When the simulation capability described in Chapter 10 and earlier in this section is combined with the ability to integrate the operating and the financial information, converting operating plans into financial terms is a straightforward matter. This simulation capability can be used to answer such questions as:

1. What will this change in product mix do to our projected inventory levels?

2. What will this change in product mix do to our projected cash flow?

3. How much more (or less) will we be spending on labor and material?

4. What will this change in volume do to our costs as we reallocate overhead? If we buy more of this product outside and make less internally, how will the new volume affect our costs as we reallocate overhead?

From the above examples, an experienced systems/data processing person can see that the amount of work involved to integrate the financial and the operating system is not overwhelming. It's a job that should take only a few man months in most companies. The information that can be produced is awesome. The power of MRP II is based on the fact that operating numbers are right because operating people are actually using the system. And these numbers can be readily translated into dollars - the language of management.

Section 4
Data Logistics

The scene: the conference room of a company where the first MRP run is about to be presented to the planners. The door opens. Two people with hand trucks bring in several boxes of paper over five feet high. The designers of the system allowed one page for each component and there were 20,000 components. Since there were six planners, they made a complete copy of the MRP output report for each planner along with a "pegging" report (5), a separate report on exceptions, etc.

Like any other system - and perhaps even more so - MRP can easily become "Many Reams of Paper." Systems designers need to take this into account. There are plenty of techniques available to get around this problem.

Output reports can be put on microfilm or microfiche, or they can be put on CRTs (Cathode Ray Tubes). Some companies like to print the items that have exception messages on hard copy. But it is important to remember that in an MRP system everything is interrelated. An exception message at one level may mean that the planner would have to look at several different items at different levels in the product structure to make a decision. So this information must be available to the planner even if it is not printed out on hard copy. It can be available through microfilm, microfiche or computer inquiry.

Data should be made available to the planners so that they can make decisions quickly. Perhaps a foreman indicates that a problem in the plating department is going to require that the main plating tank be down for two weeks to be overhauled. The planner needs to look at the detailed capacity plan, find the individual items in the plan, refer to the material plan, and trace it back up through the levels to see the items that will be affected. Some jobs will probably be sent outside to be plated; others will have to be rescheduled. The planner should have this information available quickly and conveniently to make decisions.

In most companies today - even those with the MRP output report on CRTs - tracing this information back through the system would mean going from the CRTs to printed reports back to the CRTs, etc. One of the areas that data processing and systems professionals need to work on in the future is the development of good data logistics; making information available quickly and conveniently to the users so that they can make better business decisions.

Many years ago, one of the Texas Instruments plants had a shop scheduling system that, to this day, represents one of the best possible user-oriented designs. There was a preprinted pad of paper in the room where the small dedicated computer ran the scheduling system. Anyone could inquire and indicate the field of primary interest - like a particular work center. The user could then indicate whether the secondary concern was jobs completed, jobs in the work center, or jobs coming to the work center, or all three. Other interests might be the project number the job was being run for, which ones were past due, etc. In this manner, the user could select the information required and specify how the information was to be sorted, summarized, and printed. This system existed in the middle '60's and, even today, would represent a good model of user-oriented operating information.

In the future, data logistics will be a primary area of application for the data processing and systems professional. Making the data available conveniently, quickly, and in a useful form for the people who have to use it to run the business.

Section 5
Data Processing in the Mainstream

A large pharmaceutical company has a data processing department. No one ever questions the need for this department or whether they are making an economic contribution to the business. In this company, it is assumed that computers are "good" and that to question the value of the computer department would be a sacrilege for any "sophisticated" manager. In practice, they are producing the same kind of accounting reports that had been done with manually operated accounting machines. These reports for production and inventory control are a classic example of the computerization - and sophistication - of the formal system that really doesn't work. The fact of the matter is that the company would probably operate as well, or better, if the entire computer and systems group were disbanded. But there isn't anybody in the company with enough courage to take on a political battle of that magnitude.

Too frequently data processing and systems have become a self-perpetuating entity that contributes little to the business. This isn't entirely the fault of the data processing and systems people. Managers who let this happen are really primarily to blame. Especially those who don't know enough about data processing and systems applications to use them as effective business tools, but who like to use data processing and systems jargon as a way to convey the impression that they are "modern, sophisticated managers."

A good example of poor data processing priorities in many companies was the recent fad for centralizing data processing. The idea was that it would cost less to run data processing from a centralized location with terminals than it would cost to have many small computers. (With distributed processing, the pendulum seems to be swinging the other way!)

But the point most important to consider is very basic:

BEFORE CONCENTRATING ON IMPROVING THE EFFICIENCY OF DATA PROCESSING, A COMPANY SHOULD CONCENTRATE ON MAKING THE DATA PROCESSING APPLICATIONS WORK.

Frequently, having a stand-alone computer at a given division of a manufacturing company can facilitate installing MRP. Having to tie this system in with the corporate system just adds problems that are not needed during a challenging implementation period. This does not say that the data processing operations should not be centralized. It does say that the first concentration should be on running the business more profitably. The secondary concern should be on running the data processing operations more efficiently.

A great example of loss of perspective in data processing and systems occurred in a very large company. They have a division in the midwest that does MRP II very well indeed. From a technical point of view, it is far short of perfect. They don't have as much in the way of on-line systems as they might have. They use a regenerative system rather than net change - and it takes virtually the entire weekend to run! But they run the manufacturing facilities very effectively and their system is considered to be Class A.

They had another division in California that produced computers and computer software. Everything they did was correct from a data processing point of view. The data processing and systems professionals scoffed at the other division's "crude, unsophisticated, less than professional" approaches. Unfortunately, the applications at the west coast division were very poor. They were not user oriented and they did not contribute anything to running the business. The division was liquidated in 1976.

The moral to the story: manufacturing companies do not make money in the data processing or systems department. Data processing and systems are merely a means to an end. If the choice is to run the manufacturing company efficiently or to run the data processing and systems efforts efficiently the real business professional will have no difficulty sorting out the objectives.

Data processing people are often the victim of reorganization. In the typical company, the data processing manager is moved out of the job for lack of management capability, inability to direct people, get projects done on time, etc. Then, the new data processing manager will be selected based on his or her technical credentials! This isn't to say that technical credentials aren't important. But it is important to recognize that data processing and systems in a company using MRP II becomes an important part of the organization, not a group of elite technical sophisticates who are not really accountable for a contribution to the company's progress.

For some people in data processing and systems, that's bad news. For others, that's good news. The time has come to separate the data processing professional who is a part of the business team from the pseudo professional who thinks that the company revolves around data processing and systems. In many respects, the pendulum has swung too far away from data processing and systems people. They have become isolated partly through their own mistakes, partly through management's failure to treat them as an essential part of the day-to-day running of the business. Before MRP II, in most companies, they were not a part of the day-to-day operations of a manufacturing company.

With MRP II, data processing and systems people become a vital part of operations. There is one set of numbers that the company uses to run the business. It is not just record keeping or bookkeeping. With MRP II, these numbers are the numbers that management uses to run the business on a day-to-day basis.

In the future, there will be plenty of room for the data processing professional who wants to be a systems programmer and work in other technical areas. But the managers of data processing and systems, in the future, will be chosen primarily because of their management ability and, secondarily because of their technical knowledge. One of the most successful manufacturing companies in the country promotes people from operations into data processing and systems, and then back into operations. As a consequence, their systems and data processing people are very business oriented and their business managers are very systems and data processing oriented. Their general manager, today, used to be the manager of data processing and systems. He knows how to use these tools effectively to make the business run better. With MRP II, data processing and systems will no longer be looked upon as a group of technical people with a rather nebulous mystical knowledge. They will be in the mainstream of running a manufacturing business.

Section 6
Data Processing and Systems as a Production Facility

Budget reports in many companies come out the 20th of the following month. Payroll is usually made up one week late - the pay in the envelope this Friday was based on pay cards turned in the previous week. In manufacturing it's different. The dispatch list that goes out to the shop on a daily basis in the MRP system must go out at the beginning of the shift each morning. (6) It must show the jobs that are ahead of each work center. It may show the jobs that are likely to come to the work center within the next day or two. If it doesn't come out each day, if it comes out late, if the information in it isn't up to date, it is of little value to the shop foreman who must manage his department. You can tell a company where MRP is really working: if the dispatch report is so much as an hour late, the foremen are up in arms because they don't have a current schedule to work to.

Inventory reconciliation represents a good contrast between the old way and MRP II. When the annual physical inventory was taken, if the reconciliation between actual and "book" figures came out within two to three weeks, that was considered very good. With MRP II, cycle counting is done daily. When the inventory of the sample items is taken, it is immediately put into the computer to compare it with the inventory record. The computer system must immediately identify those items where the cycle count doesn't match the book record and a recount must be taken. This isn't done several hours later or the next day. It is done as soon as the cycle count is completed.

Several companies today have on-line shop floor reporting. They have terminals in the factory - usually CRTs (Cathode Ray Tubes) - with keyboards and printers. Shop dispatchers assign jobs to operators. They get a dispatch list out of the system on request via the printer, and operators report to the dispatchers giving them counts on the number of pieces produced, scrap, rework, etc. This goes directly through the terminal to the computer where the current count is immediately compared with the previous count, to audit time reporting and count reporting.

This puts new demands on data processing because data processing is now another producing department. Data processing is the department producing information to be used in operations, not to be used just for bookkeeping. The system does not have to be "on-line real-time" to work with MRP II. Inventory records, for example, can be updated at the end of the day's activity and a "snapshot" of the current status produced for the user each morning. In a control system, as opposed to a record keeping system, timeliness is essential. In this type of system, the value of information diminishes exponentially with time.

The timing requirements for each report should be established with the users. A schedule for data processing should also be established.

When the data processing operation is viewed as a production department, the obvious question is, "Why not use material requirements planning and capacity require- ments planning to schedule it?" (For that matter, why not use MRP as a project planning technique for systems de- velopment?) The answer is that in a department of any size this would make a great deal of sense.

One data processing professional, after attending a course on MRP II said, "I'm as excited about its application in data processing as I am in manufacturing. The typical backlog in our systems development and programming area is one to three years. We need a better ability to sched- ule, prioritize, plan capacity, reschedule, and see the impact of rescheduling on our master schedule. In the past, we've given pretty poor customer service, and with better planning, I know that could be improved. When you come right down to it, we're just like a manufacturing facility that has a development shop and a production shop, and we need better planning and control in both." Because of its name - Manufacturing Resource Planning - data processing people are likely to overlook the simplest and most potentially effective tools that are available to them. Somebody should develop an MRP II program for data pro- cessing. Probably the biggest thing that will need to be changed is the name!

Once the data processing department is producing information that is really being used in operations to run the business, its operations should be planned just like the factory's operations should be planned. And it's ability to deliver a quality product on schedule should be measured just like every other department that is vital to the success of a manufacturing business.

Footnotes

1. Materials Management Worldwide, January/February, 1979, Volume III, No. 1, letter to the editor from W. Evert Welch.

2. See for example: Dearden, John, "M.I.S. is a Mirage," Harvard Business Review, January/February, 1972.

3. Manufacturing Software Systems, P.O. Box 278, Williston, VT 05495, provides a "Consumer Report" type service on computer software for MRP and MRP II. A book is available that defines the logic of the "standard system" and software reviews for the most popular software packages can also be purchased.

4. See Appendix 1, The Mechanics of Closed Loop MRP and/or Appendix 5 Glossary.

5. See Appendix 1, The Mechanics of Closed Loop MRP.

6. See Appendix 1, The Mechanics of Closed Loop MRP.

PART IV
Becoming a "Class A" User

Chapter 16
Justification

Section 1
MRP II the Potential Results

Perhaps, the most significant results that come from a successful MRP system are in the intangible areas. The quality of life improves when people have a game plan, and can work together; when foremen and purchasing people have a valid schedule and can work to it, when marketing believes what manufacturing tells them. And manufacturing feels that they are part of a team, not just the victims of an unrelenting, unrealistic, unreasonable group of sales people. The satisfaction that people get from being able to perform their jobs well may be intangible. But it is beyond the tangibles in terms of its real value.

Nevertheless, the justification should be based on tangibles, and that's not a problem with MRP. The payoffs are dramatic.

But before starting a justification, key people should be educated as shown in Figure 16-1. There are standard, live education courses available today. (1) One of these live courses on MRP II is aimed at top management. The chief executive officer and the other key executives in the major functions shown in Figure 16-1 should attend before attempting a justification.

Top Management	Five - Day
CEO	Plant Manager
VP Manufacturing	Materials Manager
VP Finance	Purchasing Manager
VP Engineering	Systems Manager
VP Marketing	
VP Administration	

Figure 16 - 1. Education

Another standard course in MRP II is called the five-day course. This week-long course is for middle management, planners, systems people, etc. Figure 16-1 also lists the people who should attend that course. Obviously, there's a degree of flexibility here. There may be additional people who should attend these courses before justification. Or a company might want their plant manager in the top management course rather than the five-day course. Nevertheless, this live education is a prerequisite to justification.

Education will be discussed in more detail in Chapter 18. But unless a company intends to go ahead with MRP, it probably isn't a good idea to educate too many people. MRP is a company game plan, and educating half the players, particularly if the company isn't committed to installing this kind of game plan, isn't going to generate a big payback. It might result in some of the people, who know that there is a better way, deciding to leave the business and go to a company where they are using or planning to use MRP.

The potential results from an MRP program were discussed in Chapter 4. The areas where they usually occur are summarized briefly in Figure 16-2. It's important to remember that each company must do its justification based on its own circumstances, and not use average figures.

1. Inventory
2. Service
3. Productivity
4. Purchased Cost
5. Traffic
6. Obsolescence
7. Overtime, etc.
8. Quality of Life

Figure 16 - 2.   Results

Occasionally, a company does so well with their informal system that it has no real justification for installing a formal system. One company, manufacturing pumps, did extremely well with their informal system. The inventory system launched orders, but their expeditors - who had an average seniority of 25 years and normally required 10 years to break in on the job - made sure that the right material was where it belonged at the right time. The plant superintendent could look at the list of incoming orders and get a pretty good idea of whether or not he needed to add more people at a particular machine. All was well and good while business continued as normal. Then they got into building nuclear pumps. The experience that the people in the company had accumulated over the years no longer mattered. It was a new ball game. And, suddenly, the company went from being the most profitable division of their corporation to the least profitable.

It doesn't happen often today, but, on occasion, a company has to face the question of whether or not they are going to wait until the situation is bad enough that they can justify MRP. As products get more complex and more of the experienced people retire, quit, or leave for other reasons, the prospects of continuing to operate effectively with an informal system diminish dramatically. Sometimes, it is better to install an MRP system before it can be justified, rather than waiting until there is a crisis.

Many companies, in fact most of them, make a good profit today without MRP. But the real issue is competition. In an industry where no one is really using MRP effectively, a company without MRP can probably get along very well. But once one airline is able to fly by instrument, the other airlines had better learn very quickly or they are going to be in an extremely difficult competitive situation. Companies like Black and Decker, Cameron Iron Works, Steelcase, and Tennant have shown that these tools, in the hands of good managers, can be a real competitive edge. In business, there is no par. There is only competition.

One of the intangibles of running a business more professionally is the competition involved in getting and keeping the best people. MRP II appeals to professional people because it is a set of tools that enables them to perform more professionally.

Section 2
A Typical Justification

Figure 16-3 shows some financial numbers for a typical manufacturing company. Annual sales are $50 million and the cost of sales is $25 million. The cost of sales is the units of sales multiplied by the factory cost. Factory cost includes labor, material, and overhead, but does not include general and administrative costs, selling costs, research and development costs, etc. A good rule of thumb in a typical manufacturing company is that the cost of sales will run between 50 and 60 percent of the actual sales dollars.

Annual Sales	=	$50 M
Cost of Sales	=	$25 M
Inventory	=	$12.5 M
Purchased Cost	=	$12.5 M
Labor Cost	=	$4.0 M

Figure 16 - 3. Typical Manufacturing Company

In the example, the inventory is 12½ million. This would be fairly typical for a company making a complex product like a crane or a machine tool in small quantities with long lead times. They would be getting about two inventory turns a year at cost without MRP. Many companies, of course, do far better than this without MRP. One cigarette manufacturer gets 18 inventory turns a year and expects 22 inventory turns a year with MRP. This is the type of thing that each company must look at on an individual basis. A company that merely purchases and assembles can have a very high inventory turnover. A company that makes a one-piece product like valves can also have a very high inventory turnover. One company makes a very complex, assembled product, but 80 percent of the dollars that go into this product are purchased components that are brought in at the very last moment and shipped right out the door, again providing for very high inventory turnover. On the other hand, a company that owns its own foundry, machines all its parts, makes an assembled product, carries them in finished goods, and has branch warehouses as well as a main plant inventory, would tend to have a far higher inventory investment. Each company must look at its own inventory investment and determine for itself whether or not this could be reduced through better scheduling.

Another test of reasonableness is that the purchased cost in a typical company will usually run about half the cost of sales. One more good rule of thumb is that labor cost - direct labor without overhead - will normally run about one-third the purchased cost. The typical company spends $3 on material for every $1 they spend on direct labor.

This is a "typical company." There are probably many manufacturing companies for whom these numbers would be very close to their real numbers.

```
Inventory Reduction × 12.5M–8.3=4.2× 10%=$420K
Customer Service    = 2.5M × 10%       =$250K
Productivity        = 4M × 8%          =$320K
Purchasing          = 12.5M × 5%       =$625K
                                       $1615K
```

Figure 16 - 4.   MRP Savings in a Typical Company

Figure 16-4 shows the potential savings from MRP. (2) A company getting two inventory turns at cost without MRP should expect to get three inventory turns at cost with MRP. A rule of thumb, based on experience, is that most companies can get about a one-third reduction in inventory due to MRP. Once again, however, it is important that each company realize that they must make this justification themselves. These numbers are provided only as an example. Certainly, no one should say that, "Because the typical company gets a one-third reduction in inventory, of course we will." That must be determined based on the judgment of the people who see the excess inventory that exists due to shortages, the material that's coming in early and not being used (material that is undoubtedly being received in place of material that's really needed, thus causing shortages). Rules of thumb are only good as tests of reasonableness.

An inventory reduction of one-third, in the example above, would equal approximately $4.2 million. The inventory savings attributed to this come out to $420,000. While interest costs have frequently been far in excess of 10 percent, the justification uses a 10 percent cost of money only. This is an extremely conservative figure for projecting future savings.

Every successful Class A or B MRP user known to the author has had a substantial improvement in customer service by making more of the right things at the right time and shipping them to the customer. This, of course, meant that inventory went down while customer service went up; an ideal situation.

In most companies, the increased profit due to improved customer service is not difficult to calculate. In the example shown in Figure 16-4, it is assumed that a sales increase of 5 percent due to better customer service is predicted by the sales and marketing people. A company making sporting firearms, for example, loses considerable sales if they do not have shotguns available when hunting season starts. A hunter who has saved his money to buy a new shotgun is surely going to buy another brand if the brand that he originally wanted is not available. Very few hunters are likely to wait until next season.

A 5 percent increase in sales at a company that does 50 million in annual sales would equal $2.5 million. Assuming that the company would conservatively expect to make 10 percent on sales before taxes, the increased profit due to MRP would be $250,000. It is important to recognize that the increased sales used in the MRP justification should be due to MRP only. In many companies, they enjoy a sales increase regularly, but the justification should consider the increase due to better customer service from MRP only.

In the typical assembly department, a 30 percent improvement in productivity is very common when MRP is introduced. In the typical fabrication area, a productivity increase of 5 to 10 percent is common. The example in Figure 16-4 uses a conservative figure of 8 percent of all direct labor which is $320,000.

MRP users have shown that when the expediting burden is off the purchasing people, they can reduce costs very substantially. Even a 5 percent reduction in purchased cost in the typical company amounts to a very large savings. Once again, this would be the additional savings due to purchasing people having more time to do a professional purchasing job rather than spending the bulk of their time expediting and submerged in paperwork.

The costs of traffic, obsolescence, overtime, etc. can be identified, but for the purpose of this example, only the areas that usually generate the heaviest payback have been used. A company doing a justification should also consider these other areas, since some of them might be very significant in particular businesses.

Nevertheless, for our purposes, the projected savings of $1,615,000 annually makes the point. MRP can produce dramatic profit improvements.

People doing the justification for their company should consider all of the areas and should come up with their own numbers. This is the reason that the key executives <u>must</u> have been educated. These are the people who will be accountable for making the <u>commitment</u> for the profit improvement that they can attain using MRP.

Section 3
The Potential Costs

Figure 16-5 shows how the costs of MRP break down. There are three basic categories:

1.   The computer and systems-associated "technical" costs.

2.   The costs of improving and maintaining data integrity.

3.   The people costs.

Most companies have the computer hardware to do MRP. As one executive said, "We are now doing with the computer what we justified it for in 1963!" However, many times some additional hardware, such as disk storage, may be required.

The situation is different with software. Most companies will have to purchase software. It is generally not recommended that a company develop all of the software for MRP themselves.

Computer	Data Integrity	People
Hardware	Bills of Material	Education
Software	Routings	Professional Guidance
Systems Work	Inventory Records	
	Work Centers	
	Master Production Schedule	

Figure 16 - 5.   Costs of MRP

Another cost in the computer area is the systems work. Most companies, however, have the people now and don't have to add additional systems people. Some, however, prefer to allocate the cost of the systems people to the MRP program. Others say this is not out-of-pocket cost and, therefore, isn't attributable to MRP. In our example, we will use allocated cost since it is a more conservative approach.

The cost of correcting the bills of material will be primarily indirect labor: the salaries and fringe benefits for the people involved. Consulting might be required at first to determine how bills of material need to be structured. This cost will fall under "professional guidance."

The job of fixing routings is very much the same as the job of fixing bills of material. In most companies, it takes considerably less time, although, for our example, we will assume that the cost of fixing the routings is the same. The standards don't have to be perfect. The important thing is that the operation sequence shows the job moving to the proper work centers. Once bills of material and routings are corrected, there should be no additional cost in doing them right the first time. There is rarely any recurring cost associated with this effort.

Most companies have some work to do in getting accurate inventory records. And, in many companies, they don't even have the proper physical layout to allow limited access. This is the biggest single cost associated with accurate inventory records: the relayout of the plant required for limited access stores.

Education should be budgeted to include both live classes and the lease or purchase of video courses that will be used to educate the large number of people necessary to make MRP work. Education will be discussed in more detail in Chapter 18.

The subject of consulting will be discussed in more detail in Chapter 17. Suffice it to say, for the purposes of this discussion, that one competent, experienced consultant who has actually lived through an MRP installation visiting once every four to six weeks is better than an army of "rented bodies" drawing flow charts and writing books of procedures.

One Time			Recurring
Computer Software	=	250K	50K
Systems Work, etc.	=	100K	30K
B/M 2 man years @ 30K	=	60K	
Routings 2 man years @ 30K	=	60K	
Limited Access Stores	=	100K	
Education	=	155K	55K
Consulting	=	20K	10K
Total	=	745,000	145,000

Figure 16 - 6. MRP Costs in a Typical Company

Figure 16-6 shows the projected costs of installing MRP in the company used for the example. The cost of the software is projected at $250,000 as a one-time cost, and $50,000 a year annually to maintain it.

Most companies don't have to add more systems people since they usually have enough of them already. Today, they are working to maintain programs that really fall into the category of "not good enough to use, but not bad enough to throw out." With MRP, they can put their efforts into doing something that will really be productive. Once MRP II is installed and many of the redundant systems are eliminated, the systems people will have even more time to work on productive projects. In this example, the extra efforts that had to be taken away from other areas and put into MRP are allocated at $100,000 as a one-time cost, and a $30,000 a year recurring cost.

The bill of material effort is assumed to take two man years at $30,000. The $30,000 includes salaries, fringe benefits, etc. for each person involved in doing the task. Routings, likewise, are assumed to take two man years, although this would be unusual in most companies.

Limited access stores has been estimated at $100,000 as a one-time cost of plant relayout. A few companies have been known to add additional stores people to get MRP up and running. But this is primarily a replacement of efforts that were previously done by foremen, superintendents, expeditors, etc. who ran around counting material, looking for material, etc. Very few companies have had to keep an additional staff of people in the stores area after MRP went on the air and people learned the new way of doing business.

The cost of identifying work centers and the master schedule is usually nil. Work centers can be identified within a week or two by a competent person.

The master schedule has to be designed properly and people have to be educated to use it. It is certainly one of the key areas in MRP, but it is not an area that costs much.

The cost of education has been estimated at $155,000 as a one-time cost and a $55,000 a year recurring cost. Education should be budgeted as a continuing activity. A good rule of thumb is that approximately seven percent of the total people should go to live classes and that these will cost around $2,000 apiece with tuition, travel, and expenses. In a company with 1,000 total people, this would mean 70 people would go to live classes for a total of $140,000, and the cost of video libraries would be approximately $15,000 a year. Each year, approximately 20 people would go to live classes to continue their education - or these might be new people who have just joined the company.

The total one-time cost then would be $745,000 for installing MRP. And $145,000 extra per year to maintain it. The savings would amount to $1,615,000 - estimated very conservatively - which represents a payout of better than 2 to 1 the first full year that MRP is in operation. Results should be expected within the first 12 months that MRP is on the air if a company is a Class A or B MRP user. Since MRP takes 15 to 18 months to install, there is a negative cash flow during the first year and a half. But from there on, the investment is far better than any other investment that management is likely to have the opportunity to make. A machine tool, for example, would be justified on the basis of a three-year payout in most companies. By these standards, an MRP system would have paid itself off almost seven times while the machine tool paid for itself once.

It's interesting, too, to look at the justification for MRP and consider that if the costs were doubled and the savings were cut in half, by any logical standards for capital investment, MRP would still be a great bargain.

There are companies that have installed MRP, but are not getting the results from it. The reasons are always the same. The bills of material aren't right, the inventory records aren't right, the master schedule isn't right. But, of course, the fundamental problems are people and education. Reinstalling MRP involves all of the costs of installing MRP with the likely exception of the data processing and systems effort.

MRP can be justified like any other investment. And there are very few that can even touch it in terms of tangible return. But the real question is not what it costs to install MRP. In most companies, the question is what they are spending day after day because they don't have it. While most manufacturing companies don't recognize it because they are so used to living in the world of the informal system, the cost of _not_ having MRP is one of the

greatest drains on profits that exists in the typical manufacturing business.

Footnotes

1. See Appendix 6 for education references.

2. We run approximately 45 live classes each year. In each of these classes, we pick a company and have them supply the numbers and do their own justification. The numbers shown are typical numbers based on hundreds of these justifications both in classes and working with clients.

Chapter 17
Implementing MRP II

Section 1
Implementing with the Right Priorities

In Chapter 7, the critical elements in implementing an MRP system were broken down into three categories:

1. Technical.
2. Data.
3. People.

They are listed in the reverse order of their significance. The computer system is like the golf club, it is a prerequisite. Most companies couldn't do MRP manually, and they need a computer system. But, like the golf club, it only gets them up on the first tee, it doesn't hit the ball.

Then they need the data areas corrected to make the closed loop system work. These are:

1. The master schedule.
2. Bills of material.
3. Inventory records.
4. Routings.
5. Work centers. (This is usually not a major effort.)

A great deal of effort is required in the typical company to get the data to a high enough level of accuracy to support an MRP system. In the previous chapter, the costs of fixing bills of material, routings, and inventory records were estimated at approximately $220,000, indicative of the magnitude of the job.

Education, of course, is the key to people understanding what is required to make MRP work. Education is the highest priority activity.

If any one sentence could best convey why most companies don't achieve the full potential of MRP, it would be this:

THEY ATTACK MRP AS A COMPUTER SYSTEM,
RATHER THAN AS A PEOPLE SYSTEM.

They spend all kinds of time choosing software when, in fact, that isn't what's going to make the difference between success or failure. Not that they don't need workable software, but most of the available software is workable. The minor differences between the good software packages will not make the difference between being a Class C MRP user or being a Class A user. But this is where the typical company will devote the bulk of their attention.

Many managers would say that they understand the right priorities, but their actions speak louder than their words. This can be demonstrated using numbers from the justification in the previous chapter.

When presented with a bill for $350,000 for computer software and systems work, they sign it recognizing that computer systems "are always expensive."

When given an estimate of $220,000 to fix bills of material, routings, and stockrooms, they are far less enthusiastic. One hundred thousand dollars to relayout the plant to have limited access stores? That's a difficult one to swallow!

When presented with an estimate of $155,000 for education, they typically balk! Somehow the idea of investing that much money in the most important resource a company has, its people, seems almost frivolous to many managers! They give lip service to "people" being the most important concern, but they show that they don't really believe it in practice.

Yet, without people who understand, everything else that is done to implement MRP will be a waste of time. It's been said before, but it must be repeated for emphasis: it's critical that during the implementation, the focus be kept on the highest priority - the people.

Section 2
Implementation and Reimplementation Steps

Appendix 3 shows a detailed implementation plan. The highlights of implementation, however, are shown in Figure 17-1.

1. First cut education
2. Justification
3. Project Leader
4. Professional Guidance
5. Project Plan – with Accountability
6. Education
7. Regular Management Review

Figure 17 - 1.   Implementation Steps

Reimplementing an MRP system, and many companies nave this problem, isn't much different from implementation. Most of the companies that tackled MRP as a computer system have only the technical part of MRP implemented, and need to go back and do all the other implementation steps over again. If a company is reimplementing MRP, they should check off the steps in the detailed implementation plan that have been accomplished and are really working, and then go through it just as if they were implementing MRP for the first time.

The first-cut education prior to justification and the justification itself were covered in Chapter 16. Suffice it to say that MRP should be tackled like any other business proposition: looking at the costs, looking at the potential returns, and having managers sign off on the results that they can generate.

Once the justification has been done and the project has been approved, the next step is to pick a project leader. The four most common mistakes in picking a project leader are:

1. Using a systems person. The issue here is straightforward: accountability. Systems people are an indispensable part of the project team. But the project manager must be a user. No one in systems can be held accountable for making the system work in operations after it's on the air. Only a user can do this. It's important to re-

member that the responsibility for the paybacks rests with line management. The project manager is simply the representative, the delegate of the chief executive officer.

2. Using an "outsider" as the project leader. A lot of companies tend to think that MRP is some kind of a computer technique, and if they can only get the right "expert" from outside, all will go well. But this isn't where the real MRP challenge lies. The best project leader is one who currently has a title like materials manager or plant manager and has been with the company for many years, knows the products, the problems, and the people. It is easier to teach a person who knows the company, the products, and the people MRP than it is to teach an MRP "expert" about the company, the problems and the people. A company in upstate New York was surprised to hear this specification for a project manager, but picked their man based on these qualifications. Six months into the project they understood why he was the right man. He did an outstanding job of working with the shop people - people he knew - to show them the "why" and the "how" of keeping inventory records correct. That doesn't say that an outsider can't be a part of the MRP project team. It does say that this is a very poor choice of person for the project leader's job.

3. Picking a "boy to do a man's job." One company in California had been floundering around with MRP for many years. They went through several project managers, but each time a crisis came up, they would remove the project manager and have him back fighting fires. The most recent project manager was a young man six months out of college! A man with outstanding potential, but simply not enough credibility to convince foremen, general foremen, buyers and other experienced company people that they were going to change their behavior and do business in a more professional manner.

4. Trying to use a part time project leader. Today, unfortunately, the firefighting problems will always be the compelling problems. When a project leader isn't full time, MRP installation

drags on interminably. The typical question is, "The person we would like as project manager is indispensable. How can we run without him during the project?" And the answer to that is very straightforward. In the event this "indispensable" person got hit by a trolley car and was in traction for six months, the company would not be liquidated. It would continue to run. What an opportunity to put in an understudy while the project manager works full time on the project getting it on the air. And the understudy should understand exactly what's going on: that this is a temporary position to see if the understudy can fill the position temporarily vacated by the project manager.

Few companies would build a new factory and have a part time project manager, someone from the systems group as a project manager, or a young man six months out of college as the project manager! Certainly, the qualifications for the manager of a project to run the business in a new way inside the old bricks are at least equal to the qualifications required for the manager of a project to run the business the old way inside new bricks.

Experience has shown that very few companies are able to put an MRP system on the air successfully without some professional guidance. Experience has also shown that very few MRP successes ever took place when a large consulting firm sent in a group of consultants to install MRP for the client. Unfortunately, the way most consultants work is exactly the wrong way to make MRP work. The group of people they supply are usually systems/technical people. And they tend to take the initiative away from the user. Above all, the system must be a company system; a system that belongs to the users. The motivation of a large consulting firm, where people get paid and get their bonuses based on the number of "billing days" they can produce, is to do exactly what the client doesn't need. That's why so many consulting jobs simply result in a half a dozen large books full of flow charts and procedures that nobody ever uses.

Nevertheless, installing an MRP system successfully is a new experience for most of the people in any company. An outside consultant can say the right things to management when they need to be said. Very few insiders can do this without sometimes having to "put their job on the line."

So the best kind of consulting is to get someone who will come in once every four to six weeks and act as the "catalyst," not try to perform the "reaction" for the client. Even in dealing with a large consulting firm, it would be better to have one of the more experienced members of the firm, who has actually installed a successful MRP system somewhere else, come in occasionally than to have that person supervise a group of people to install the system.

But the most important single consideration in getting any consultant is experience. It's difficult to believe how many hardheaded business men have hired consultants to advise them on subjects like MRP without ever finding out where the person who will consult to them has done it successfully. MRP is a far more effective way to run a manufacturing business. Consultants are always looking for the latest "buzz words" and "gimmicks" to sell their services. As a consequence, virtually every consulting firm that has anything to do with manufacturing is talking about MRP today. Unfortunately, while many of them have letters behind their names to indicate that they are "certified," this certification was based on a written test, not on checking to see what kind of results their clients were able to produce. There are many other consultants who have had this kind of success. These are the people to provide professional guidance.

Many successful MRP users have taken the detailed project plan (discussed in Appendix 3), crossed out a couple of topics that did not apply, written in a couple of topics that were peculiar to their own situation, and started the project promptly. It is important to remember, however, that no project plan is valid without the names of the line managers who will be accountable for attaining results next to each of the topics on the project plan.

Teaching a company to operate in "formal system mode" is a real challenge. Like learning to fly an airplane, it is not an extension of experience. No one who has ever installed an MRP system successfully ever said, "We did too much education!" No one who has done it unsuccessfully failed to say, "We didn't do enough education!" The education task is a formidable one, yet it can be handled using the live outside classes and the video education courses that are available today. Education is a sufficiently significant task so that the next chapter is devoted to the subject.

There should be a regular management review of the project plan with the top management people - the CEO and the top managers in each of the major functions - sitting down at least every two weeks to make sure that the project is moving along on schedule. At that time, the project manager and people accountable for various parts of the project will review the progress and problems with management.

The project manager will have a number of people on the project team. Some professional systems people, and other people will move in and out of the project as it progresses. Accounting people, for example, should be sitting in, reviewing the project, and getting their information ready to tie in with MRP so that the system can embody the functions of MRP II when it goes on the air. But their need for full time participation probably won't come until considerably later in the project.

During implementation, it's important for line managers to talk with their people and get feedback on their attitudes. The best approach to take to installing an MRP system successfully could be called the "sandwich" approach. The most critical people are the people at the top of the company and the people on the firing line, the foremen, buyers, etc. Those who have never worked in a factory are likely to take foremen and buyers for granted. But that is a serious mistake. These are the people who make schedules happen. No scheduling system is going to work well unless the foremen want it to work well.

Yet, in most companies, the foremen are given very little education and are considered to be fairly insignificant in making MRP work. Look at the attendance at a typical professional society seminar on MRP, for example. Very few foremen are ever invited to attend, even though the subject of the entire seminar is scheduling. If the foremen, general foremen, shop superintendents, etc. don't understand MRP and don't see the value it will have for them, the chances of it being successful are very slim indeed. And MRP can be explained to foremen as long as it is kept straightforward and the elegant simplicity of MRP is not obscured with a bunch of fancy techniques that don't have any significance in the real world. Any foreman can understand that if the system can tell him what to work on the beginning of this month to prevent a shortage the end of next month, life is going to be just a little more tolerable in the factory.

The other problems that are common in an MRP system include:

1. Engineers who aren't interested in making bills of material that the operating people can use.

2. Marketing people who don't want to get involved in developing a master schedule.

3. Financial people who want to keep their own set of records and remain aloof from MRP.

These are all management problems. They are natural, normal problems that are likely to occur in any company. And it's management's job to be sure everyone understands what MRP II is really all about so that each knows how to play his or her position on the team.

That's why the "sandwich approach" is a good one to keep in mind. Everyone has to be educated to understand MRP because it's a new way of running a business. But the top management and line supervision are the most critical ones. The others can be educated fairly readily, especially if people at the top really provide the leadership to run the company more professionally.

Section 3
The Pilot and the Cutover

There are three methods for converting to a new system:

1. The "cold turkey" approach.
2. The "parallel system" approach.
3. The "pilot" approach.

The "cold turkey" approach, according to some theoreticians, "motivates people to sink or swim." The system will be put on the air all at once and this forces people to make it work. A great approach - <u>in theory</u>! In practice, very few people have drowned from lack of motivation. Drowning people are among the most highly motivated in the world. Their problem is not motivation; they are overwhelmed. <u>No company should ever put a system on the air cold turkey</u>. A few companies have done it successfully, but the problem boils down to a question of the odds and the stakes. Even if there are nine chances in ten that it could be done successfully, the stakes, in the event of failure, are incredibly high. Foremen have heard about computer systems over and over again. With some understandable skepticism, they listen to the description of MRP and what it can do for them. It makes sense. Nevertheless, their experience tells them that this is probably one more computer fiasco. And, if it turns out to be a fiasco because the cold turkey approach was taken, the chances of making MRP work in the near future are very remote. Those consultants most experienced in installing MRP successfully consider the cold turkey approach naive and irresponsible.

The "parallel" method is another one that sounds good in theory. It certainly appears to be a conservative approach. The idea of the parallel method is that the old system and the new system will be run in parallel and the old system will be in place until such time as the new system starts to work properly.

In the real world, there are two very serious problems with this approach. In the first place, there probably aren't enough people around to run two systems. And the effort should be put into making the new system work, not perpetuating the old system.

Secondly, MRP is a computer system that couldn't possibly be done manually. Manually we simply did not have the massive data manipulation capability. Consequently, running systems in parallel doesn't work. The old system will say "order more" while MRP says "reschedule out, you don't need it." The parallel approach can be made to work when transferring manual inventory records to a computer because manual inventory records <u>could</u> be kept successfully with a pencil and they can be done on a computer. The advisability of running parallel systems, even where they <u>can</u> be done, is highly questionable. But trying to run an MRP system in parallel with the old system simply doesn't make sense. The basic rule is:

> <u>The most significant systems to put on a computer are those that couldn't possibly be done manually. Thus, by definition, there is no way to run them in parallel with the old system.</u>

The "pilot" approach is the approach that most of the Class A and B users have used in putting in MRP. There is a lot of confusion about this method. People ask, "How can we tell if it's really working when we only have one product line on the system?" "What is the best product to pick? The easiest one or the most difficult one?" Or, "What if we don't have a product line with entirely unique components?" All of these questions ignore the two fundamental issues of the pilot:

1. Using it to make sure that MRP can predict the shortages for the product line used in the pilot. As long as no shortage list is needed to determine what material is <u>really</u> required and <u>when</u> it is required, the MRP pilot is satisfying this requirement

2. People understanding. Does the planner, or planners, whose product lines are being used in the pilot understand MRP's simple, fundamental logic?

Most companies installing MRP find that a good planner who is using it as a pilot will be the best salesman for MRP. In a company making pharmaceuticals, one of the best planners was picked for the pilot. She had recently been transferred into production and inventory control from the quality control department. Her comment after she had been working the pilot for several weeks was, "Production and inventory control was just massive confusion to me when I first came here. They ordered once a month, they expedited once a minute. Very few orders seemed to have the right dates on them. It was a confusion of redundant, often conflicting, systems. MRP is simple, it makes sense."

The pilot is primarily a test of the people and their understanding. Once that understanding has been demonstrated, MRP can be extended to other product lines, and finally, the entire material requirements planning system can be installed.

Figure 17-2 shows an MRP implementation schedule. The schedule begins the day the project manager signs off on the project plan. The pilot MRP system should be on the air on the first product line within nine to twelve months. Within twelve to fifteen months, MRP should be installed across the board. Nothing is more demoralizing than dragging out the time from pilot to full MRP. By month 15 to 18, the closed loop system including purchasing, capacity planning, and dispatching should be installed. By month 18 to 24, the financial function should be tied in with MRP so that the company has an MRP II system.

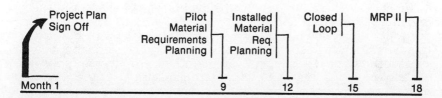

Figure 17 - 2. Implementation Schedule

Many people look at a project plan with a schedule like this and think it is unrealistic. In practice it's not. Some of the best MRP installations have not only hit this schedule, but, in some cases, beat it. Of the critical elements discussed in the beginning of this chapter, the ones that are most likely to be in the critical path in implementing an MRP system are:

1. Developing the computer software.
2. Fixing bills of material.
3. Fixing routings.
4. Fixing inventory records.
5. Educating people.

Obviously, work centers must be correct. But that's not usually a great problem in most companies. The master schedule must be correct and must be managed properly. That is a challenge in running an MRP system, a challenge that some companies with MRP on the air for many years are still struggling with. But it isn't a time-consuming implementation step.

If there is a problem in hitting the implementation schedule shown in Figure 17-2, every effort should be exerted to find out which of these items is in the critical path. And what needs to be done to complete the critical items sooner and get MRP installed more quickly.

One important reason for implementing MRP with all deliberate haste is financial. The payback from the justification in the previous chapter was $1,615,000. If the implementation takes an extra year, that is the amount of money which will have been lost and can never be recaptured.

But there's an even more important reason for installing MRP as quickly as possible. This kind of project requires a group of enthusiastic people who are going to work long hours to make it happen. A company can't hire a bunch of outsiders to fix their bills of material, fix their inventory records, and educate their people. They have to do that themselves. This means that they will be doing this while also keeping the shipments going out the door. The enthusiasm to support this kind of effort can only be sustained for a year to eighteen months. If the project drags on, the enthusiasm will be gone and the project will limp along forever.

And it's important that the emphasis be kept on shipments while the system is being installed. If the shipments don't continue to go out the door, many of the people installing the system won't be around to enjoy the benefits of a new system. In a manufacturing company, shipments are the lifeblood of the business and cannot be ignored while a new system is being installed.

The key measures to be monitored before installation were discussed in Chapter 7, but it's important to remember that they must be considered "go/no go." In other words, MRP should not be installed even on a pilot basis if the company doesn't come up to these standards in three critical areas of data integrity:

1. Inventory record accuracy 95 percent.
2. Bill of material accuracy 98+ percent.
3. Routing accuracy 95+ percent.

No MRP implementation should be attempted with record accuracy below these standards. The records will NOT get better after the system is installed.

One company installed MRP before their inventory records were really accurate. Their theory was that the order point system that they had didn't work very well and they needed something better. They felt that MRP would be better, even with the same poor records that had been used with the order point system, because MRP is inherently a far better system. Unfortunately, this ignored the fundamental issue. They did not have an order point system. The order point does not address the question, "When do you really need the material?" Their real system was a shortage list. When they put MRP on the air with poor inventory records, their real system was still a shortage list. They were very fortunate they had the kind of management leadership and shop supervision that could bring them back from a traumatic false start to finally make MRP work. Very few companies that get off to a bad start ever really make it as Class A or B MRP users.

These are the other key points to be sure of before installing MRP:

1. That top management really understands. This is an absolute must. The project should be stopped if top management refuses to take the time to learn about MRP II. It will not generate much in the way of success without top management knowing how to run the business with the new tools.

2. That first-line supervision really understands.

3. That a standard MRP logic is being used in the system.

4. That the system is being kept as simple as possible for the users.

5. That virtually all of the people in the company have been educated by the time the pilot goes on the air. Education will be discussed in more detail in the following chapter.

6.   That the pilot approach for cutover is going to be used, and no excuse will be accepted for running the risks involved in going "cold turkey."

7.   That the CEO has told the people who report to him, and each line manager has told those who report to them, "Tell me ahead of time if you see any problems with MRP, and let's work them out together. Don't come to me afterwards and say, 'I told you so.' <u>You</u> will be accountable for the success of MRP."

A word of caution: when MRP is first installed, there is a real potential for starving the plant and the vendors. It used to be said in installing a new inventory control system that inventory would go up temporarily. This was true because inventory systems in bygone days concentrated only on "when to order." When the new system went in, the things that needed to be ordered got ordered right away. The things that were not needed had to be worked off from the inventory. But MRP is a scheduling system, not an ordering system. The minute it is installed, it will indicate that many orders need to be rescheduled because they are not needed right away. This could cause a serious disruption in plant production rates and in vendor production rates. The inventory reduction should be planned in an orderly manner, and MRP can easily accommodate this as long as people are aware of the problem ahead of time. When the capacity planning and the orders for vendors show that there's going to be a very sharp drop in activity, the master schedule can be reviewed and managed to spread this inventory reduction over a period of time rather than making it abruptly causing disruptions in the factory and with the vendors.

If there is ever a question about whether MRP is working or not, there's a simple way to find out. MRP is a series of simulated shortage lists. If the shortage list today that results from physically pulling material out of the stockroom does not match up with what shows on the MRP report today, the master schedule, the bill of material, or the inventory record must be wrong. There's a simple rule to understand: <u>MRP is a simulation of reality</u>. As long as it simulates reality, it always works.

Section 4
How to do it Wrong

The number of ways to put MRP in wrong is almost limitless. All of them stem from one fundamental misunderstanding many people have; they think that MRP is a computer system and that somehow the "system" will make the business run better. Here are some favorite approaches to doing it WRONG:

1. Hire a "turnkey" consultant. This is the kind of thing that some consultants really believe they can do. Install a system where the user supposedly simply has to "turn the key" and the system works. That may work well in other areas, but it does not work for MRP. An MRP system simply generates a piece of paper or an image on the tube. If the people don't work hard to use it, it isn't going to succeed. Management cannot subcontract their responsibilities to a "turnkey" consultant.

2. Hire a software company or a computer hardware manufacturer to do the job. Unfortunately, in practice, the systems engineers from the computer hardware companies have an abysmal track record - with a few notable exceptions. This is not to say that this type of technical consulting is not useful. But it certainly does not replace the professional guidance from a consultant who will go right to the president and tell him what he's doing wrong in installing MRP. For obvious reasons, a company that makes its living by selling software or hardware tends not to want their people to make too many waves with the president. The major issue is still the same. Most of these people are technical people, and when they look at the critical elements involved in installing MRP, their instincts will be to concentrate on the technical areas - not the people areas - where, after all, they probably aren't very qualified.

3. Hire some young MBAs out of college to install the system. Unfortunately, in a rapidly developing technology, as one college professor put it very aptly, "We are probably always going to be twen-

ty years behind what's happening in the real world." Very few college professors today really understand MRP II. (1) Even fewer understand it as a people system rather than a computer system. Most college graduates have to learn that simplicity, not the sophistication they were probably taught, is the only thing that works. Fortunately, experience has shown that they do tend to learn this very quickly when they get into the real world.

4. <u>Let the systems people do the job</u>. There is no way that systems people can be held accountable for the success of MRP. All too often naive or ambitious systems people are ready to do the job "because if we don't, nobody else will." But, if it isn't going to work, letting the systems people do it will be a bad experience that will jeopardize doing it right at a later date.

It's obvious that each of these favorite mistakes stems from people's compulsion to believe that MRP is some kind of computer magic. But there is no magic in the computer. The real magic in MRP is people.

Section 5
The Odds for Success

MRP II can be highly successful. The companies that understand the important things - the proper priorities and the implementation steps - will be successful with MRP. One young man who started working in consulting after successfully installing and operating an MRP system showed what could be done. Of his first eight clients, seven were either Class A or B MRP users within the first few months after they had the system installed. (The eighth company had some management problems that proved insurmountable. MRP will not fix this.) Most of the clients of this consultant who are Class B are well on the way to becoming Class A MRP users. (2)

Most companies attack MRP as a computer exercise, and the main result is that they get to exercise the computer. Those who see it as a serious management challenge in running a manufacturing business more professionally, and install it properly, can expect a <u>100 percent chance of success</u>!

Footnotes

1. One Harvard Business School professor said MRP
    applies primarily "to assembled products." A dead
    giveaway that he still thinks of it as an inventory con-
    trol technique! "How Managers Can Know All and
    Control Inventory," Christian Science Monitor, October
    16, 1981.

2. See the Checklists in Appendix 2 for further dis-
    cussion on Class A,B,C, and D MRP.

Chapter 18
The Education Task

Section 1
The Key Element in Success

The justification done in Chapter 16 showed a total cost of $745,000 to install an MRP system. The bulk of this cost was in computer and systems work, fixing bills of material, routings, and inventory records. Education accounted for about 20 percent of the total cost. Yet, all the rest of the investment in MRP will be wasted if the education job is not done properly. It is the most highly leveraged part of the MRP investment.

The education job is the one that is usually underestimated, underbudgeted, and not understood. Consequently, it is the cause of most of the problems with MRP systems. People say that the problems are inventory record accuracy, bill of material accuracy and bill of material structuring, an overstated master schedule, etc., but almost all of these problems can be traced back to lack of understanding. The typical company installing an MRP system should plan to educate better than 90 percent of all of the people in the company - 100 percent would be better!

Machine operators certainly should be given education so that they understand MRP. One company gave them one-hour education sessions each month while MRP was being implemented. When people hear that a new computer system is coming in, the first thing that they think of is the number of people who are going to be laid off as a result. It's true that MRP can result in greater productivity, but it usually results in greater market penetration at the same time. Most companies that install MRP don't have to lay people off because they enjoy a sales increase as a result of better customer service. But this needs to be explained to people in the factory. They need to understand that MRP will result in more of the right material being available at the right time. They need to understand, for example, that this means no more "shopping trips" through the stockroom. They need to understand what MRP is, how to use it, and, especially, the new set of values.

Without some understanding of MRP, resistance is normal. But MRP is simple in its logic. It addresses problems people in manufacturing companies have experienced. In one company, before they installed MRP, management was putting pressure on the assemblers in the surgical table department to increase their productivity. Their response was a grievance stating that until such time as management provided the parts so that the surgical tables could be built the way they were designed to be built, management had no right to ask them to increase their productivity. If unions understood what MRP was all about, it would become a contract requirement! The logic of MRP is simple and compelling. But people have to be taught what it is or they'll think it's just one more computer exercise!

In Chapter 16, the education of a few key people before justification was discussed. Once a company has decided to go ahead with an MRP program, then the critical mass - virtually everybody in the company - must be educated.

Section 2
Educating the Critical Mass

There are three apparent methods for handling education:

1. Attendance at professionally run live classes.
2. Having an "outside expert" run live classes "in-plant."
3. Using video education.

Certainly key people, and especially those who are going to teach others, should attend live classes. There are two types of classes today that are considered basic. Many others give more detail in areas like purchasing, distribution, MRP and accounting, etc. The two major programs are a top management course and a course for planners, foremen, supervisors, systems people, etc. The top management class is two and a half days and the other class usually is a week in length and, therefore, is commonly called "The Five-Day Class." It is taught by a number of people and is considered the standard class in the field.

Live classes get people away from their jobs which allows them to discuss their problems with other people from other companies. They learn that all companies have the same problems and that their company is not "unique." This gives them a far broader perspective than if the "outside expert" approach were used.

Even if a live class is run locally, it's better to have people stay at the class location overnight. The objective is to get them away from the job and day-to-day problems in order to learn some new concepts.

The only pitfall in choosing live classes is to make sure that the instructors have actually done it in practice. Once again, as in consulting, many people who are not qualified have gotten into the field.

The same is true with the top management class. There are classes available that are excellent. There are others that put the primary emphasis on the technology of MRP - the least important thing that management needs to know on the subject. Once again, the test is: where has the instructor actually succeeded in doing it in the field? Where are the successful companies that have attended these courses and turned their knowledge into an MRP success? There is more information on these educational programs in Appendix 6.

The second approach, bringing in a consultant to run in-plant education, should be avoided. On the surface, it seems very appealing. "Why not have the instructor come to the company rather than send many people to the instructor?"

In practice, it just doesn't work. It would be difficult to find a company that is a Class A user where they have used "live in-plant education" as the way to get their people educated. Plenty have tried it, but to the author's knowledge, none have succeeded. The problems with this approach to education are:

1. It reinforces the popular parochialism: "We're unique, we're different."

2. There is something unexciting about getting a notice and being told to be in the auditorium to hear some "outside expert" talk about MRP.

3. Most people look at the speaker in the auditorium as "one more consultant" selling his bill of goods. A far different attitude exists in the classroom.

4. The general attitude toward the consultant in the auditorium is, "What does he know about the window shade business? He probably never made a window shade in his life." The "outside expert" approach to education does little to give the kind of "peer confirmation" that exists in a live class.

5. The "outside expert" approach to education is a one-shot deal rather than continuing education to support a more professional approach to management. It's like trying to give people "smart pills." It's far better to have a few key people go to live education courses and follow this up with continuing education using video programs.

6. The most tempting education to do "in-plant" is top management education. And it is a terrible mistake to take this kind of short cut in educating the people who really have to make MRP work. No matter how good the instructor is, he

is "on their turf" when he is talking to top management in their own company. Having heard plenty of consultants before, top management is usually looking for some kind of panacea and the meeting is often dominated by the CEO rather than the instructor. The meeting can also quickly degenerate into talking about specific company problems rather than getting educated. It is far better to have top management go away, get the business off their minds temporarily, and participate with other members of top management from other companies in genuine education.

There is plenty of money to be made by consultants and educators running live in-plant education. Some consultants claim that they do not do "in-plant" education because they insist that it be done off site in a motel, country club, or on a college campus. But this doesn't address any of the problems discussed above. The only problem that it does solve is that of secretaries slipping notes in. And imaginative secretaries can usually figure a way to do that no matter where the course is held!

The most experienced professionals refuse to do "in-plant education in spite of the money. Experience shows it just is not an effective way to go about it.

The third method is the way to educate the critical mass: video courses as an in-plant education method. The video courses generally contain the same material as that taught in live classes, and can be tailored into education courses for machine operators, foremen, marketing, engineering, accounting, planners, buyers, etc. Once again, it's important to make sure that the video courses are of the highest quality. Too many people tend to think that MRP education consists only of teaching people things.

Education is not just a "fact transfer." Education about MRP is capturing people's imaginations to show them how a simple system, a formal system that they have never experienced before, can be made to work for them if they will make it work. The primary purpose of MRP education is to transfer facts along with an enthusiasm and commitment for doing a far more professional job. Without that enthusiasm, the fact transfer is worthless.

The track record of the video instructors, and the ability of the course content to interest people, as well as to teach them facts, should be a very serious consideration. In education, there is good and there is better. But because people are the key to success, only the best is a good investment. And results is the only criterion for judging what is best.

In addition to live classes for key people, video courses must then be used to educate virtually everyone in the company. Those who supply video courses also supply the course outlines tailored to an individual company's requirements. This consists of a book showing how many sessions will be given to the group in marketing, for example, what subjects will be covered, what video tapes will be used, when the sessions will start, and how long they will last (1)

One of the pitfalls with video education is that it can too easily become, "Let's all go watch the movies." A well-structured video course would have the following general format:

1.   Questions and answers from last session - 5 to 15 minutes.
2.   Review of reading - 5 to 10 minutes.
3.   Video - 15 to 30 minutes.
4.   Review and discussion - 30 to 60 minutes.

While a person from a training department or the personnel department can set up the classes and handle most of the logistics, the responsibility for education is a line responsibility. In the first place, this makes the education far more meaningful. Secondly, no one learns as much as the teacher. Video education can be used in "chain letter" fashion so that each person who is educated has the responsibility for educating the people who work for them. They should at least be present during the discussion session, and frequently throughout the entire video education session to make sure that their people understand the material that is being taught.

Here again, the video education is a far more powerful format than in-plant training by an "outside expert." Consider a foreman who is going to a class taught by his plant superintendent who has been to one of the live classes. The plant superintendent will have credibility that an outside consultant/educator could never have. And that is the challenge: to make MRP credible, to teach people that this is for real; that this is not another game being played by the computer experts, but is, in fact, a different way of life for people in a manufacturing company.

It is the responsibility of each manager or supervisor to educate the people who work for them, and to evaluate how well these people are comprehending the material that is being taught. Giving formal tests is not always the best way to find out if people are learning from the courses. Formal tests smack of being in "high school" again. This evaluation is something the manager should be able to do by talking with the people who have been through these programs. One-on-one discussion is usually a far better method than formal "testing."

The most important issue of all in education is that it be taken seriously. There are a lot of education programs that are interesting, and maybe even fun, but don't have a lot to do with the way the job is being done on a day-to-day basis. It is as important for people to get educated in handling MRP as it is for a crew to learn how to fly that particular airplane. Whether it will fly or not will depend on the skill of the people. The line managers and supervisors have the responsibility for making sure that their people get educated. Attendance at video classes should be mandatory with make-up done later - usually on the person's own time - if any class is missed. There is always an excuse for not going to an education program. But when the skill of any member of the team can seriously impair the ability of the rest of the team to use MRP properly, attendance at education courses cannot be looked upon as an optional task to be done after the "important" tasks have been finished.

Section 3
Training the Users

There is an important distinction between education and training. Education teaches people "why" and some of the "how" while training gets into the details of "how." People often ask, "We are nine months away from installing an MRP system; isn't it too early to educate the foremen?" It is too early to train the foremen in how to handle a dispatch list, but it's not too early to educate them so that they know what a dispatch list is and why MRP will require keeping numbers accurate, etc. Education can never be done too early; training can.

The training for an MRP program should be done just prior to installation. The best approach to training is the "conference room pilot." Here, actual output reports are given to planners, foremen, buyers, etc. and they are taught to use the reports. They are taught to interpret them, to make changes, etc. There are really two conference room "dry runs." One is a program test. This is to make sure that the programs are working properly, that data has been handled properly, and that the numbers come out the other end properly.

Then there is a real user conference room "pilot." It shows for the users exactly what the output forms will look like, exactly how to interpret them and how to work with them. Everything is real except that the system isn't actually being used. This should go on for a few weeks until the users are comfortable with the output, the forms, the CRT displays, and the transactions. This is the real "training" part of installing an MRP system.

Section 4
Changing our Attitudes

If someone walked into the data processing department and said, "You people need education," they would be interested in what kind of education, what subjects would be covered, etc. Education is a normal way of life in data processing. If the same person walked up to the plant manager and said, "You need education," he would probably be offended. His response would most likely be, "What do you mean? I've been here 20 years!"

Education in manufacturing was not taken very seriously in the past. It was often considered a fringe benefit. "Let's send Charlie off to a seminar. He might meet some nice people and get <u>one</u> good idea!" Manufacturing simply was not a profession where there was a defined body of knowledge. It was a case of learning a few things in college and then "on-the-job training." The colleges generally taught either "mathematical analysis" - or used case studies. Either approach may very well help people to think more analytically, but it does not teach them a body of knowledge. Teaching specifics in the manufacturing area that were nonmathematical (managing a manufacturing enterprise on a day-to-day basis does not involve much higher mathematics) was considered by many of the educators to be "vocational training" and beneath the level of college education; "We teach them to think!"

Some of the colleges today are definitely beginning to learn what MRP and MRP II are all about and are beginning to teach it. Many of the others are not even particularly interested. But, after all, it isn't easy to teach solutions to people who don't understand the problems. Teaching them to think may well be the most important concern for the colleges.

We would, however, be in a very bad situation if the medical profession considered someone competent because they had a degree involving subject matter that only taught them to "think analytically," and then gave them "on-the-job training" and let them discover everything by themselves. A profession is a profession because there is a defined body of knowledge, and that is what's happening in the manufacturing field today. As manufacturing becomes more and more of a profession, education will become a normal part of day-to-day activity and not just a one-shot "send Charlie to a seminar" activity.

Footnotes

1. See Appendix 6 for sources with further information on video libraries.

Chapter 19
Operating with MRP II

Section 1
Using the Tools to Manage

MRP II provides the missing link that enables management to use the principles discussed in Chapter 6. Once objectives have been set, policy must be established and detailed planning done to implement the policy. Most of this planning will take place at the production planning level (discussed in Chapter 8), and the master scheduling level (discussed in Chapter 9).

But it's important to stress, once again, that the system will do nothing but generate paper or an image on a tube. It's what people do with this information that will determine whether MRP II is considered "a success" or not. And, unfortunately, even in the 1980's there is a great deal of misinformation around. Consider this quote from an article about MRP:

> The real intelligence of the overall materials management process has been usurped from middle level planner/managers and disbursed throughout the MRP software with control concentrated at the top level - the master schedule. With MRP, he who controls the master schedule, controls the production and material coverage processes and has a truly challenging and rewarding job. However, the middle managers now find themselves in a different role of <u>reacting</u> to the dictates of MRP rather than <u>planning</u>. These people must possess the education and intelligence to understand and cope with MRP, but they are no longer called upon to use their intelligence in a challenging and creative manner. Their new role of following instructions provided by MRP is perhaps more suitable for a new class of employee, the <u>superclerk</u> or an <u>automaton</u>. (1)

This is the kind of ridiculous nonsense being broadcast by consultants who have brushed up against MRP, perhaps even seen a Class C system, but certainly never seen a Class A or B system operating. In practice, <u>it just does not work that way</u>.

Consider the way the capacity planner, the material planner, and the master scheduler would work together in managing with the system. The capacity planner might find, for example, that there was a potential overload in a given work center. A detailed capacity plan would show the individual jobs involved by part number. Going to the material planner, the capacity planner could find out what these components would be used for and which ones were most critical. Working with the master scheduler they could determine how important it was to get additional capacity by subcontracting or working overtime and also what jobs would be affected by their decisions. If it was determined that additional capacity was needed, the capacity planner would then work with shop supervision to see how this could best be obtained.

If there is an emergency order that must be shipped, MRP simply generates that information. It doesn't say how material will be obtained in shorter than normal lead time. It doesn't determine which jobs will be pushed aside to get this job through. It only identifies the jobs that are currently scheduled within the capacity, and leaves the choice up to people. MRP does not decide to work overtime, fly material in, or change vendors because of poor delivery performance. This kind of action has to come from the people - the same people who always made these kinds of decisions before. The difference is not that they are now "superclerks," the difference is that they now have the information to make these decisions far better than they could before. And they see the problems coming sooner so they can spend their efforts keeping out of trouble, rather than getting out of trouble.

MRP II is fairly new. Consequently, most of the emphasis so far has been on installing MRP properly, and using it as a planning tool. Undoubtedly, more and more emphasis will be placed on execution in the future because that, in the final analysis, will make the difference between the good users and the excellent users.

Section 2
Management Policy

Before there was a formal system for executing management policy, management policy was rarely expressed in
formal terms. With a system that translates high level
plans into detailed plans for the entire company, policy is
essential.

Before the formal system was available, jobs would just
be expedited through the shop with the attitude, "Let the
chips fall where they may." Today, an MRP system enables
people to look at the potential consequences to see whether
overtime may be needed, whether another job may have to
be rescheduled out, and to plan ahead of time rather than
simply reacting. Establishing policy ahead of time is simply
a case of deciding where the boundary lines are before the
ball goes into play rather than debating the boundaries
constantly.

Master scheduling is a good case in point. Without a
written policy, there is no master schedule. Probably 80
percent of the companies operating with MRP today don't
have a master scheduling policy, and then they wonder why
MRP doesn't work as well as it should!

Before the formal system worked, there was very little
that could truly be done to implement policy. When MRP
does work, policy can be implemented very effectively - as
long as there is policy to be implemented. It would be fair
to say that in most companies what manufacturing believes
to be the policy on changing schedules, for example, is not
what marketing believes to be the policy. It's up to
management to specify, working with manufacturing and
marketing, what a reasonable policy is.

There are many areas where it is important to have
policies where very little formal policy existed in the past.
Among them are:

1. Business planning policy, spelling out the fre-
    quency of updating the plan, tying it in with the
    production plan, and who must sign off on the
    plan.

2. Production planning policy. This was discussed
    in Chapter 8. In a manufacturing company, the

production plan is where everything starts. It establishes the production rate which will determine how much finished product is produced (affecting the amount of inventory in a make-to-stock product line or the amount of backlog in a make-to-order product line), how much material will have to be purchased and manufactured, and how much labor will be required. In a manufacturing company, the production plan should be signed off by the top operating executive because it will govern the levels of inventory, customer service, manpower, and, ultimately, cash flow.

3. Master scheduling policy. This was discussed in Chapter 9.

4. Policy concerning the planning department. Very few companies recognize the true function of this department: to make valid plans that others will be held accountable for executing. These plans, of course, will be derived from the production plans via the master schedule. These people should be measured on making valid, equitable plans. The people who have to sign off on these plans should be measured on execution. The job of the planning people is to plan, monitor, and call attention to the problem areas so that the execution will take place.

5. Capacity planning policy. The capacity requirements plan determines the number of standard hours required to produce the material to meet the master schedule, the production plan, and ultimately, the business plan. The shop management people should be required to sign off that they can meet the capacity required, or point out ahead of time that they can't.

6. Scheduling policy in the factory. The dispatch list gives the shop foremen a schedule for each work center each day. Policy should establish their responsibility for meeting the schedule, their prerogative for changing the sequence of jobs in order to save setups, for example, when this will not impair their ability to meet the schedule, and the responsibility for feeding back information ahead of time when the job cannot be completed as scheduled. (The "anticipated delay

report" is discussed later in this chapter and shown in Figure 19-1.)

7. Scheduling policy for purchasing. The purchasing department schedules the outside factory, and the policies for operating the purchasing department should be similar to those that are used by the people who operate manufacturing.

8. Policy about engineering's role. They will be required to provide and maintain valid documentation on product structure (bills of material) and operation sequences (routings). Ground rules for making engineering changes should also be spelled out. An engineering change committee should be identified (see Chapter 13). Engineering should also be required to sign off on schedules for customer orders that need to be engineered, new product introduction, and the provision of partial and completed documentation for highly engineered products.

9. Policy about marketing's role. It should specify the kind of forecasts they should be making, the type of accuracy expected (see Chapter 9), and the communication that must exist between marketing and manufacturing.

10. Policy about the financial department. They should be required to provide input to the MRP II system to keep costs up to date as labor and material costs change, and to keep overhead allocation up to date as production rates change.

These are just some of the policies required by the formal system.

Above all, management needs to insist that people tell the truth. In the past, the inventory control department ordered material from purchasing and put dates on the purchase orders that were earlier than they really needed. They didn't believe that purchasing would bring the material in on the date specified anyway! Purchasing knew that these dates were unrealistic. They didn't bother to try to bring the material in on those dates unless there was a phone call to expedite them! These were the habits that developed in the world of the informal system where the system couldn't possibly tell the truth. MRP II is a formal system that <u>can</u> tell the truth. But people have to <u>learn</u> to tell the truth so that the system can provide them truthful information to manage the business better.

Many people ask, "What can MRP do?" or, "Can we do this with MRP?" The answer is simple: since MRP is a simulator, it can do anything because it can simulate anything. MRP is not moral (good), it's not immoral (bad). It is amoral (doesn't know the difference). MRP cannot recognize a lie. It assumes that people will tell the truth - that must be one of the basic tenets of management policy that is expressed - <u>and demonstrated</u>.

Section 3
Performance Measures

In the past, management measured the shipments against the shipping budget, measured customer service, and measured inventory turnover. These are the <u>effects</u> and it's very important to measure them. But, in the world of the formal system, it's equally important, if not more important, to measure the <u>causes</u> like inventory records, bills of material and routings. These are the basic pieces of data that must be accurate if the formal system is to work.

The key measures, then, are:

1. Inventory (95 percent accuracy).

2. Bills of material (98 to 99 percent accuracy).

3. Routings (95 percent accuracy).

4. The master schedule (95 percent by item produced within the month).

5. Shipping dollars (100 percent shipped within the month).

6. Delivery performance (95 percent delivery against the original promise date each week).

7. Output by key work center (±5 percent each month).

8. Shop delivery to schedule (95 percent each week).

9. Vendor delivery to schedule (95 percent each week).

10. Engineering delivery to schedule (95 percent each week).

11. Forecast accuracy (depends on product; 90 percent 60 days in advance is typical).

The means for measuring inventory record accuracy, bill of material accuracy, and routing accuracy were discussed in earlier chapters. The recommended percentages are based on experience. These are the levels of accuracy that the successful users of MRP II have had to maintain to keep the system operating properly.

The master schedule should be measured each month to see what percent of the individual items in the master schedule were actually produced. Ninety-five percent is a typical bogey for many companies. Of course, some items might be pushed out and others pulled in; and thus, the shipping dollar objective of 100 percent was still attained even though the master schedule performance was only 95 percent.

Delivery performance by item is really a matter of the demands of the marketplace upon a company. Some companies in the instrument manufacturing business, for example, are halfway between make-to-stock and make-to-order. They assemble a batch of instruments when they have some orders on hand, and if a customer happens to place their order at the right time, their delivery will be very quick. On the other hand, if they place an order right after a batch of this particular instrument has been produced, delivery will be several weeks or even months. Some make-to-stock companies in the pharmaceutical industry, for example, or industries like cosmetics, couldn't live with a delivery performance as low as 95 percent. They would expect 98 to 99 percent of the line items ordered to be shipped. Delivery performance of 95 percent for the typical make-to-order company, however, would probably be quite satisfactory in most industries. This means that 95 percent of the orders are being shipped out the door as promised to the customers. It is also sometimes valuable to measure the percentage of customer order promises that meet the customer order request dates in a make-to-order business.

The input/output report is a monitor on capacity (see Appendix 1) that measures the number of standard hours produced by each work center against the plan. This can vary week to week, but over a four week period, for example, should be within ± 5 percent because producing even 5 percent below the plan every week would mean that the material was not being produced to meet the material requirements plan, and, consequently, the master schedule would not be able to be met.

The shop and vendors should be expected to deliver 95 percent or better of the orders on time. Obviously, there are times when there will be scrap or orders that have to be pulled up for one reason or another and that is expected in the 95 percent delivery bogey.

Engineering should be expected to deliver to the same type of performance bogey in a company operating with a formal system. Engineering should be measured against this objective.

Forecast accuracy is probably one of the most difficult things to measure and can vary tremendously from company to company. A company making popular records, for example, can be expected to have great difficulty forecasting. One making very stable items that sell year after year would expect the forecasts to be fairly accurate. A typical measure might be that 90 percent of the items forecast 60 days in advance would be within ± 5 percent of the forecast by individual item, product family, or option usage rate.

The specifics of delivery performance and forecast accuracy can vary considerably company to company. Inventory record accuracy, bills of material, routings, and attainment of the master schedule <u>cannot</u>. An MRP system requires these fundamentals to be correct if it is going to produce truthful information for planning and control purposes.

Because there hasn't been a valid plan to measure performance against in the past, performance measurement hasn't truly been used or understood as well as it should have been. These three aspects of performance measurement are the ones that seem to cause the most confusion:

1.   <u>Auditing</u>. Every performance measure must be audited two ways:

   a.   The causes of the problems must be identified so that they can be fixed. Inventory record accuracy, for example, is measured by cycle counting. When the errors are found daily, the <u>reasons</u> for the errors should be identified and reported, and efforts directed to correct the problems.

   b.   The manager of each major function should periodically audit the way the function is being measured. It's a good idea to have people measure themselves, but it's also important to make sure that they are measuring themselves correctly. The planning manager, for example, should go down to the stockroom and participate in the cycle counting periodically to make sure it is being handled properly.

2. The need for tolerance. Tolerance must be established for each performance measure. Tolerance is used in cycle counting. Usually, the items in inventory are broken down into a few groups and the expected accuracy is determined by group. A number one "audit category" group would be an item like an engine for a riding sweeper. One company uses ten per year of a particular engine at a cost of $600 apiece. This would not qualify as a high annual dollar usage "A item." But it is still expected that engines can be counted accurately. If the count was wrong by one unit, it would be considered to be an error.

The open purchase order file is another good example of this type of tolerance. There are many components that are used in high volume, and if 10,000 are on the purchase order or on the vendor schedule, and 9,998 are received, this is not a problem. On this type of item there could be a tolerance of up to 10 percent. On the other hand, if some specialized forgings are being ordered for a particular customer order and there are ten on the purchase order and only nine are received, the vendor cannot be credited with delivery on time. The point is very simple: any performance measure requires a reasonable tolerance.

3. The difference between planning and measurement. This quote is often heard: "Corporate won't permit us to change the business plan during the year." That, of course, is patently ridiculous. What if sales don't materialize? If the company stays with the original plan, too much inventory is bound to result. The confusion comes from the difference between a plan for measurement, and a plan for operations. It's important at some point in time to "take a snapshot" of the plan to measure performance against. The way this is

done with the master schedule was discussed in Chapter 9. But it's important also to have an operating plan that changes to respond to changes in the real world, or the operating plan will not provide valid input to the rest of the planning system.

People talk a lot about planning, but, undoubtedly, not enough about monitoring and auditing. This quote about one of the successful MRP users, Cameron Iron Works, makes the point well. (2) "Neither Cameron - nor any other successful user of MRP - will concede that the system is easy to implement or to successfully maintain. As has been pointed out previously, education and training for managers and operators is a must from the early stages of the project. And once the system is set up, constant monitoring and auditing of the process is vital."

Once a formal system works properly, there is a plan that people can be held accountable for achieving. Performance measurement is the means to implementing accountability for the execution of the plan.

Section 4
Executing the Plan

MRP is not a computer decision model. It is a simulation that tells people "what will happen if." The results will depend upon how people execute these plans.

There should be "sign offs" wherever this is practical. The foreman should sign off on the level of production that he can provide to meet the plan. From there on, he is accountable for meeting it unless he indicates that there is some kind of problem.

One of the concepts that needs to be conveyed to people using MRP is the principle that "silence is approval." If a schedule is sent out to the vendor and there is no feedback, the vendor has accepted the schedule. If the foremen do not report problems from the factory floor in meeting the schedule, they are indicating that they will meet it.

The foremen cannot be expected to sign off on every dispatch report. This is a good example of "silence is approval." If they do not report back that there is a problem, they are expected to meet the schedule on the dispatch report.

Another concept that is vital to the "closed loop" approach is the feedback to indicate when there are significant deviations from the plan as with the input/output report (shown in Appendix 1) that is used to monitor capacity. Performance measures will indicate when output is not meeting the plan. The output control report will show the specific work centers and how many hours behind schedule the work center actually is. (This, by the way, is an excellent example of the necessity for valid planning if performance is to be measured. In the past, it was considered "normal" to have every department in a manufacturing organization behind schedule even though shipments were going out according to plan! This, of course, was due to the order launching and expediting discussed in Chapter 2).

Feedback is essential to control. Anticipating problems is just as essential.

One of the tools for managing with MRP II is shown in Figure 19-1. This is an anticipated delay report sent back from the factory floor by the foremen. (There should also be one from the purchasing department supplied by the vendors.) This report shows that shop order number 19712 is not going to be completed on schedule because of the broken fixture. It is now the responsibility of the planner to work with the master scheduler and identify the implications of this missed schedule. It may turn out, for example, that this is for a penalty contract and, as a result, everything possible will have to be done to get the broken fixture repaired immediately. Even if it means working around the clock Saturday and Sunday.

Work Center 1600					Day 406
SO No.	Part No.	Due Date	Cause	New Date	Action
19712	44318	421	Fixture Broke	Vendor's Best is 428 Will Ship 450	

Figure 19 - 1.   Anticipated Delay Report

It's important that the feedback from the factory be organized. A lot of information coming to management people in a disorganized fashion doesn't help in executing the plan.

One report that can be extremely valuable is shown in Figure 19-2. (3) Each week each planner identifies the five or six biggest problems that exist. The planners, then, get together with the planning manager and identify the "top ten" problems that need to be brought to management's attention because they cannot be fixed by the planners and the foremen working together. This report becomes the agenda for the weekly manufacturing meeting. The planning department identifies the manager responsible for each of the critical problem areas. This manager is notified the day before the manufacturing meeting that his problem area will be one of the "top ten." This is an effective means of separating the "vital few" from the "trivial many" and constantly focusing management's attention on what the problems are, assigning responsibility to those who must fix them, and monitoring the execution to see that they do get fixed. Since the manager responsible has indicated what the solution to the problem is, and signed off on executing it, problems tend to get solved. If the problem isn't solved, it will show up on next week's report with that manager's name still beside it. People can't continually make excuses. In practice, this kind of report has rapidly separated the competent managers from those who were able to get by in the past because their performance couldn't really be measured in the confusion caused by informal systems.

From: Prod. Cont. Mgr.	cc:	Chief Industrial Engr.
To: Plant Manager		General Foremen(4)
Week no. 13		Quality Control Mgr.
		Purchasing Agent
		Production Planners (2)

Summary of activity:

1. Current finished goods inventory = 56,000 pcs. — one week below 72,000 pcs. goal.
2. Service level last week = 96% vs. 98% goal.
3. Incoming business 22% ahead of forecast for 1st quarter. Marketing revising forecast; due Monday.

Summary of major problems	Recommendation	Action
1. New people in Elect. Subassembly not producing acceptable product.	Continue overtime to meet prod. reqt's. Q.C. aid foreman in finding specific operators responsible and retaining.	Replacing one girl. Adding temporary supervision. J.P.V.
2. Popco switches still one month behind scheduled deliveries.	Second source.	Buyer to visit Popco weekly. 3 potential suppliers bidding this week. F.W.W.

Figure 19 - 2. Weekly Summary of Activity and Problems

Too many people don't like to face up to reality. Too many planning people don't have the courage to tell management people what reality is. One company that has had an MRP system for years still has a bad reputation with their customers for on-time delivery. Top management doesn't really understand the MRP system and sees it as some kind of black magic being done by "experts" on the computer. They still insist on their prerogative of jamming things into the master schedule and don't want to be told what the ramifications are. The consequence is that the expedited items do go out on schedule, but the company has a dismal reputation for meeting customer promises.

One company found themselves far behind schedule in August, and with their inventory of automotive service parts far below the desired level. Overtime over the Labor Day weekend was recommended to the plant manager who, of course, was not in favor of bringing people in over the holiday weekend. By deciding <u>not</u> to work overtime, the "other decision" was to have customer service lower than the desired level through the end of November. When the "other decision" was explained to the plant manager, over-time was scheduled even though it was a distasteful de-cision

Good managers thrive on MRP because they pride themselves on their good performance. Now, they have a way to really measure their own performance. Nothing that's happened in our manufacturing businesses before MRP II has done more to enable good managers to show what they can really do.

Section 5
System Continuity

One of the biggest problems with any system is keeping it operating. Nevertheless, there are very few companies that have had Class A or B MRP systems who have degenerated to Class C or D. Many companies do, however, suffer a little relapse within a year or two of implementing MRP successfully. They get a little overconfident. They get a little careless about things like inventory record accuracy. They slip into old habits. Most of the companies that have had this happen, however, quickly recognize that they are drifting back to doing it the hard way.

One blind alley for an MRP system that's not working properly is to change software. Typically, the problems are not in the software. The problems are master scheduling, data integrity, and education of people. Before going through the trauma of changing software, management should insist that the real problems be identified to determine if the software is going to solve these problems. People are always quick to blame the system when they have problems, rather than working to make the system work properly.

And excuses like, "MRP isn't flexible enough for us" shouldn't be accepted either. What's the alternative? There is no other system that simulates reality in a manufacturing business. And there is certainly nothing inflexible about a system that operates on a computer in nanoseconds. Systems people may have built in some inflexibilities and these should be "built out" quickly. On the other hand, "system inflexibility" may just be an excuse for people not wanting to face reality. If an emergency order must be forced into the schedule, the system can be used to identify what other orders will have to be pushed aside. That is not inflexibility. If there isn't additional capacity available, that's simply reality. People should not be allowed to blame the system for their own aversion to facing up to the tough decisions.

There are a few key steps in system continuity:

1. Make sure that the system is working by monitoring key data like inventory record accuracy, bills of material and routings, and also how well

the master schedule is being met. If the factory has to operate to a shortage list, it's a sure sign that something is wrong with the master schedule.

2. Identify the _real_ problems. They will be most likely due to people who have not been educated or need to be re-educated.

3. Make sure that education is a continuing function. At an All Star Executive Conference (May 18 and 19, 1981, Los Angeles, California), executives from six companies that have been successful using MRP were asked, "What would you do differently if you were to do it over again?" _Every one of them_ said, "Start the education earlier, educate more people, and do a better job of continuing the education."

4. Be sure that key managers, in particular the president or general manager (especially if they are new to the company or the division), are educated to understand MRP. This point has been made before, but it must be emphasized:

    > There is nothing that will kill a system quicker than a manager who doesn't know how to manage with a formal system, and starts operating based on reflexes developed from operating with an informal system.

In the early years of computer systems, the problem of system continuity plagued the designers. One questioned, "Will the business manager of the future be able to learn enough about the internal logic of a complex system? This is an intriguing question to which there is no satisfactory answer known at present." (4) Today, the answer to that imagined problem has become very clear: the manager _will_ understand MRP because it is a _standard set_ of tools for running a manufacturing business, because it is _simple_, and because _education has become a way of life_ for the professionals who run our manufacturing businesses.

Footnotes

1. "MRP: Who Needs It," _Datamation_, May, 1979.

2. Paul Cathey, "Manufacturing Mastery Made Possible By MRP," _Iron Age_, March 10, 1980.

3. Figure 19-2 is used with permission from _Production and Inventory Control: Principles and Techniques_, George Plossl and Oliver Wight, (Englewood Cliffs, N.J.: Prentice Hall, 1967, p. 327).

4. Joseph A. Orlicky, _The Successful Computer System_, McGraw Hill, 1969, p. 174.

Chapter 20
Beyond MRP II

Section 1
Managing a Better Way

As we have examined and re-examined our manufacturing economy more and more, people have concluded that one of the keys to greater success and greater productivity is managing our human resources better. Having the tools to do that is one thing, but along with that, a different attitude is developing. And that is going to make the environment for these tools far better than it was before in most manufacturing companies.

One of the key words that we are beginning to hear over and over again is "trust." (1)

Why, after all, do we have unions? Why must there be an adversary relationship between management and labor? <u>The problem is one of trust.</u> The worker, who feels a manager has no concern for his family and their well-being, will seek protection in a union. Unfortunately, that brings its own set of problems because frequently political problems within a union are as great a cause of strife as problems between the union and the company. And, of course, as always, it's the working person who suffers.

Why did we have this problem of trust? The Industrial Revolution started in England where there always was a great class distinction. There was the "upper class," the "middle class," and the "lower class" or "working class." The English upper class traditionally looked with disdain upon working people and, consequently, treated them as chattel. As capitalism developed, an adversary relationship between the "owners" and the "workers" developed. This attitude spread to the United States. As recently as 1979, John Z. DeLorean said, "In fact, among all layers of management at GM, there are those with outright contempt for the working person. To them, the worker is devoid of integrity and purpose. It is deep-seated. Its psychological roots may be in the fact that many GM managers came from working class families in the depression, and now that they have 'made it,' they reject this past and its contradiction with the present. Not all feel this way, but enough do that it effects the company's union dealings." (2) The attitude at General Motors has changed dramatically today based on some bad experiences and reinforced by some good ones.

To the casual visitor who is looking at Japanese man-ufacturing for the first time, it appears that everybody follows the boss' orders. But it isn't really that way. The Japanese are a very homogeneous group of people with a great deal of mutual respect. They practice management "by concensus." Everybody is informed of what's going on. They are given the respect of being told, and, for that matter, <u>asked</u> about any new approaches the company is going to take or problems that the company has to solve.

In a Japanese company, lifelong employment for many employees is considered to be the norm. In American companies, we tend to hire people when we need them and lay them off when we don't. And the consequence is that we have unions that insist upon a "guaranteed annual wage."

In the capitalist world we started out with management exploiting labor. The natural consequence was unions to protect the working people. The ultimate reaction was communism where capitalism is revoked, and government is for and by the workers who have "thrown off their shackles."

In the meantime, of course, the Japanese showed us how capitalism could be handled with great respect for the individual. They showed how we could run manufacturing businesses and treat the workers with respect and dignity. Give them the assurance, the trust, that they had jobs that would not be suddenly wiped out by the whim of some irresponsible manager. This trust provided an excellent foundation for real teamwork. It's a lesson for every capitalist country.

Even the communists have proved that you cannot manage without trust. In 1980 in Poland, the workers went on strike against the government, <u>a government that was supposed to be run by the workers</u> who had once revolted against capitalist management. They went on strike because they no longer felt they could <u>trust</u> their leaders.

The art of management is really still in its infancy. People have been doing it for centuries, but little real, practical knowledge has been identified and passed on to others. Even today, we understand very little about what makes a good manager. An executive from one of the large construction equipment companies told about their problem with absenteeism. In one division, the shipping department had a strikingly low absenteeism rate. When asked why that was true, the workers (in probably one of the lower paid jobs in the company) said, "We wouldn't let our fore-man, Jack, down. People come to work even if they're sick because of Jack." Time and again, we see managers who think that being a manager is being a boss. A boss can get people to do things because they must. <u>But the best managers aren't bosses, they are leaders.</u> People will fol-low a leader and do far more than they have to because they have confidence and trust in this person.

Section 2
Managing with Better Tools

Today, a lot of better tools and approaches for managing our manufacturing businesses are being discussed. Among them are:

1. Participative management.

2. Theory Z. (3)

3. CAD/CAM (Computer Aided Design/Computer Aided Manufacturing).

4. Quality circles.

5. Management By Objectives (MBO).

6. MRP II: Manufacturing Resource Planning.

Unfortunately, those who talk about each of these management tools tend to ignore all the others. That's just a sign of the adolescence of managing a manufacturing business as a profession. All of the tools are valid, all of them support each other. None of them are mutually exclusive.

A company must start with a valid business philosophy and approach to management. That's what participative management and Theory Z are all about.

The philosophy of the business should be highly visible and clearly understood. The objectives of the business should be clearly understood. Overall objectives should be broken down into shorter term supporting objectives, and accountability assigned. That's management by objectives.

MRP II is just a set of tools for taking these objectives and making them more refined, detailed plans. These plans can then be conveyed down through the organization so that they can be executed by all of the functions in the organization. The emphasis of MRP II is planning: the foundation of teamwork, the company game plan.

CAD/CAM is simply a technology that allows the computer to help the people in engineering, not only in the design phase, but in preparing the documentation and, in some cases, even the detailed instructions for numerically controlled machines. Here, once again, the engineering and manufacturing people, because of the new technology, are working far more closely together. This is exactly the kind of teamwork that MRP II helps to make practical. And the preparation of this kind of data in this manner will, undoubtedly, make a contribution to the data integrity required by MRP, and to having the product made as it was intended to be, which will be a real contribution to quality.

Better scheduling can give supervisory people more time to work on making the product right the first time. Better scheduling means less firefighting in the factory, less rush crisis and substitutions because of delivery problems. This means that workers will have a better chance to make their contribution through quality circles. And quality circles, of course, are an excellent example of participative management. Better quality contributes to better shipping performance, just as better scheduling contributes to better quality.

We have not yet done a very good job of showing how it all fits together. The better tools are available today and management should look at them as mutually supportive. Because they are!

Section 3
Managing Competitive Energy

In the typical American company, the engineering people often look upon manufacturing and marketing as "the competition." The financial people often take the attitude that they are the "watch dogs" trying to "catch" other members of management when they are wrong. We have not done a good job of focusing the competitive instincts of people in the right direction.

Human beings will compete. They play tennis, football, golf - or they watch somebody else play it. By nature, we are competitive. When competition isn't directed against the real competition, it will normally be directed against the closest people.

The president of one company said, "I don't understand why my people don't seem to generate the enthusiasm that I'd like them to have. I keep telling them how we're doing on return on investment and net profits, but they don't seem very interested." Of course they're not. Very few of them are stockholders. That isn't the game that they're playing. That isn't how their competitive instincts are going to be brought out and directed properly.

In too many manufacturing companies today, the people who run the machines, the supervisors, the foremen, don't even know who the competition is. And that's what they really need to know: who are they competing against? Is it another company? Is it a Japanese company? How is the other company doing? What new products are being brought out in order to compete? One of the best managed companies in the United States today has a showcase of all of their competitors' products in the main tunnel going into their factory. Their management continually directs the attention of their people to the REAL competition so that they can concentrate their energies on the competition rather than each other.

"It's not just nostalgia," lamented one man in his fifties. "When I was growing up, this country had purpose, pride and spirit like we've never had since." And he never even discussed the obvious reason: In the early 1940's, we all knew who the "bad guys" and "good guys" were. Things haven't been as simple since. Back then, we worked together enthusiastically. We knew who the competition was. We had a common purpose.

Man will compete. Management must direct that competition positively rather than negatively.

(Postscript: After working in two other companies for a total period of fourteen years, I joined IBM in 1965. One of my first impressions was that we were all on the same team. Not that there wasn't some problem with politics as there is in all companies, but it was so much less. The whole concept was, "We're in it together. We're out to sell our product against the competition. The competition is Honeywell, Burroughs, and Univac, not the other IBM'er." The whole thing came home very vividly one day when a salesman was complaining about an order that he had lost in the Hartford, Connecticut area to one of the competitors. I finally asked how many manufacturing installations that competitor had in Hartford, and his reply was, "This will be the first one, and if I have my way, the only one." I reminded him that IBM was operating under a consent decree because of antitrust laws, and that it probably wasn't too bad a thing. His reply was, "That's the lawyers' problem. I'm in marketing. We did a disservice to the IBM Corporation by letting a competitor sell to that account. And we did a disservice to the account because they bought an inferior product from an inferior company. They simply won't get the results that they would have gotten with our support." When people know who the real competition is, the best of them will perform even better. OWW)

Section 4
The New Breed of Capitalist

In 1957, the new Chevrolet had two spears for hood ornaments and a horn that any casual observer would recognize as a deadly instrument in the event of a collision. How in the world could anybody put spears on the hood of an automobile without recognizing that some child would someday be hit by a car?

There's no question that those who are anti-business can point to many things that business people have done that are irresponsible: spoiling the environment, producing unsafe products, placing profit ahead of social responsibilities. We all know these things have happened.

But the responsible people in the business community today recognize that these things have backfired. Today, the government is involved in product safety. We now have breakaway hood ornaments. They could easily have been instituted by industry. But industry didn't, and the government did. The breakaway hood ornaments are a good thing, but along with them have come many other things such as annoying bells and buzzers. We now have congressmen designing products and the net result is not good for the consumer or for industry.

We have government imposing work safety regulations that could have been instituted by industry. And, once again, we have proved that there is nothing that business can do that government can't do worse.

Some people think that caring only about the bottom line is being a "hardheaded businessman." In fact, it's being a shortsighted business man. Business must take the initiative to take more social responsibility, to do a better job of leveling employment, to do more for worker job enrichment. And that's starting to happen today. It must happen. It's not just a case of social responsibility. It's enlightened self-interest.

But business people have a lot to do to demonstrate the contribution they make to society and to get the message through to others in the community. One of the newspapers recently carried a letter from a reader who wanted to know, "Which business executives get the most outrageous salaries?" The newspaper answered and listed the ten highest paid executives in the country. They did it with a straight face without mentioning the fact that some rock stars make over seven million dollars a year, that several baseball stars make over a million dollars a year, or that one of the stars of an evening soap opera makes two million just for the soap opera activities, not counting his other forms of income like endorsements. Surely, we should consider the social contribution of the people who head the industries that provide us with our goods and our jobs to be worth as much as a baseball player or a rock star.

James Fallos, in the article "American Industry, What Ails it, How to Save it," said, "In this age when production matters and when our international affluence can no longer be taken for granted, our economic and social rewards have come unmoored from measures of true productivity." He goes on to quote Robert Reich, the Director of the Office of Policy Planning at the Federal Trade Commission, saying, "Economic life has yielded more and more of its prizes to those who can work the legal and financial angles, or can guess right in speculation, rather than those who work at improving a product or making a sale." (4)

There is no question that our system must reward the producers better than it does. How can we expect young people to go into manufacturing when they can make twice as much money taking a job on Wall Street? It's about time we started giving our respect and the proper recognition and rewards to the producers, to those who make the pie, rather than those who slice the pie or those who entertain us.

And we've got to show young people that manufacturing is a worthy and very exciting field to get into. Before the knife existed, there was no body of knowledge about surgery; there were no professional surgeons. The simple set of computer routines we call MRP II provides us today with the one critical element we never had before: a standard set of tools - the prerequisite to a standard body of knowledge that is the foundation of any profession. No longer is each new generation destined to repeat the mistakes of the past. Managing a manufacturing enterprise is becoming a profession today, a profession that offers a great deal of job satisfaction through working with people and leading people. A profession that has a profound impact in a free economy.

With this kind of new and more professional approach, our manufacturing economy, our capitalist philosophy, and our democracy can not only survive, they can thrive. Those who don't understand the relationship between the maintenance of a stable economy and democracy have forgotten what economic chaos in Germany in the 1920's resulted in during the 1930's.

Yes, <u>Time</u> magazine said it well, "Without economic freedom, there can not be personal freedom." (5) <u>And personal freedom is the ultimate human dignity</u>.

Footnotes

1. Some of this text was taken from "The Management of Trust," _Fortune_, February 23, 1981, sponsored by the Oliver Wight Companies.

2. J. Patrick Wright, _On A Clear Day You Can See General Motors_, (Grosse Pointe, Michigan: J. Patrick Wright Enterprises, 1979).

3. William Ouchi, _Theory Z_, (Reading, Massachusetts: Addison - Wesley Publishing Company, 1981).

4. _Atlantic Monthly_, Volume 246, September, 1980, pp. 35-50.

5. "Capitalism: Is it Working?," _Time_, April 21, 1980

APPENDICES

Appendix 1
The Mechanics of Closed Loop MRP

Section 1
The Closed Loop System

The logic of the closed loop MRP system is extremely simple. It's in every cookbook. The "bill of material" says, "Turkey stuffing takes one egg, seasoning, bread crumbs, etc." The routing says, "Put the egg and the seasoning in a blender." The blender is the work center. The master schedule is Thanksgiving.

But, in manufacturing, there is a lot more volume and a lot more change. There isn't just one product. There are many. The lead times aren't as short as going to the corner store. The work centers are busy rather than waiting for work - because some of them cost a third of a million dollars or more - and it simply is not wise economically to let them sit idle and to have excess capacity. In addition, the sales department will undoubtedly change the date of Thanksgiving several times before it actually arrives! And this isn't through perversity. This is because the customers want and need some things earlier or later.

The volume of activity in manufacturing is monumentally high; something is happening all the time. And change is the norm, not the exception.

But the point is that the logic of MRP is very straightforward indeed. Figure A1-1 shows the closed loop system.

The production plan is the rate of production for a product family typically expressed in units like, "We want to produce 1100 Model 30 pumps per week." The production plan is made by taking into account current inventory, deciding whether inventory needs to go up or down during the planning period, projecting the sales forecast, and determining the rate of production required to maintain, raise, or lower the inventory level. For a make-to-order product, as opposed to a make-to-stock product, the "order backlog" rather than the inventory is the starting point for the production plan.

Figure A1-2 shows a typical production plan. Figure A1-3 shows a business plan which is simply an extension of the production plan into dollars. The complete business plan in a manufacturing company will include research and development and other expenses not directly related to production and purchases. But the core of any business

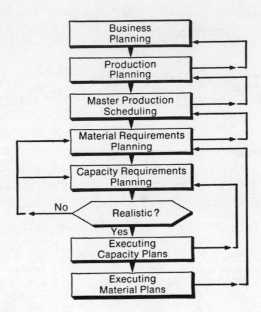

Figure A1 - 1. MRP II

plan in a manufacturing enterprise is the production plan. With MRP II, the production plan and business plan are interdependent and, as the production plan is updated, it is extended into dollars to show it in the common denominator of business - money.

Month Ending		Sales (thousands)	Production (thousands)	Inventory (thousands)
3/31	Plan			
	Actual			60
4/30	Plan	30	35	65
	Actual	25	36	71
6/30	Plan	30	35	75
	Actual			

Figure A1 - 2. Production Plan

The closed loop MRP system then takes a master schedule ("What are we going to make?"), "explodes" this through the bill of material ("What does it take to make it?"), and compares this with the inventory on hand and on order ("What do we have?") to determine material requirements ("What do we have to get?").

Month Ending		Sales (thousands)	Production (thousands)	Inventory (thousands)
3/31	Plan			
	Actual			6,000
4/30	Plan	3,000	3,500	6,500
	Actual	2,500	3,600	7,100
5/31	Plan	3,000	3,500	7,000
	Actual	3,800	3,200	6,500
6/30	Plan	3,000	3,500	7,500
	Actual	3,200	3,700	7,000
12/31	Plan	3,000	3,500	10,500
	Actual			

Figure A1 – 3. Business Plan

This fundamental material requirements planning logic is shown in Figure A1-4. Figure A1-5 shows the bill of material. For this example, a small gasoline engine for a moped is the product being manufactured. The bill of material shown in Figure A1-5 is what's known as an "indented bill of material." This simply means that the highest level items in the bill of material are shown farthest left. For example, the piston assembly components are "indented" to the right to indicate that they go into that assembly. Therefore, in this example, they are at "level 2."

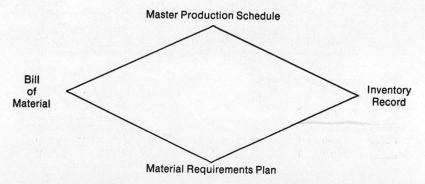

Figure A1 – 4. MRP Logic

A bill of material "in reverse" is called a "where-used" list. It would say, for example, that the locating pins go into the crankcase half-left, which goes into the engine.

Part Number	
87502	Cylinder Head
94411	Crankshaft
94097	Piston Assembly
91776	Piston
84340	Wristpin
81111	Connecting Rod—Top Half
27418	Connecting Rod—Bottom Half
81743	Piston Rings Compression (2)
96652	Piston Ring Oil
20418	Bearing Halves (2)
59263	Lock Bolts (2)
43304	Crankcase Half Right
28079	Crankcase Half Left
80021	Locater Pins (2)

Figure A1 - 5. Moped Engine Bill of Material

Figure A1-6 shows a master schedule for engines that is similar to the one shown in Chapter 9. In a make-to-stock company, the master schedule would be very similar, but it would take into account the inventory on hand.

Master Production Schedule
Engines

	Week							
	1	2	3	4	5	6	7	8
Master Schedule	80	0	100	0	0	120	0	120
Actual Demand	40	40	30	30	30	40	40	20
Available to Promise	0	0	10	0	0	40	0	100

Figure A1 - 6. Master Production Schedule

Section 2
Material Requirements Planning

Figure A1-7 shows the material requirements plan for the crankcase half-left and also for the locater pin that goes into the crankcase half-left. The projected gross requirements come from the master schedule plus any service parts requirements. "Scheduled receipts" are the orders that are already in production or out with the vendors. The projected available balance takes the on-hand figure, subtracts requirements from it, and adds scheduled receipts to it. (In Figure A1-7, the starting on-hand balance is 120 for the crankcase half-left.) This calculation projects future inventory balances to indicate when material needs to be ordered or rescheduled.

Material Requirements Plan
Crankcase Half — Left

LEAD TIME = 4 WEEKS ORDER QUANTITY = 200		Week							
		1	2	3	4	5	6	7	8
Projected Gross Requirements		80	0	100	0	0	120	0	120
Scheduled Receipts				240					
Proj. Avail. Bal.	120	40	40	180	180	180	60	60	-60
Planned Order Release					200				

Material Requirements Plan
Locater Pin (2 Per)

LEAD TIME = 4 WEEKS ORDER QUANTITY = 500		Week							
		1	2	3	4	5	6	7	8
Projected Gross Requirements					400				400*
Scheduled Receipts									
Proj. Avail. Bal.	430	430	430	430	30	30	30	30	-370
Planned Order Release					500				

*Requirements from Another Crankcase

Figure A1 - 7. Material Requirements Plan

The material on hand and on order subtracted from the gross requirements yields "net requirements" (60 in week 8 for the crankcase half-left in Figure A1-8). This is the amount that is actually needed to cover requirements. When the net requirements are converted to lot sizes and backed off over the lead time, they are called "planned order releases."

The "planned order releases" at one level in the product structure - in this case 200 "crankcase half-left" - become the projected gross requirements at the lower level. The 200 unit planned order release in period four for the crankcase half-left becomes a projected gross requirement of 400 locater pins in period four since there are two locater pins per crankcase half-left.

Most MRP systems also include what is called "pegged requirements." This is simply a way to trace where the requirements came from. For example, the pegged requirements for the locater pins would indicate that the 400 in period four came from the crankcase half-left and that the 400 in period eight came from another product. Pegged requirements show the quantity, the time period, and the higher level item where the requirements are coming from.

MRP — Rescheduling
Crankcase Half — Left

LEAD TIME = 4 WEEKS ORDER QUANTITY = 200	Week							
	1	2	3	4	5	6	7	8
Projected Gross Requirements		80	0	100	0	0	120	0	120
Scheduled Receipts					240				
Proj. Avail. Bal.	120	40	40	-60	180	180	60	60	-60
Planned Order Release					200				

MRP — Locater Pin (2 Per)

LEAD TIME = 4 WEEKS ORDER QUANTITY = 500	Week							
	1	2	3	4	5	6	7	8
Projected Gross Requirements					400				400*
Scheduled Receipts									
Proj. Avail. Bal.	430	430	430	430	30	30	30	30	-370
Planned Order Release					500				

*Requirements from Another Crankcase

Figure A1 - 8. MRP — Rescheduling

Figure A1-8 shows the same crankcase half as in Figure A1-7. Note, however, that now the scheduled receipt is shown in period four. This means that the due date on the shop order or the purchase order is week four. An MRP system would generate a reschedule message for the planner to move the scheduled receipt from week four into week three to cover the requirements in week three.

Note, also, that the fact that the scheduled receipt for the crankcase half needs to be rescheduled does not affect the requirements for locater pins. The locater pins have already been released into production for the crankcase halves that are on order. The "requirements" for locater pins are for planned orders that have not been released yet.

The bill of material is the instrument for converting planned order releases at one level into projected gross requirements at a lower level. The bill of material for the crankcase half-left, for example, would show that two locater pins per crankcase half were required.

Section 3
Capacity Planning and Scheduling

   Capacity planning for the manufacturing facility follows the same general logic as the material requirements planning shown in Figure A1-4.   Figure A1-9 shows this capacity requirements planning logic. The remaining operations on released shop orders and all of the operations on planned order releases are "exploded" through the routings (like bills of material for operations) and posted against the work centers (like an inventory of capacities).   The result is a capacity requirements plan in standard hours by work center showing the number of standard hours required to meet the material requirements plan.   This capacity requirements plan shows the capacity that will be required to execute the master schedule, and consequently, the production plan.

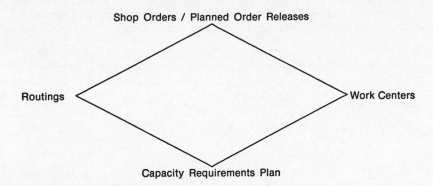

Figure A1 - 9.   CRP Logic

   It's important to note that everything in a closed loop MRP system is in "lock step." If the capacity to meet the material requirements plan can't be obtained either through a company's own manufacturing facilities, subcontracting, or purchasing material on the outside, obviously the master schedule will have to be changed.   But that is the last resort.   The objective is to make the master schedule happen.

   Operations scheduling involves assigning individual schedule dates to the operations on a shop order using scheduling rules.   Scheduling rules would typically be similar to these:

1. Allow two days for inspection. (This is a matter of judgment.)
2. Round the standard hours up to the nearest day.
3. Allow X days for queue time.
4. Release work to stockroom one week prior to first operation.

Calendar						
AUGUST						
S	M	T	W	T	F	S
1	2	3	4	5	6	7
8	9	10	11	12	13	14
15	16	17	18	19	20	21
22	23	24	25	26	27	28
29	30	31				

Figure A1 - 10.   Calendar

Scheduling with a regular calendar is extremely awkward. For example, if a job was to be completed on August 31 (see Figure A1-10) and the last operation - inspection -was scheduled to take two days, the previous operation would have to be completed on August 27, not August 29 (Sunday) or August 28 (Saturday). The scheduler would have to reference the calendar continuously to avoid scheduling work on weekends, holidays, during plant vacation shutdown week, etc. Figure A1-11 shows a "shop calendar" where only the working days are numbered. This allows the scheduler to do simple arithmetic like "subtract two days from day 412," thus the previous operation is to be completed on day 410. Shop calendars are in very common use in manufacturing companies today, but they do have drawbacks. People don't relate to these calendars as easily as they do to a regular calendar. And, of course, they are awkward in dealing with customers who don't use the

Calendar						
AUGUST						
S	**M**	**T**	**W**	**T**	**F**	**S**
1	2 391	3 392	4 393	5 394	6 395	7
8	9 396	10 397	11 398	12 399	13 400	14
15	16 401	17 402	18 403	19 404	20 405	21
22	23 406	24 407	25 408	26 409	27 410	28
29	30 411	31 412				

Figure A1 - 11. Calendar

same shop calendar. Therefore, the shop calendar dates must, once again, be translated back to regular calendar dates. There is a simple solution to this problem with today's computers. A shop calendar can be put in the computer and the computer can do the scheduling using the shop calendar, but print the schedule dates out in regular calendar days. If a company has a shop calendar, there is no reason to discontinue using it if people are used to it. On the other hand, there is no need to introduce the shop calendar today when the computer can do the conversion.

Figure A1-12 shows a shop order for the locator pin. This will be used as an example of operations scheduling and, in this example, a shop calendar will be used in order to make the arithmetic of scheduling clear. The due date is day 4l2 and that is determined, in the case of the locator pin that goes into the crankcase half-left, from the material requirements plan.

Operations scheduling works back from this need date to put scheduled finish dates on each operation using scheduling rules like those discussed above. Inspection will be allowed two days. Thus, finish turn must be completed on day 410. It is assumed that the work center file in-

Shop Order NN. 18447
Part No. 80021 — Locater Pin
Quant. 500   Due: 412   Release 395

Oper.	Dept.	Work Center	Desc.	Setup	Per Piece	Std. Hrs.	Finish
10	08	1322	Cut Off	.5	.010	8.5	402
20	32	1600	Rough Turn	1.5	.030	16.5	406
30	32	1204	Finish Turn	3.3	.048	27.3	410
40	11		Inspect				412

Figure A1 – 12.   Shop Order NN. 18447

dicates that there are two shifts working in work center 1204 (two shifts at 8 hours apiece equals 16 hours), thus the 27.3 hours required for finish turn will take two days. Planned queue time in this example is assumed to be two days ahead of finish turn. Rough turn must be completed four days earlier than the finish turn must be completed, and its scheduled finish date, therefore, is day 406. The standard hours are calculated by multiplying the quantity by the time per piece and, in this case, adding in the setup time. Where machine operators do not set up their own machines, it might make sense to keep this separate.

It is important to recognize that Figure A1-12 shows the information that would be in the computer. <u>The finish dates would not appear on the shop paperwork that was released to the factory</u>. The reason is that material requirements planning would be constantly reviewing the need date to see if it had changed. If, for example, the left crankcase halves are scrapped because of a problem with the castings, and the best possible date to have a new lot of castings for the crankcase halves is day 422, the master schedule would be changed to indicate that. The shop order for the locater pins in the computer would be given a new finish date of 422 and operation 30 would then become 420, operation 20 would become 416, etc.

Capacity requirements will now be posted against the work centers using the routine shown in Figure A1-9. A capacity plan, as shown in Figure A1-13, will be the result. This capacity plan has, of course, been cut apart to show

Part No.	SO No.	Qty.	Week 396-400	Week 401-405	Week 406-410	Week 411-415	Week 416-420
91762	17621	50		3.5			
80021	18447	500			16.5		

Work Center   1600

Includes Planned Orders

Total Std. Hrs.			294	201	345	210	286

Figure A1 – 13.   Capacity Requirements Plan

it in the figure. It would include many more shop orders as well as the planned order releases from MRP, in reality. The locater pins are shown here as a released shop order. (Note: there is no released shop order for locater pins in Figure A1-8. It would show as a "scheduled receipt" if there were.) One of the great values of MRP is the fact that it projects "planned order releases." These planned order releases are used to:

1. Generate lower level material requirements.
2. Generate capacity requirements.
3. Determine when lower level material - both purchased and manufactured - must be rescheduled to earlier or later dates.

This ability to see capacity requirements ahead of time is especially important to good manpower planning. Seeing the capacity requirements coming rather than seeing the backlogs of work out on the factory floor enables factory supervision to do a far better job of leveling production, resulting in less overtime, and less need to hire and lay off people on a short term basis.

Figure A1-14 shows a summary of the capacity requirements over an eight-week period. In practice, this would typically be projected over a far longer period. The summary is drawn from the capacity requirements plan illustrated in Figure A1-13 which would also extend much farther into the future than the five weeks shown. A typical manpower plan would extend three to six months into the future and would be calculated weekly. A "facilities plan" that would be used for determining what

**Capacity Requirements
Summary (in Standard Hours)**

Week	4-Week Total	4-Week Average	Hours	Week	4-Week Total	4-Week Average	Hours
1	294			5	286		
2	201			6	250		
3	345			7	315		
4	210	1050	263	8	257	1108	277

Figure A1 – 14. Capacity Requirements Summary (in Standard Hours)

new machine tools were needed would be calculated typically once every two to three months and extended three to four years into the future because of the lead time for procuring machine tools.

The most important information for a foreman is the average hours that he must plan to turn out. This production rate is usually calculated as a four-week average because the individual weekly hours are not particularly significant. The variations between these hours are more random than real. Figure A1-13 shows one reason why this happens. The 16.5 hours for part number 80021, the locator pin, are shown in the week bracketed by days 406 and 410. Referring back to Figure A1-12, it can be seen that these 16.5 hours are <u>actually going to be in work center 1600 Tuesday of the previous week</u>!

Many people have tried to develop elaborate computer load leveling systems because they were alarmed by the weekly variation in the apparent "load" shown in the capacity requirements plan. These variations are random. They are exaggerated by the fact that capacity plans are usually done in weekly time periods, and any foreman can attest to the fact that the hours never materialize exactly the same way they are shown on the plan. The most important thing to know is the average rate of output required so that <u>manpower</u> can be planned accordingly.

In Figure A1-14, the four-week averages are 263 standard hours for the first four weeks and 277 for the second four weeks, or an average of 270 standard hours per week. Now the capacity planner must determine whether that capacity requirement can be met. The first step is to find out what the output from the work center has been over the last few weeks. This is called "demonstrated capacity." (This term was coined by Dave Garwood and is very useful in describing the present capacity of a work center as opposed to its potential capacity when all shifts are manned, etc.)

It is the job of the capacity planner to then determine whether or not the current capacity is sufficient. Or, what needs to be done to get the capacity to meet the plan. Or - as a last resort - to feed back information that the plan cannot be met.

If the plan cannot be met, the master schedule and, perhaps, even the production plans will have to be changed. If, for example, a company has one broach and it is the only one of its type available because it was made specifically for this company, it could well become a bottleneck. If the capacity plan indicated that more hours were required at the broach than could possibly be produced, the master schedule would have to be changed to reflect this.

Once again, however, it's important to emphasize that this is the last resort. The job of the capacity planner is to get the capacity that is needed to meet the plan. And that is an important point to emphasize. If there is any problem that exists in practice with capacity planning, it is the fact that people expect the computer to do the capacity planning rather than recognizing that all it can do is generate numbers that will be given to an intelligent, experienced person - the capacity planner - to use in working with other people to fix capacity problems.

Once it is agreed that the capacity requirements can be met, an output control report as shown in Figure A1-15 is set up. Three weeks have passed since the one in the figure was made, and the actual standard hours produced - shown in the second line of the figure - are falling far short of the required standard hours at work center 1600. The deviation in the first week was 20 hours. In the second week, it was 50 hours - for a cumulative deviation of 70 hours. In the third week, it was 80 hours, giving a total cumulative deviation of 150 hours. This is a true control report with a plan and feedback to show where actual output in standard hours compares with the plan. It shows

Output Control
Work Center 1600
Week No. 4
(in Std. Hrs.)

Today

	Week 1	Week 2	Week 3	Week 4
Planned	270	270	270	270
Actual Std.	250	220	190	
Deviation	–20	–70	–150	

Figure A1 – 15. Output Control

the deviation from the plan. The 150 hour deviation in week three indicates that 150 standard hours of work required to produce material to meet the master schedule has not been completed.

The amount of tolerance around the plan has to be established. If it were determined, for example, that the company could tolerate being one half week behind schedule, the tolerance in Figure A1-15 would be 135 standard hours. When the deviation exceeded 135 standard hours, that would require immediate attention to increase output through overtime, adding people, etc. Whenever the planned rate in the output control report is changed, the deviation will be reset to 0.

It's a good idea to show input to a work center as well as output. That way, when a work center is behind on output because a feeding work center has not given them the work, it can be detected very quickly since the input report will show the actual input below the planned input. This is called an input/output report.

The capacity planning and output control reports are concerned with capacity. The dispatch list shown in Figure A1-16 is concerned with priority. The dispatch list is generated daily - or as required - and goes out to the shop floor at the beginning of the day. It shows the sequence in which the jobs are to be run according to the scheduled date for the operation in that work center. The movement of jobs from work center to work center is put in to the computer so that each morning the foremen can have an

Dispatch List Work Center No. 1600				Day 405
Shop Order No.	Part No.	Qty.	Scheduled Date	Std. Hours
17621	91762	50	401	3.5
18430	98340	500	405	19.2
18707	78212	1100	405	28.6
18447	80021	500	406	16.5
19712	44318	120	409	8.4
			Total Hours	76.2

Figure A1 – 16.   Dispatch List

up-to-date schedule that is driven by MRP. If part 80021 had been rescheduled to a new completion date of day 422 as discussed above, its priority would drop on the dispatch list because its scheduled date would now be 416. This would allow part number 44318 to be made earlier. The dispatch list gives the foremen the priority of jobs so that they can pick the proper job to start next. Since the dispatch list is driven by MRP, it tells the foremen the right sequence in which to run the jobs to do the best job of preventing predicted shortages.

Section 4
The MRP Output Reports

The figures in this chapter represent the major reports that are used in a closed loop MRP system. Referring back to Figure A1-1, the functions of the production plan (Figure A1-2), the master schedule (Figure A1-6), the material requirements plan (Figures A1-7 and A1-8), and the capacity requirements plan (Figure A1-13) are illustrated. The output control report (Figure A1-15) is the means for monitoring output against the plan to be sure that capacity plans are being executed. The dispatch list (Figure A1-16) is the report for the factory to use in executing the material plans. Vendor scheduling, as discussed in Chapter 11, is the way the material requirements plans are executed with the "outside factories."

It is important to emphasize the feedback functions in a closed loop system. For example, if vendors are not going to ship on time, they must send in an anticipated delay report as soon as they recognize that they have a problem. This anticipated delay report was shown in Chapter 19. In the past, ship dates were not valid. The typical company had many past due purchase orders with the vendor. With MRP - if it is properly managed - dates will represent real need dates, and, thus, it is important to feed back information as quickly as possible to indicate when these dates cannot be met. This, of course, is also true for the factory, where the anticipated delay report should be a regular part of their feedback to the closed loop system.

A closed loop MRP system is a fairly modern development. Many companies talked about material requirements planning for years and did explode bills of material on a computer. But, it was the advent of the modern computer with its great processing speeds and storage capabilities that made modern MRP practical. The ability to break requirements down into weekly, or even daily, time periods rather than showing them in monthly increments, for example, helped MRP to become a scheduling system rather than just another order launching system (even though it is superior to the order point as an ordering system). The ability to plan requirements weekly - or even daily - made MRP a practical scheduling tool. Before 1971, it would be hard to find any closed loop MRP system in existence.

Master scheduling was not well understood. Capacity planning and dispatching were tried, but were usually ineffective because the priority planning wasn't valid. Computers of the day couldn't keep schedules up to date and the people using them didn't understand how to master schedule properly to do this. Closed loop MRP is truly a product of the computer age.

Appendix 2
The Checklists

Section 1
The ABCD Checklist

The ABCD Checklist is for companies that are currently operating MRP systems and want to measure their effectiveness. Companies that are implementing MRP should see Section 2 of this appendix.

A Class A MRP user is one that uses MRP in a closed loop mode. They have material requirements planning, capacity planning and control, shop floor dispatching, and vendor scheduling systems in place and being used.

And management uses the system to run the business. They participate in production planning. They sign off on the production plans. They constantly monitor performance on inventory record accuracy, bill of material accuracy, routing accuracy, attainment of the master schedule, attainment of the capacity plans, etc.

In a Class A company, the MRP system provides the game plan that sales, finance, manufacturing, purchasing, and engineering people all work to. They use the formal system. The foremen and the purchasing people work to the schedules. There is no shortage list to override the schedules and answer the question, "What material is really needed when?" - that answer comes from the formal MRP system.

Companies using MRP II have gone even a step beyond Class A. They have tied in the financial system and developed simulation capabilities so that the "what if" questions can be answered using the system. In this type of company, management can work with one set of numbers to run the business because the operating system and the financial system use the same numbers.

Technically, then, an MRP II system has the financial and operating systems married together and has a simulation capability. But, the important point is that the system is used as a company game plan. This is what really makes a company Class A.

A Class B company has material requirements planning and usually capacity requirements planning and shop floor control systems in place. The Class B user typically hasn't done much with purchasing yet and differs from the Class A user primarily because top management doesn't really use the system to run the business directly. Instead, Class B users see MRP as a production and inventory control system. Because of this, it's easy for a Class B user to become a Class C user very quickly. Another characteristic of the Class B company is that they do some scheduling in the shop using MRP, but their shortage list is what really tells them what to make. Class B users typically see most of their benefits from MRP in inventory reduction and improved customer service because they do have more of the right things going through production. Because they haven't succeeded in getting the expediting "monkey" off the backs of the purchasing people and foremen, they haven't seen substantial benefits in reduced purchase costs or improved productivity - and they still have more inventory than they really need.

A Class C company uses MRP primarily as an inventory ordering technique rather than as a scheduling technique. Shop scheduling is still being done from the shortage list, and the master schedule in a Class C company is typically overstated. They have not really closed the loop. They probably will get some benefits in inventory reduction as a result of MRP.

A Class D company only has MRP really working in the data processing department. Typically, their inventory records are poor. If they have a defined master schedule, it's usually grossly overstated and mismanaged, and little or no results have come from the installation of the MRP system. Ironically, except for the education costs, a Class D company will have spent almost as much as a Class A company. They will have spent about 80 percent of the total, but not achieved the results.

The ABCD Checklist is a way to measure how well a company is operating their MRP system. A few thousand companies have MRP, but probably only 50 to 75 are Class A MRP users as of 1981. There are another 200 to 300 that are Class B users and doing very well. And even Class C companies usually get a payback from MRP. But each of these companies that is not Class A should try to find out what the problems are and fix them. Inevitably, fixing the problems amounts to establishing proper objectives, assigning accountability, educating people, measuring performance, handling data properly, managing the master schedule properly, etc.

Technical	YES	NO

Technical

1. Time periods for master scheduling and material requirements planning are weeks or smaller.
2. Master scheduling and material requirements planning run weekly or more frequently.
3. System includes firm planned order and pegging capability.
4. The master schedule is visibly managed, not automatic.
5. System includes capacity requirements planning.
6. System includes daily dispatch list.
7. System includes input/output control.

Data Integrity

8. Inventory record accuracy 95% or better.
9. Bill of material accuracy 98% or better.
10. Routing accuracy 95% or better.

Education

11. Initial education of at least 80% of all employees.
12. An ongoing education program.

Use of the System

13. The shortage list has been eliminated.
14. Vendor delivery performance is 95% or better.
15. Vendor scheduling is done out beyond the quoted lead times.
16. Shop delivery performance is 95% or better.
17. Master schedule performance is 95% or better.
18. There are regular (at least monthly) production planning meetings with the general manager and his staff including: manufacturing, production and inventory control, engineering, marketing, finance.
19. There is a written master scheduling policy which is adhered to.
20. The system is used for scheduling as well as ordering.
21. MRP is well understood by key people in manufacturing, marketing, engineering, finance, and top management.
22. Management really uses MRP to manage.
23. Engineering changes are effectively implemented.
24. Simultaneous improvement has been achieved in at least two of the following three areas: inventory, productivity, customer service.
25. Operating system is used for financial planning.

Figure A2 – 1.   ABCD Checklist

The first section in the checklist is the technical section. A company must have a system that is technically capable of allowing them to be a Class A MRP user. The system will not make them Class A, but, without a properly designed system, it's hard to see how a company could achieve Class A status. The paragraphs below are numbered to correspond with the items in the ABCD Checklist, Figure A2-1.

(1) The time periods for the master schedule and the material requirements plan should be in increments of weeks or smaller. There are people who try to do MRP in monthly time periods, for example, and there is no way that they can be better than a Class C user because a factory cannot be scheduled in monthly increments. Knowing what is needed "this month" doesn't help very much. At the very least, the factory - and the vendors - need to know what is needed this week. It would be better, of course, to know this day by day rather than week by week. But weekly is a bare minimum requirement for a Class A user.

(2) The master schedule and the material requirements plan need to be run at least weekly. This is the minimum frequency that will allow a company to be a Class A user. In a net change system, it's practical to run every day, and that is a better, more responsive system. A regenerative system, however, must be run at least once a week if it is to be a scheduling system rather than just an inventory ordering system.

(3) Two features that should be in an MRP system - not to add "bells and whistles," but to give users control over the system - are: "firm planned orders" and "pegging." Firm planned orders allow people to take a planned order and establish the timing or the quantity of this order rather than letting the computer do it. An example would be a part that is made in-house on numerically controlled machines in three weeks and takes a subcontractor six weeks, because the subcontractor does not have numerically controlled machines. The lower level material will have to be planned to be available at an earlier date, and this is where the firm planned order can be very useful. In addition, it has other uses in representing the real world where production is being leveled, thus jobs are being moved into earlier time periods, where lead time is being collapsed in order to get jobs out in time, etc. "Pegging" means that the system provides the information to answer the question, "Why did the computer tell me to do that this time?" The pegging report tells where each requirement came from at the higher level and allows the user to trace

requirements right back to the master schedule and, ultimately, into customer orders to determine the impact of any
schedule changes or other problems. Without these tools,
the degree of user control over the system is not sufficient
to consider it a Class A system.

(4) The master schedule must be managed and must not be
generated automatically. During the '60's, master scheduling wasn't well understood at all. Somehow, people felt
that the master schedule would be input via some forecasting system or customer orders, and that this would be
the driving force behind material requirements planning.
That never worked for a very simple reason. It was not a
representation of the real world. The master schedule must
be very visible to management so that it can be managed
properly.

(5) A Class A MRP system should include capacity requirements planning and control. That means that the standard
hours of capacity requirements by work center are determined from the system.

(6) A Class A system should have a daily dispatch list to
transmit the shop schedule that is driven by the material
requirements plan to the factory. The dispatch list should
be daily because jobs move on a daily basis. If the dispatch list is generated any less frequently than daily, shop
foremen have to cross out jobs that have already moved,
add in jobs that have come in since the dispatch list was
made out, etc., and it will probably not be used properly.

There should be vendor scheduling as well as dispatching. The vendors should get a schedule at least once
a week to tell what material is really needed and when it is
really needed.

(7) The input/output control report is the way to monitor
capacity to make sure that the required capacity is being
attained. In an MRP system, everything relates to everything else. The capacity plan must be attained in order to
make the material that's required for the material requirements plan: in order to meet the master schedule, in order
to meet the production plans, in order to meet the business
plan.

(8) In the area of data integrity, inventory record accuracy is one of the most important and, at the same time,

one of the most challenging areas. Our experience in working with Class A users is that a company needs to have 95 percent of the items within counting tolerance. Methods for measuring inventory accuracy are discussed in Chapter 6, but if a company is not above 95 percent, they cannot be considered to be a Class A user.

(9) Bill of material accuracy is another vital support to an MRP system. The methods for measuring bill of material accuracy were discussed earlier in Chapter 13.

(10) Routing accuracy is critical. It's important that the routings specify what work center a job moves to. The routing itself is far more important than the time standards. If a job has a poor standard, it doesn't matter a great deal when the input/output approach is being used. If it takes 10 hours to run the job according to the standard, but it really takes 15, 10 hours will be planned and 10 hours will be credited. The problems will show up in labor efficiency, and of course, will have to be addressed. But from a capacity planning and control point of view, precision in the standards is not a requirement. Precision in the operation sequence is. And this accuracy should be up to at least 95 percent.

Work centers are not considered as a critical item in measuring the effectiveness of the system. Not that there can't be problems in work center identification. Some companies try to identify every machine as a work center. Others apply a work center number to an entire "cost center" defined by accounting. The entire screw machine department may be a cost center from an accounting point of view, but "00" Brown and Sharpe machines are considerably different from eight spindle New Britain Gridleys from a capacity planning point of view. Nevertheless, very few companies have failed with MRP because of their work center identification problems. This should be done right, but if it isn't done right the first time around, it can usually be corrected quickly for capacity planning purposes.

(11) The next section on the checklist deals with the people and their education. If 80 percent of the people in the company, and this includes the total population, have not had some form of education, a company should not consider itself Class A. Obviously, results are the real criterion, but the results just aren't likely to be there without this

amount of education. This certainly means top management has had at least 15 to 20 hours of education. And this should have taken place in a live class with the CEO, and those reporting to the CEO. This should not be the "outside expert" doing in-plant "training." Every foreman and lead man should have some education, and machine operators should have about 1 hour a month of education using video courses. There is more about education in Chapter 18, but the issue here is that massive amounts of education have to be done to make a company a Class A user. The recommended hours of education are just a guideline. The important point is not the number of hours, but the amount of understanding that results from the education.

(12) It's important, too, that education be an ongoing program, not just a "one shot deal" where a few people get educated to put MRP on the air and from there on it's assumed that the system will run properly. Just like airline pilots who need regular updates - not just to learn new techniques, but also to make sure that bad habits aren't developing - the professionals who run manufacturing businesses must make continuing education part of their job. Another reason for continuing education is the new people coming into a company. They need to be taught how to run the business using an MRP II system.

The next section deals with the real test: how well a company is able to use MRP.

(13) The shortage list is a dead giveaway that the formal system is not working. An MRP system should predict the shortages so that they can be prevented rather than identify them after they actually exist.

(14) Vendor delivery performance should be 95 percent or better. This means that vendors are delivering on time 95 percent of the time specified on the vendor schedule. Some tolerance can be established here for the quantity being delivered, etc., but the important point is to measure this delivery performance. Did the vendors send as much as was needed when it was required?

(15) There should be vendor scheduling out beyond the quoted lead times. People who only order from their vendors as far out as their lead times will inevitably get involved in the lead time syndrome when vendors start to develop backlogs. Scheduling out beyond the quoted lead

times and asking vendors to confirm that they can handle the material and capacity requirements can prevent the lead time syndrome, particularly if a company uses MRP and gives vendors realistic dates rather than order launching and expediting which will generate a phoney backlog.

(16) Shop delivery should also meet the 95 percent delivery criteria. Ninety-five percent of the shop orders should be completed on time.

(17) Master schedule performance should be 95 percent or better. This means that the individual items in the master schedule week by week should be completed to a minimum of a 95 percent objective (this measure is by item). Total dollars should equal 100 percent.

(18) There should be regular formal communication if a company is to be a Class A MRP user. These production planning meetings are in addition to the normal weekly manufacturing meetings that just include manufacturing people.

(19) There should be a written master scheduling policy that is adhered to. No company can consider that they have master scheduling without a master scheduling policy. There should be an anticipated delay report, feedback from the shop and from vendors on particular jobs that will not be completed on schedule. This is a critical element in a closed loop system where "silence is approval."

(20) Originally MRP was a way to order material - a better way - made possible by the computer. And since the thrust of inventory management in the '50's and '60's was to establish "when and how much to order," many people installed MRP as a better inventory control technique - a better "ordering" technique. If it is not used to keep need dates up to date in the factory and with the vendors, a company, by definition, is a Class C MRP user at best.

(21) MRP must be understood by people in manufacturing, marketing, engineering, finance and, of course, by the CEO. That may sound like a subjective area to measure, but, in fact, it's not. If the engineering people see the bill of material as something that's basically "theirs" and resent having to provide the basic data to run a manufacturing business, they don't understand. If the marketing people think that MRP is fundamentally a "production and inventory control system for manufacturing" rather

than seeing it as a tool for marketing, <u>they</u> don't understand. If the financial people maintain a separate system because they don't understand MRP II and don't realize that it is a way to have the operating and the financial systems using the same numbers, <u>they</u> don't understand.

(22) If management's approach to controlling inventory is to sign every requisition for over $500, <u>they</u> don't understand. If the accepted way to get a "hot job" through production is to go down and tap a foreman on the shoulder and tell him to give it "the old push," the manager doesn't understand. If management people feel that the way to reduce inventory is to issue an order to "cut the inventory by 20 percent" (which will work, of course, but it may take the company three years to recover from the customer service problems that are generated as a result!), then <u>they</u> don't understand. The master schedule is the tool for reducing inventory, increasing inventory, improving customer service, getting "hot jobs" through, etc. A management that understands MRP realizes that they have a far more powerful tool for making things happen than they ever had before. It's important, too, that the people who implement MRP make sure that management sees it as a "can do" system rather than one more "inflexible" computer system.

(23) Before MRP was available, it was difficult to plan and implement engineering changes. MRP won't do this, but it certainly provides the tools for people to do this.

(24) A company putting in MRP may not reduce inventory. Some have chosen to keep inventory the same or even increase it because they felt their biggest opportunity was in the area of better market penetration through better customer service. Other companies didn't have an opportunity to do a lot to improve productivity. Some manufacturing companies are more process than fabrication and assembly oriented, and productivity may not be a great benefit in some process environments (although it certainly is in many). Nevertheless, a company that has installed and is operating MRP successfully should certainly expect to see an improvement in two out of three of these vital areas.

(25) Once MRP is generating the proper numbers, they should be tied in with financial planning. Not too many companies are doing this today, but the standards are

always improving as the most effective users of MRP learn new ways to use the tools better. Today, a company should definitely be tying the financial and operating systems together. Tomorrow, they will not be able to be considered Class A if they don't.

How to Use the Checklist

Go through the checklist, and try to honestly evaluate where your company stands. This should involve at least two or three people, and there are some instances where partial credit would be appropriate. Question 3, for example, could have half credit (two points since the questions each rate four points). Question 21 is another one that could generate partial credit.

A Class A user would be one where the company rated 90 points or higher on the checklist. From 70 to 90 makes a company a Class B user; from 50 to 70, a Class C user; and below 50, a Class D user.

Each company has to use this as a guide in evaluating themselves. If, for example, a company doesn't have any real manufacturing, but only purchases and assembles, then Questions 5 and 6 would not apply, and full credit would be given even though the company doesn't have capacity planning and a daily dispatch list.

When the weakest areas in the company are identified, then the important issue is to fix the problems. And the problems always come back to people, and their understanding at one level or another. For example, if inventory record accuracy isn't good, that may be because the stockroom people don't understand. It may be because their supervisor doesn't understand, or it may be because the plant manager to whom the stockroom reports doesn't hold people accountable for inventory record accuracy because the plant manager doesn't understand. Understanding is a case of education, and management conveying a message to people about running a business more professionally.

Section 2
The Implementation Checklist

This checklist was developed to help people who are currently implementing MRP. Using this checklist, they can measure whether or not they are really on the track and are likely to get the results from MRP. Note that in this checklist, the numerical valuations are <u>DEDUCTED</u> from the total. It doesn't take many wrong moves to keep an MRP system from working.

1. Do you have a *full time* project leader, a *user* who will be *accountable* for making the system work after it's on the air? 20

2. Have the following top management people been educated in the Top Management Class?
   General Manager 20
   Marketing 10
   Manufacturing 10
   Engineering 10
   Finance 10

3. Have the following people been educated in the five-day class?
   Materials Manager 20
   Production Control 10
   Systems, Data Processing 10
   Purchasing 10
   General Foremen 10

4. Have you educated at least 80 percent of *all* of the people in the company? 15

5. Do you have a project plan for implementing MRP? 20

6. Do you have a regular management review of the implementation plan?... 10

7. Do you have professional guidance from a consultant who has actually *done it?* 10

8. Does your plan call for implementation in 18 months or less? 10

9. Do you plan to cut over with a pilot approach? 20

10. Has top management assigned accountability for inventory accuracy, bill of material accuracy, master scheduling, etc? 20

11. Are you planning to use a standard MRP system? 20

Figure A2 – 2. Implementation Checklist

(1) A company implementing MRP needs a full time user as the project leader. This is because someone with the dual responsibility of installing a new system, and also trying to do the day-to-day firefighting, simply won't get the system installed. The system must be installed by a user who will

be accountable for making it work afterwards. There's no way a systems person can be held accountable.

(2) There has been too much talk about management "support." Support without understanding is a liability. In particular, the general manager must understand the new ball game, the new set of values that must be instilled throughout the organization, he must set objectives for inventory accuracy, bill of material accuracy, and master schedule performance; and <u>measure</u> people against these objectives. If he or the people he's measuring don't understand, the chances of success are very low.

(3) Certainly, the people who are going to be using the system, especially the purchasing people and general foremen, need to know what the system is all about and why they should be using it.

(4) MRP is a different way to run a business. All the computer can do is generate paper. If a "critical mass" of people have not been educated, it simply won't work. Eighty percent is a bare minimum number. The most successful companies wind up educating between ninety and one hundred percent of <u>all</u> of the people in the company, including machine operators. No one has ever said they did too much education. The only practical way to do this is with video-assisted instruction. <u>Having a consultant do in-plant education is an ineffectual one-shot approach.</u> Responsible consultants won't do this type of education for any price. When a general foreman goes back from the five-day class and teaches his people using the video courses as we've outlined in the implementation plan (Appendix 3), the effect is far more powerful.

(5) Without an organized approach to installing MRP, it simply isn't likely to happen.

(6) If management doesn't review the project and make sure it stays on track, it will probably never get completed.

(7) For virtually every company installing MRP, it's a new experience, and there is a learning curve. Professional guidance can be very helpful. But MRP has become the buzzword and the consultants have all jumped in. It's critical to pick a qualified professional who has <u>actually done it himself</u>. This kind of consultant will probably only come in one day every month or six weeks. He should be

the catalyst, not the reactor. The test of any consultant is very simple. <u>Find out where he has actually done it.</u>

(8) Because MRP requires a concentrated effort to install, it's important to install it in a minimum amount of time. The key items in the critical path in installation are typically:

    a.   Developing and implementing the software.
    b.   Fixing inventory records.
    c.   Fixing bills of material.
    d.   Fixing routings.
    e.   Educating people.

Some companies are able to do all of this in a twelve-month period depending on how much work their inventory records require, etc. Others take up to two years. It's important that a company try to take eighteen months or less since it's difficult to keep management's attention for any longer period of time. There are always new problems, a new plant being built, a new product being developed, a strike, a serious decline in business, a dramatic increase in business - all of these take management's attention away from installing MRP. So the name of the game is concentrate on it, do it, and get it done. The chances of ever installing MRP if you plan to take over two years are very slim indeed. The secret to taking less time is to identify the items in the critical path and "break the back of the learning curve."

(9) In theory, there are three ways to install an MRP system:

    a.   The "cold turkey" approach.

The theory here is that this motivates people to "sink or swim." In practice, people don't drown through lack of motivation, and the "cold turkey" approach almost always results in overwhelming people and keeping MRP from ever getting off the ground. The "cold turkey" approach is not recommended <u>under any circumstances</u>.

    b.   The "parallel" approach.

The theory here is to get it working manually and then put it on the computer. Anything that works manually probably never should be put on a computer. The reason

MRP can produce such dramatic results is that it's something that can't be done manually. So there's no way to install an MRP system in parallel.

c. The "pilot" approach.

Here, one planner's product lines are picked and MRP is installed on these products. Obviously, MRP's priority planning effectiveness in the shop cannot be used as a way to evaluate the effectiveness of the pilot since other items are still being scheduled with the old system. In many companies, it's impossible to find a product line that doesn't have some components common to other product lines. This is no problem; these items should be ignored during the pilot. There are two tests of a pilot:

1. Do the people understand what they are doing? It is not a test of the computer software. This should have been tested long before. The test is whether the people know how to use what comes off the computer.

2. Does the MRP report effectively "predict the shortages?" This can be checked by physically pulling the material from the stockroom, making up a physical shortage list, and comparing it with shortages In MRP. If the master schedule, the bills of material, and the inventory records are correct, what the people pull physically to support this week's production will match 100 percent with the shortages in the MRP output report; then the pilot is working.

(10) One of the best tests of management's approach to MRP is inventory record accuracy. The informal system operating with a shortage list does not require accurate records. The formal system must have them or it will not work. Keeping accurate records is a management problem, not a computer systems problem. It requires that top management assign accountability for inventory accuracy and measure performance using cycle counting as a way to do a "statistical quality control" check on inventory transactions.

(11) In the old days, companies believed that they were unique, and each tried to develop a special system to solve their special problems. Today, we recognize that the problems of scheduling are universal, and that only standard systems work. Before the airplane flew, people drew pic-

tures of all kinds of airplanes. After it flew, most airplanes looked the same. If any system is to work, it will inevitably have to look like the other systems that already work.

A company can interpret its score in the same way as with the classifications in the first checklist. After deducting points (assuming this is necessary), people can get a pretty good idea of just what class a company will likely be after the system goes on the air. <u>If this checklist shows that this company is headed the wrong way, now is the time to stop.</u> In most companies, the foremen and many of the other people on the firing line have already experienced several abortive attempts at using the computer in manufacturing. MRP <u>can</u> work, but if it is installed poorly and everybody is demoralized, the road back is an extremely difficult one. It would be far better to stop the installation right now if the company is not ready to install MRP properly. Whenever there is a system that has not been installed successfully, there is always someone who thought that they could "cheat a little" and get by. Systems for running businesses are very unforgiving. A little cheating will result in failure.

Appendix 3
The Implementation Plan

Appendix 3
The Implementation Plan

This implementation plan was developed by Darryl Landvater, President of Manufacturing Software Systems, Inc. It has been updated to include the financial functions that would be included in an MRP II system. In its earlier form, it has been used by hundreds of companies as a road map for implementing MRP successfully.

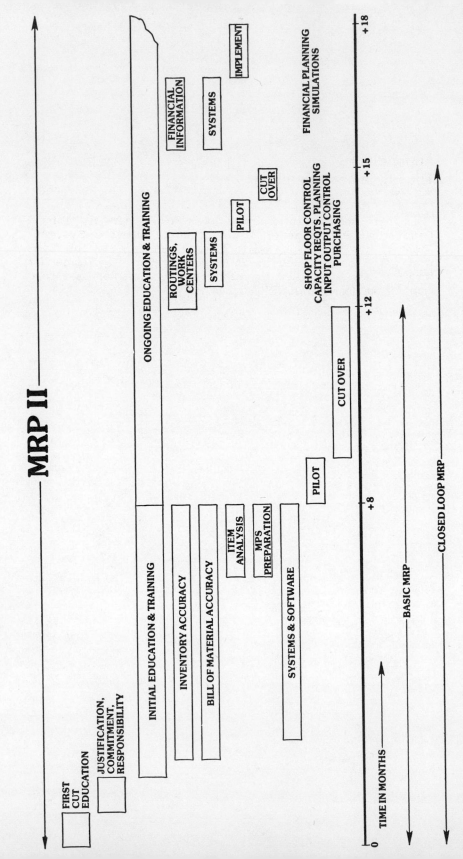

MRP II

MRP II DETAILED IMPLEMENTATION PLAN

More and more people are asking for information on the implementation and operation of MRP systems. These people are not interested in being sold on MRP. MRP systems work. The proof is available and companies are using them every day. People who understand the fundamentals and the logical simplicity of MRP are looking for a proven way to implement the system.

This detailed implementation plan is a road map to help people implement MRP systems. The implementation plan outlines the basic functional areas needed to implement MRP. These functional areas are then broken down into specific milestones. This listing of broad functional areas and specific tasks provides a very practical plan.

PEOPLE USING MRP

The implementation plan is also meant for companies using an MRP system. There are many companies which have the technical part of an MRP system in place. Yet, they are not using the system well. The implementation plan can help these companies. The jobs in improving an MRP system are the same as the jobs to implement it correctly. The only difference is that some of these jobs may have already been done. If so, they can be deleted from the plan.

MRP II

MRP, which started out over ten years ago as a better way to order material has evolved into MRP II. MRP II is a total company wide system. It is a way to get all the people in the company working to the same game plan; to the same set of numbers. A company can now plan material, capacity, finance, marketing strategy, etc. all with the same system. In addition, all these things can be simulated to provide the management of the company with real planning capability.

This version of the implementation plan includes the steps for MRP II.

Finally, the implementation plan has been put on video tape. The course MRP: Making It Work, available from Oliver Wight Video Productions, Inc., uses this implementation plan as the core of the section on implementing MRP. Each of the points in this implementation plan are expanded significantly and explained in that video course.

USING THE PLAN

The implementation plan is a generalized framework applicable to nearly any company. Its two primary uses are:

1. To provide a clear statement of priorities -
   to separate the vital and trivial, and keep
   them in perspective.
2. To provide a road map for implementation.

The implementation plan is organized to constantly focus attention on the items that have the greatest impact on the potential for success. The people part of an MRP system is fully 80% of the system. The system will only work when people understand what it is, how it works, and what their responsibilities are. For this reason, the education and training are listed at the front of the implementation plan. The computer software and programming effort is not as likely to be something which prevents the success of an MRP system, and so this topic is covered later in the plan.

The other purpose is to provide a detailed schedule of events that have to be accomplished in order to implement the system. The most effective way to use the plan is to tailor the plan to each company and then use it as the agenda for management reviews of implementation progress.

PRACTICALITY

This implementation plan is not a theoretical exercise. In the six years since the first version of the plan was developed, it has been used successfully by a number of companies. Whether these companies would have been successful without the plan, I cannot say. But it does work, it is practical, and those who have used it swear by it.

TAILORING THE PLAN TO YOUR COMPANY

The implementation plan is a general framework stated in terms of departments and job titles. The departments and job titles should be replaced by the names of the people within the organization who will be responsible for the tasks.

The implementation plan also contains an approximate time frame for scheduling the tasks under each of the functional topics. The scheduled due dates for the tasks in implementation are given under the heading "DATE." These due dates were developed based on the dependence of some tasks on others. The times on the plan, +3 and +7 for example, are months relative to a starting point. A time of +3 means the task should be completed three months after the start date. The start date used in the plan is the date that formal commitment is given to the project.

The plan should be rewritten to include calendar dates in place of the scheduled completion dates in months. Columns should also be added for the scheduled start date, the actual start date, and the actual completion date. The scheduled start dates are not on the generalized plan since the size of the different tasks will vary from company to company. The actual start and actual completion dates should be included on the plan to indicate the progress or lack of it during the management reviews of implementation.

The comments column on the implementation plan is meant to give a short explanation of the phases of the plan and tasks that make up each phase. Some people choose to leave these explanations in the final version of the plan, others leave them out. In either case, additional comments on the progress of the tasks should also be included as the plan is periodically updated. These comments would indicate, for example, the results of the cycle counts, or any other information about one of the items in the plan.

A company may also have to add or delete tasks from the implementation plan to account for situations that are a part of the implementation, or work that has already been done. As an example of an item that would be deleted from the plan, a company may have already enclosed the stockrooms and may have started cycle counting. In this case, it makes no sense to count 100 parts as a starting point. As an example of an item that would have to be added to the plan, a company may have to convert to a different

computer to do MRP. In this case, the conversion from one
computer to the other should be included on the detailed
implementation plan.

Figure 1 is an example of the implementation plan
before and after it has been tailored to a company. This
example includes replacement of departments and job titles
with people's names, the inclusion of calendar dates with
columns for scheduling dates, and some comments on tasks
that are working.

MRP DETAILED IMPLEMENTATION PLAN

TASK	RESPONSIBLE	DATE	COMMENTS
A. Measure 100 parts as a starting point.	Stockroom Mgr.	+1	This will help assess the work that needs to be done to bring the inventory records to 95%.
B. Map out limited access to the stockroom areas.	Stockroom Mgr.	+1	Lay out any stockroom changes that are necessary to insure limited access.
C. Provide the tools for limited access and transaction recording.	Top Management Stockroom Mgr. Team Leader DP Mgr.	+3	A fence, enough stockroom people, adequate space, counting scales, transaction forms, labels, skids, etc.

TASK	RESPONSIBLE	– SCHEDULED – START	DUE	– ACTUAL – START	DUE
A. Measure 100 parts as a starting point.	R. Ferris	6/20/80	6/27/80	6/20/80	6/24/80
Results indicate that the inventory accuracy is 63%.					
B. Map out limited access to the stockroom areas.	R. Ferris K. Miller	6/1/80	7/1/80	6/5/80	
Lay out any stockroom changes that are necessary to insure limited access. Main and spare parts stockrooms to be enclosed and third stockroom to be consolidated into the existing stockrooms.					
C. Provide the tools for limiting access and transaction recording.	D. Roser R. Ferris K. Miller H. Arner	7/15/80	9/1/80		
A fence, enough stockroom people, adequate space, counting scales, transaction forms, labels, skids, etc.					

Figure 1

MRP DETAILED IMPLEMENTATION PLAN

TASK	RESPONSIBLE	DATE	COMMENTS
1. **First cut education.**	Top Management P&IC Shop Management	−1	What is MRP and how does it work. Why should we as a company commit to it? The courses should be the equivalent of the following courses offered by Oliver Wight, Inc. P.O. Box 435 Newbury, New Hampshire 03255 (800) 258-3862 or (603) 763-5926
	Top Management P&IC Shop Management		MRP II: Manufacturing Resource Planning For Top Management MRP II: Manufacturing Resource Planning—5-Day
2. **Justification, commitment, and assignment of responsibility.**	Top Management P&IC Shop Management	0	Formal commitment to the project.
A. Prepare justification.	P&IC Shop Management	0	Cost/Benefit
B. Commit to the project.	Top Management	0	
C. Set up implementation team and team leader.	Top Management	0	Implementation team leader is full time. His responsibility is to make the MRP system work by coordinating and managing the project.
D. Schedule periodic management project reviews.	Top Management	0	Approximately every month. To include all those responsible for parts of the project currently active.
E. Schedule periodic visits from a consultant with experience in implementing successful MRP systems.	Top Management	0	The consultant should have successfully implemented a system or worked with successful systems. Schedule visits from once a month to once every three months.

MRP DETAILED IMPLEMENTATION PLAN

TASK	RESPONSIBLE	DATE	COMMENTS
3. Detailed education and training.	Team Leader	0 – +8	This phase of the plan is aimed at the people part of the system.

The objective of this part of the plan is to give the people operating the system an understanding of the system and the means to use it effectively. Education and training must translate the general principles of MRP into the specifics of operation at the company.

The plan separates education and training. Education is broad based understanding of MRP which is essential. Training is the detailed knowlege of reports, forms, etc.

The education and training are structured in levels. People in the company attend outside courses. These people then serve as teachers and train their own people.

A. Outside courses for people who will be teachers at the in-house courses.		+1 + 3	The courses should be the equivalent of the following courses offered by Oliver Wight, Inc. & Oliver Wight Education Associates, Inc. P.O. Box 313 Newbury, New Hampshire 03255 (800) 258-3862 or (603) 763-2061
	Team Leader		MRP II: Manufacturing Resource Planning - 5 day
	Steering Committee Chairman		MRP II Implementation Class
	P & IC Mgr.		MRP II Implementation Class
	Purch. Mgr.		MRP II: Manufacturing Resource Planning - 5 day
	Plant Supdt.		MRP II: Manufacturing Resource Planning - 5 day
	Stockroom Mgr.		MRP II: Manufacturing Resource Planning - 5 day
	Engineering Mgr.		MRP II: Manufacturing Resource Planning - 5 day
			MRP II: Manufacturing Resource Planning for Top Management
	Sales/Marketing Mgr.		MRP II: Manufacturing Resource Planning for Top Management
	DP Mgr.		MRP II: Manufacturing Resource Planning - 5 day

MRP DETAILED IMPLEMENTATION PLAN

TASK	RESPONSIBLE	DATE	COMMENTS
B. Purchase or lease the MRP video courses for in house education.	Team Leader	+1	These video courses will serve as the framework for all the educational courses in the following educational plan. The current library consists of 53 videotapes, approximately 33 hours of videotaped education on MRP. The MRP video library is available through: Oliver Wight Video Productions, Inc. P.O. Box 278 Williston, Vermont 05495 (802) 878-8161
C. Teachers course. Video education.	Team Leader	+1½	The team leader and all teachers go through the video courses to translate the general principles of MRP into the specifics of operation at the company. *Attendees:* All teachers. *Length:* Approx. 80 hrs.
D. Top Management course. Video education.	Team Leader	+2·+8	*Attendees:* Pres., all VPs, Plant Superintendent, others as appropriate. *Length:* Approx. 40 hrs.
E. Production and inventory control Video education.	P&IC Mgr.	+2·+8	*Attendees:* All people in P&IC. *Length:* Approx. 80 hrs.
Outside workshop	Master Scheduler	+3	Outside master scheduling workshop for one or more master schedulers. The workshop should be the equivalent of the one offered by Oliver Wight Education Associates, Inc.

MRP DETAILED IMPLEMENTATION PLAN

TASK	RESPONSIBLE	DATE	COMMENTS
In house training.	P&IC Mgr.	+7-+8	*Attendees:* All people in P&IC. *Coverage:* All forms, reports, and documents that will be used by the people in P&IC. This includes a dry run of the system, sometimes called a "conference room pilot," to gain experience in using the reports and transactions.
F. Purchasing. Video education	Purch. Mgr.	+2-+8	*Attendees:* All people in purchasing. *Length:* Approx. 45 hrs.
Outside worskshop.	Purch. Mgr. Buyers	+5	Outside purchasing workshop for one or more buyers. The workshop should be the equivalent of the one offered by Oliver Wight Education Associaties, Inc.
In house training.	Purch. Mgr.	+7-+8	*Attendees:* All people in purchasing. *Coverage:* All forms, reports, and documents that will be used by the people in purchasing. This includes a dry run of the system, sometimes called a "conference room pilot," to gain experience in using the reports and transactions.
G. Shop foreman. Video education.	VP Mfg. Plant Supdt.	+2-+8	*Attendees:* All shop foremen. *Length:* Approx. 40-45 hrs.
Outside workshop.	Shop Foreman	+5	Outside shop floor control and capacity requirements planning workshop. The workshop would be the equivalent of the one offered by Oliver Wight Education Associates, Inc.
In house training.	Plant Supdt.	+7-+8	*Attendees:* All shop foremen. *Coverage:* All forms, reports, and documents that will be used by the shop people. This includes a dry run using the documents.

MRP DETAILED IMPLEMENTATION PLAN

TASK	RESPONSIBLE	DATE	COMMENTS
H. Stockroom people. Video education.	Stockroom Mgr.	+2-+4	*Attendees:* Anyone who will be making inventory transactions. *Length:* Approx. 15 hrs.
Outside workshop.	Stockroom Mgr.	+3	Outside inventory accuracy workshop for one or more stockroom managers. The workshop should be the equivalent of the one offered by Oliver Wight Education Associates, Inc.
In house training.	Stockroom Mgr.	+3	*Attendees:* Anyone who will be making inventory transactions. *Coverage:* All forms, reports, and documents that will be used in the inventory transaction system.
I. Sales and marketing. Video education.	Sales/Mktg. Mgr.	+3-+8	*Attendees:* All sales and marketing people. This course is usually divided into two courses. One for those people in-house and one for those in district sales offices. *Length:* Approx. 25-30 hrs.
In house training	Sales/Mktg. Leader +8		*Attendees:* All in-house sales and marketing people. *Coverage:* All forms, reports, and documents used in master scheduling and forecasting applicable to the sales marketing people.

MRP DETAILED IMPLEMENTATION PLAN

TASK	RESPONSIBLE	DATE	COMMENTS
J. Engineering. Video education.	Engr. Mgr.	+2-+8	*Attendees:* Anyone who will be working with bills of material or routings. *Length:* Approx. 30-40 hrs.
Outside workshop	Engr. Mgr.	+3	Outside bill of material structuring workshop for the engineering manager and several of the engineers who will be structuring bills of material. The bill of material workshop should be the equivalent of the workshop offered by Oliver Wight Education Associates, Inc.
In house training.	Engr. Mgr.	+5	*Attendees:* Anyone who will be working with bills of materials or routings. *Coverage:* All forms, reports, and documents that will be used to maintain bills of material and routings.
K. Data processing. Video Education.	DP Mgr.	+2-+8	*Attendees:* Anyone who will be working with the MRP programs or files. *Length:* Approx. 55 hrs.
L. Finance. Video education.	Mgr. Finance/ Accounting	+2-+8	*Attendees:* All people in finance. *Length:* Approx. 35 hrs.
Outside workshop.	Mgr. Finance/ Accounting	+2-+8	Outside finance and accounting workshop for one or more managers of finance and/or accounting. The workshop should be the equivalent of the one offered by Oliver Wight Education Associates, Inc.
M. Lead men and set up men.	Shop Foremen	+2-+8	*Attendees:* All set up or lead men *Length:* Approx. 20 hrs.

MRP DETAILED IMPLEMENTATION PLAN

TASK	RESPONSIBLE	DATE	COMMENTS
N. Distribution center managers. Video education	Distribution Mgr.	+2-+8	*Attendees:* All distribution center or branch warehouse managers. *Length:* Approx. 20 hrs.
Outside workshop	Distribution Mgr. DC Mgrs. Master Scheduler P&IC Mgr.	+3	Outside distribution resource planning workshop for the manager of distribution, one or more distribution center or branch warehouse managers, one or more master schedulers, P&IC manager. The workshop should be the equivalent of the one offered by Oliver Wight Education Associates, Inc.
O. Distribution center employees. Video education	DC Mgrs.	+3-+8	*Attendees:* All distribution center employees. *Length:* Approx. 15 hrs.
P. Introduction to all direct labor employees.	V.P. MFG Plant Supdt.	+3+8	*Attendees:* All direct labor employees. *Length:* Approx. 2 hrs.
Q. Anyone else affected by the system and not covered in the courses above.	Team Leader	+8	*Attendees:* As required. *Length:* As required.
4. Inventory accuracy.	Stockroom Mgr.	+8	This phase of the plan is aimed at bringing the inventory accuracy to 95% of the items within the counting error. This must be accomplished before the pilot program can be started. This includes distribution centers or branch warehouses.
A. Measure 100 parts as a starting point.	Stockroom Mgr.	+1	This will help assess the work that needs to be done to bring the inventory records to 95%.
B. Map out limited access to the stockroom areas.	Stockroom Mgr.	+1	Lay out any stockroom changes that are necessary to insure limited access.

MRP DETAILED IMPLEMENTATION PLAN

TASK	RESPONSIBLE	DATE	COMMENTS
C. Provide the tools for limited access and transaction recording.	Top Management Stockroom Mgr. Team Leader DP Mgr.	+3	A fence, enough stockroom people, adequate space, counting scales, transaction forms, labels, skids, etc.
D. Assign responsibility for the inventory accuracy.	Top Management	+3	The inventory manager and his people are now responsible for the inventory accuracy. Change job descriptions where necessary.
E. Start counting a control group of 100 parts.	Stockroom Mgr.	+3	Control group parts are counted once every ten days. Any inventory errors are investigated to find the cause of the error.
F. Each ten days a report is published showing the results of the control group.	Stockroom Mgr.	+3 on	The report should show the history of the inventory accuracy and the cause of the errors.
G. Start cycle counting all inventory items.	Stockroom Mgr.	+5 on	All parts are counted periodically. A simple method would be to count A and B items twice a year, and the C items once a year.
H. Bring the inventory accuracy to 95% of the parts within counting error.	Stockroom Mgr.	+8	As measured by the results of cycle counting the items in inventory, and not based only on the control group items.
5. **Bill of material accuracy.**	Engr. Mgr. P&IC Mgr.	+8	This phase of the plan is aimed at bringing bill of material accuracy to 98%. The tasks in this phase must be completed before the pilot program can begin. Both design and production engineering should participate in structuring the bills of materials,

MRP DETAILED IMPLEMENTATION PLAN

TASK	RESPONSIBLE	DATE	COMMENTS
A. Measure 100 bills of material as a starting point.	Engineering	+3	This will help assess the work that needs to be done to eliminate errors from the bills of material.
B. Decide and assign responsibility for the accuracy of bills of materials.	Top Management	+3	This may involve centralizing some responsibilities and setting up procedures to control the flow of documents if these are not already present.
C. Verify the bills of materials for correct part numbers and quantities per assembly.	Engineering	+8	This requires either a line by line audit or an exception system, like stockroom pulls, to point out bill of material errors. Either method must highlight and correct any errors in component part numbers or quantities per assembly.
D. Verify the bills of materials to show the correct structure of the product.	Engineering	+8	This requires restructuring the bills where necessary to show: 1. The way material moves on the shop floor. 2. Raw materials on the bills of material. 3. Modules or self-consumed assemblies where needed.
E. Decide on and implement bill of material policies.	Top Management Engineering P&IC	+5	Policies: 1. Engineering change procedure. 2. Documenting new or special products.
6. Item analysis			
A. Measure 100 items as a starting point.	P&IC Purch. Team Leader	+1	This phase of the plan covers the verification or assignment of the ordering rules. The parts are checked for correct lead times, ordering quantities, and safety stock (if applicable) This measurement will help assess the work that needs to be done.

MRP DETAILED IMPLEMENTATION PLAN

TASK	RESPONSIBLE	DATE	COMMENTS
B. Agree upon and assign responsibility for the ordering rules.	P&IC Purch.	+2	Responsibilities depend on how purchasing fits into the organization and whether or not the planner/buyer concept is used.
C. Verify or establish ordering policies.	P&IC Purch.	+8	Decide between fixed order policy or lot-for-lot ordering. Dynamic order policies like part period balancing are not recommended.
D. Verify or establish order quantities and order modifiers.	P&IC Purch.	+8	Assign order quantities for fixed order policy items. Modifiers should be assigned where they are appropriate.
E. Verify or establish lead times.	P&IC Purch.	+8	*Manufactured parts:* 1. Use simple scheduling rules. 2. Be consistent. *Purchased parts:* 1. Use current lead times.
F. Verify or establish safety stock levels.	P&IC Purch.	+8	*Independent demand items:* 1. Consistent with the master schedule policy. *Dependent demand items:* 1. In special circumstances.
7. Master Production schedule preparation.	Top Management Marketing P&IC Shop Management	+8	This phase of the plan covers the work required to set up a working master production schedule. Must include resource requirements planning.
A. Develop a production planning function.	Top Management Marketing P&IC Shop Management	+6	Production planning is basic strategic planning to develop a statement of production which is in families of products and by months.

MRP DETAILED IMPLEMENTATION PLAN

TASK	RESPONSIBLE	DATE	COMMENTS
B. Develop a master scheduling function.	P&IC	+6	Master scheduling takes the production plan and translates it into a specific statement of production. The master schedule is a statement of production in specific item numbers and by weeks.
C. Develop a master schedule policy.	Top Management Marketing P&IC Shop Management	+6	The master schedule policy should cover the following points for both production planning and master scheduling: 1. Procedure for changing the production plan or master production schedule. This procedure should include who can request a change, how the proposed change is investigated, and who should approve it before it is implemented. 2. Periodic reviews of the forecast and actual sales, also the master schedule and the actual production. The purpose of these reviews is to determine whether or not the production plan or master production schedule should be changed.
D. Begin operating the production plan and master production schedule.	Top Management Marketing P&IC Shop Management	+8	The first production plan and master production schedule are developed.

MRP DETAILED IMPLEMENTATION PLAN

TASK	RESPONSIBLE	DATE	COMMENTS
8. Systems work and software selection.	DP Mgr.	+8	This phase of the plan outlines the work that needs to be done in selecting software and accomplishing the systems work and programming for the MRP system.
A. Review and select software to be used.	Data Processing P&IC Shop Management	+2	Software should be evaluated using the software evaluations from: Manufacturing Software Systems, Inc. P.O. Box 278 Williston, Vermont 05495 (802) 878-5254
B. Systems work, programming, and testing of inventory transactions.	Data Processing	+5	Issues, receipts, cycle counting.
C. Systems work, programming, and testing of bills of material.	Data Processing	+6	Normal bill of material functions.
D. Systems work, programming, and testing of scheduled receipts.	Data Processing	+6½	Scheduled receipts: 1. Manufacturing orders. 2. Purchase orders. 3. Distribution orders.
E. Systems work, programming, and testing of the MRP logic.	Data Processing	+8	Any modifications that need to be made.
G. Systems work, programming, and testing of the master schedule system.	Data Processing	+8	Master scheduling and production planning support.
H. Agree on time schedules and cutoff times.	Data Processing	+6	Times for reports, transactions and cutoff times for transactions to the system.

MRP DETAILED IMPLEMENTATION PLAN

TASK	RESPONSIBLE	DATE	COMMENTS
9. Pre-installation tasks.	P&IC Mgr. Team Leader	+8	This phase of the plan covers the tasks that immediately precede the pilot program. Must include some form of shop dispatching.
A. Set up planner structure and part responsibilities.	P&IC	+8	Which planners are responsible for which groups of parts. Decide among vertical or horizontal responsibility: 1. Vertical-product line oriented. 2. Horizontal-department oriented.
B. Set up procedures for handling both top down and bottom up closed loop planning.	P&IC Shop Foremen Purchasing.	+8	Specific procedures for rescheduling, order release, and feedback of anticipated delays.
C. Physical clean-up.	P&IC Shop Foremen Purchasing	+8	Physical clean-up of the shop floor to insure that each open order has the required component parts, and that all parts on the floor are on an open order. Parts not covered by a shop order should be returned to the stockroom. All manufacturing orders and purchase orders should be verified.
10. Pilot program.	Everyone involved so far.	+8 + 9	This is the pilot program. It is a trial run of the system on one or a group of product lines that total several hundred part numbers. The purpose is to verify that the system is giving correct information.
A. Monitor the critical measurements.	Team Leader	+8 - +9	Verify that the system is providing correct information and that people are comfortable using the system

MRP DETAILED IMPLEMENTATION PLAN

TASK	RESPONSIBLE	DATE	COMMENTS
11. Cut over	Everyone involved so far.	+9-+12	This phase of the plan outlines the sequence that is used to move from the pilot program to full implementation on all product lines.
A. Group the remaining product lines into three or four divisions.	P&IC	+9	Divisions should contain product lines that are similar or share common parts.
B. Bring each division onto MRP, one division at a time.	P&IC	+9-+12	As each division is put onto MRP, set up planner coverage so the product lines involved get intense planner coverage until they are quieted down.

END OF FIRST MAJOR SECTION IN IMPLEMENTATION

TASK	RESPONSIBLE	DATE	COMMENTS
12. Training for shop floor control, capacity requirements planning, input output control, and purchasing.	Shop Management	+15	This phase of the plan outlines the training for shop floor control, capacity requirements planning and purchasing. This training has the same objectives and the same basic course outline as the MRP training covered previously.
A. Shop Foremen. In house training.	Plant Supdt.	+15	*Attendees:* All shop foremen. *Coverage:* All forms, reports and documents that will be used in the shop floor control and capacity requirements planning systems.
B. Planners In house training.	P&IC Mgr.	+15	*Attendees:* All planners that will be working with the shop people. *Coverage:* All forms, reports, and documents that will be used in the shop floor control and capacity requirements planning systems.

MRP DETAILED IMPLEMENTATION PLAN

TASK	RESPONSIBLE	DATE	COMMENTS
C. Shop dispatchers. In house training.	Shop Foreman	+15	*Attendees:* All shop dispatchers. *Coverage:* All forms, reports and documents that will be used in the shop floor control and capacity requirements planning systems.
D. Purchasing. In house training.	Purch. Mgr.	+15	*Attendees:* All purchasing people. *Coverage:* All forms, reports and documents that will be used in vendor follow-up and vendor negotiation.
13. Routing accuracy.	Shop Foremen Prod. Engr.	+15	This phase of the plan outlines the work that needs to be done to get routing accuracy to 95%.
A. Measure 100 routings as a starting point.	Shop Foremen Prod. Engr.	+10	This will help assess the work that needs to be done to eliminate errors from the routings.
B. Decide on and assign responsibility for the accuracy of the routings.	Top Management	+11	This may involve centralizing some responsibilities or defining areas of responsibilities if these do not already exist.
C. Verify that the routings show the operations correctly.	Shop Foremen Prod. Engr.	+15	This requires either a line by line audit of the routings or an exception system to point out routing errors. Either method must highlight and correct the errors in the routings. The routings should be verified for the following: 1. The correct operations and work centers. 2. The correct operation sequence. 3. A reasonable standard that can be used in scheduling.

MRP DETAILED IMPLEMENTATION PLAN

TASK	RESPONSBILE	DATE	COMMENTS
14. Work center identification.	*Shop Foremen* Prod. Engr.	+ 15	This phase of the plan outlines the simple steps that are required to define and classify the work centers.
A. Identify work centers.	Shop Foremen Prod. Engr.	+ 15	Decide which machines or groups of machines will be called work centers. In some cases a single machine will be a work center. In others, a group of similar machines will be a work center.
B. Establish an approximate work center capacity & desired Q.	Shop Foremen	+ 15	The work center capacity should be developed simply. This is typically done by using the acutal output over the last month or so to give the demonstrated capacity for the work center.
15. Systems work.	DP Mgr.	+ 15	This phase of the plan outlines the systems work and programming that must be done for shop floor control and capacity requirements planning.
A. Systems work, programming, and testing of shop floor control.	Data Processing	+ 15	Shop floor control functions.
B. Systems work, programming, and testing of capacity requirements planning.	Data Processing	+ 15	Capacity requirements planning functions.
C. Systems work, programming, and testing of input output control.	Data Processing	+ 15	Input output control report.
D. Systems work, programming, and testing for purchasing.	Data Processing	+ 15	Vendor follow up and vendor negotiation reports.

MRP DETAILED IMPLEMENTATION PLAN

TASK	RESPONSIBLE	DATE	COMMENTS
16. Implementation of shop floor control.	Shop Foremen P&IC	+15 - +16	The implementation of shop floor control uses a pilot program since new transactions and disciplines are being used on the shop floor.
A. Implement shop floor control on a pilot group of parts.	Shop Foremen P&IC	+15	The pilot should be large enough to provide one hundred or so shop orders. It is also helpful to use a product line that will create shop orders under shop floor control in all departments.
B. Implement shop floor control on the remaining items.	Shop Foremen P&IC	+15½	Cut over remaining items.
17. Implement capacity requirements planning input/output control, and purchasing.	Shop Foremen P&IC Purch. Mgr.	+16	This is a simple implementation. Capacity requirements planning, input/output control and purchasing negotiation reports are simple started.

END OF SECOND MAJOR SECTION IN IMPLEMENTATION

MRP DETAILED IMPLEMENTATION PLAN

TASK	RESPONSIBLE	DATE	COMMENTS
18. **Training for financial planning and simulation.**	Mgr. Finance/ Accounting, P&IC Mgr.	+18	This phase of the plan outlines the training for financial planning and simulations. This training has the same objectives and the same basic course outline as the MRP training covered previously.
A. Finance and Accounting. In house training	Mgr. Finance/ Accounting	+18	*Attendees:* People in finance and accounting. *Coverage:* All forms, reports and documents that will be used.
B. Production and Inventory Control In house training	P&IC Mgr.	+18	*Attendees:* People in P&IC. *Coverage:* Differences between simulations and normal operation of the system.
19. **Develop financial planning numbers**	Mgr. Finance/ Accounting	+18	These numbers are used to do inventory projections, cash flow projections, and fixed overhead allocations. Numbers include: 1. Cost by item. 2. Labor costs. 3. Machinery operating costs. 4. Fixed overhead allocations by work center, group of work centers, or departments.

MRP DETAILED IMPLEMENTATION PLAN

TASK	RESPONSIBLE	DATE	COMMENTS
20. Implement financial planning and simulations.	Mgr. Finance/ Accounting P&IC Mgr.	+18	No pilot is needed. Begin running the programs and verify the numbers before using for decisions. Types of simulations available include: 1. Changed master production schedule: A. Material impact. B. Capacity impact. C. Financial impact. D. Marketing impact. 2. Make/Buy simulations. 3. Different forecast — same MPS. 4. Sales promotions — same or different MPS. 5. New product introductions.

Darryl Landvater
MANUFACTURING SOFTWARE SYSTEMS, INC.
P.O. Box 278
Williston, Vermont 05495
(802) 878-5254

Appendix 4
The Order Point Inventory Model

Section 1
How "Scientific Inventory Management" Evolved From Order Launching and Expediting

Before computers came along, order launching and expediting was all that <u>could</u> be done. An inventory system ordered material, and then put dates on the shop orders and purchase orders. And the expeditors used the shortage list to determine what material was really needed.

There are two basic kinds of ordering systems:

1. The order point type system.
2. The material requirements planning system.

The order point type system establishes a "level" of inventory that "triggers" a reorder based on average usage. The material requirements planning system looks at future production schedules, breaks these down into components and raw material, takes into account the material currently on hand and on order, and orders the balance of the material needed to meet these production schedules. This, of course, is what we call MRP - Material Requirements Planning - today.

Every ordering system devised falls into one of these two categories; order point or material requirements planning. The well-known "min-max" system simply establishes a minimum (order point) and a "maximum" which is an "order up to" level. The maximum is really the sum of the order point plus the order quantity. Other systems that have rules such as "keep a sixty-day supply on hand and on order at all times" are merely variations of the order point system.

Before the computer was widely available, the biggest problem that was perceived with order points was just plain keeping them up to date so that they reflected current demand. Updating average usage rates regularly was a major challenge before the computer was available.

MRP, however, presented even greater challenges in a manual environment. A typical approach to MRP was to plan requirements quarterly (this was the so-called "quarterly ordering system"). The task was so immense using people, pencils, and desk calculators, that it was difficult to calculate requirements more frequently. With all the changes that go on continuously in a manufacturing environment, this was not even a good ordering system.

Neither approach did a good job. In fact, in many situations it didn't matter much which system was used because neither really worked. The shortage list was inevitably the real schedule.

Keeping order points up to date so that they reflected current usage was a serious problem in the manual system environment. Doing material requirements planning quickly enough so that it was even a good ordering system was also a serious problem. It was obvious that the inventory control people weren't able to do their ordering very effectively, and in the early days of computers, that appeared to be the important problem that had to be addressed - making the ordering system work properly.

As the operations research movement gained momentum after World War II, an ideal place for the application of operations research - mathematical, analytical techniques - seemed to be inventory management. The books of the day stated that the questions of inventory management were, "How much to order?" and "When to order?" The answer to the question "when to order" was to be addressed by the order point that would scientifically determine when to "trigger" a replenishment order.

Section 2
The Order Point Inventory Model

The basic order point formula is:

Order Point = Demand x Lead Time + Safety Stock

If the demand is estimated to be 100 units a week, lead time is estimated to be six weeks and a two-week safety stock is desired, the order point would be constructed as follows:

100 x 6 + 200 = 800 (order point)

When the inventory on hand and on order for a particular item is below order point, then more material must be ordered. The idea, of course, is to order when there is enough material to last until the new supply comes in.

If the forecast were perfect and the material came in at the end of the lead time every time it was ordered, no safety stock would be required. Obviously demand during the lead time period will frequently be greater than predicted and, for that matter, lead times could be longer than average.

Figure A4-1 shows the concept of statistical safety stock. It assumes a normal distribution of demands. If 600 is the average demand over lead time, the actual demand over a number of the most recent lead time periods is compared with this to calculate the average deviation from demand called the "mean absolute deviation" or simply "MAD." The MAD is an approximation to a standard deviation. The difference is that MAD is simpler to calculate because it doesn't involve the square root computations of the standard deviation.

Looking at Figure A4-1, it can be seen that 600 is the average demand over lead time. If material is ordered when the inventory level reaches 600, 50 percent of the time there would be an out-of-stock situation before new material was received. By putting in safety stock based on the measurement of the historical deviations from forecast - the MAD - a "scientific" determination of the amount of safety stock required to keep from going out of stock before new material is received could theoretically be calculated. Statistical tables, for example, indicate that one mean ab-

solute deviation will give approximately 80 percent service.
In other words, no safety stock would give 50 percent
service, while adding one mean absolute deviation as a
safety stock would give 80 percent. Two mean absolute
deviations, however, would give 95 percent service. (1)

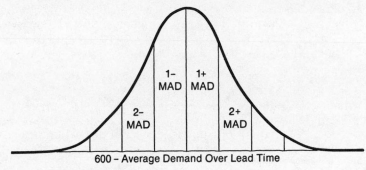

Figure A4 – 1.   Statistical Safety Stock

Figure A4-2 shows graphically the function of safety
stock as it is assumed to happen by the order point model.

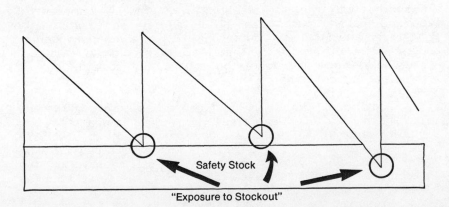

Figure A4 – 2.   The Function of Safety Stock

There is no need to go into the order point theory in more depth. It is covered in literally hundreds of books. Unfortunately, it has had a very poor record in practice because it is not a valid model of most real world conditions.

Section 3
The Assumptions of the Order Point Model

The order point model makes certain assumptions that severely restrict its application in practice. An inventory "model" is supposed to be a representation of reality, and the order point model makes assumptions that are, in many instances, very much contrary to reality. Among these are:

1. Demand is independent.
2. Demand is continuous.
3. Lead time is known and fixed.
4. Due dates, once established, will remain correct.
5. Stock should be replenished when it is used and there should always be stock on hand.
6. When to order is the big question.
7. Precise computations of safety stock are very important.
8. There is no need to look beyond the current order cycle because material will always be available and capacity will always be available.

The order point assumes that each item can be reviewed and ordered independently. This, of course, is not true for the bulk of the items carried in inventory. Consider the four parts that go into a ball bearing: the outer race, the inner race, the balls, and the retainer. Each of these parts is needed in inventory at the same time. They cannot be considered to be "independent items" when they are "dependent" items. They are dependent upon the assembly date. Each component is required on the date the assembly is to be built. They are also dependent upon each other. If the outer race cannot be made because of a problem in the grinding department, the inner race, retainer, and balls are not needed on the original assembly date. Material to make the outer race such as the bar stock also has a dependent demand. It is only needed when the bar stock will be scheduled to be used in the turret lathe to make the outer race. The concept of independent versus dependent demand was first developed in 1965. (2) It states that requirements planning techniques must be used for dependent demand items, and order point can only be used for independent demand items.

Figure A4-3 shows schematically the way a finished goods item might have many small independent demands. A component going into a higher level item would have a few large dependent demands.

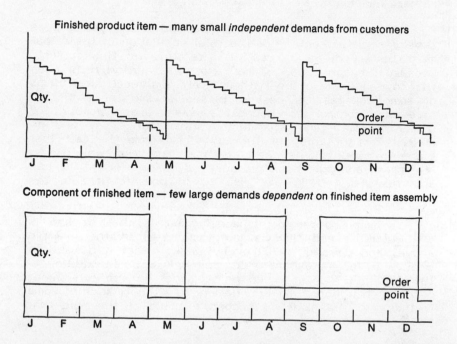

Figure A4 – 3. Independent versus Dependent Demand

But there is more to this than is immediately apparent. Consider a company with a main plant warehouse supplying many branch warehouses. Demand at the main plant warehouse is not independent. It is <u>dependent</u> upon <u>when</u> the inventory will be replenished at the branches and in what quantities. A company manufacturing bottles tries to keep an average month's supply on hand for their biggest users including a brewery. They base this on average usage and are constantly in trouble. The demand back at the bottle manufacturer is really <u>dependent</u> upon the bottling schedules at the brewery. They would be far better off to get these bottling schedules for the next few weeks from the brewery each week, convert them into their bottles, and schedule their plant accordingly. This production schedule would have to be revised weekly as the schedules at the brewery changed weekly, but under any circumstances, it is far more effective to <u>calculate</u> dependent requirements rather than to try to <u>"forecast"</u> them.

The number of independent demand items that exist is a very small percentage of the total population of items that must be scheduled. Yet, the literature on this subject, because the application of mathematical analytical techniques fits so handily into the mathematical, analytical curriculums of some colleges, is heavily biased toward the statistical inventory control approaches. There are probably 100 books on statistical inventory control for every one on MRP. Part of this, of course, stems from the fact that planning requirements seems rather pedestrian while doing statistical analysis has the aura of being "scientific and analytical." And if the real world doesn't fit into the theoretical model - get a bigger hammer!

A simple order point model assumes that demand is <u>continuous</u>. Lead time is six weeks, as in the example above, and demand is 100 every week. What if demand in week 5 is for an export order for 2000 units in addition to the 100 units? The order point model has no convenient way of handling "lumpy" demands without adding some features to the model. A good example of the rule that "poor systems breed more systems."

Perhaps the most significant assumption that the order point model makes is that <u>lead time is known</u> and fixed. Lead time is assumed to be "six weeks," for example. (3) In the real world, lead time is anything but "known and fixed." A manufactured part may have a normal average lead time of six weeks, but if it is needed badly because of a penalty contract, a "blow out" at an oil well, or because there is an AOG (Aircraft on the Ground), lead time will be shortened. The typical product that takes a normal lead time of six weeks to make can be made in 24 to 48 hours if it is hand carried from operation to operation and everything possible is done to make it on an expedite basis. By the same token, every time some job is made in less than normal lead time, other jobs will get pushed aside and will take more than normal lead time. And that is exactly what the MRP model represents. Looking at Figure A4-1, it can be seen that the 600 average demand during lead time will be met or exceeded 50 percent of the time. Demand during lead time will be 600 or less about 50 percent of the time! The order point inventory model ignores this and tries to protect against a stockout only for times when demand will be equal to or greater than the average.

MRP starts out with an assumed lead time of six weeks. It then issues reschedule messages to the planners to tell them to make the material or take delivery of purchased material earlier (reduce the lead time), or to make or take delivery later (to increase the lead time). This is a faithful representation of what has always been done in the real world of manufacturing and purchasing.

It would be hard to conjure up many situations in the real world where lead time is truly known and fixed. And the really important thing is to keep priorities valid, not to assume a fixed lead time when the lead time can vary substantially.

Having made the rather broad assumption that lead time is known and fixed (when, in reality, a theoretical six-week lead time item might have actual lead time of three days or three months), the so-called "scientific inventory management" model then goes on to multiply the demand by that lead time! "If demand is 100 a week, lead time is 6 weeks, demand during lead time equals 600." And this lead time is also used to adjust the safety stock! (The mean absolute deviation is usually calculated over a weekly or a monthly time period and then adjusted for the lead time using tables or formulas that account for the fact that this adjustment is not linear.) Having taken a figure which, in practice, can be something between 48 hours and several months and called it "six," it is now used to multiply or adjust the other factors in the formula to come up with an order point which is then called a "scientific inventory model"!

The order point model assumed that due dates would be established based on lead time. An item with a six-week lead time would be ordered when it hit the order point and the due date would be at the end of the lead time.

Ironically, the order point didn't even establish the due date for independent demand items correctly most of the time. Consider an example where the order point is 850 (100 per week usage, 6 week lead time, 250 safety stock). If a demand triggered the order point and the amount on hand and on order was 600, the due date would still be week 6. If the on hand and on order was 300, the due date would _still_ be week 6.

There was nothing in the order point model per se to cope with the need to _update due dates_. This was a common failing in all the early attempts at inventory management. The quarterly ordering system assumed that material could be ordered once a quarter and that nothing significant would change. The order point assumed that things could be ordered when they hit the order point and that no significant changes in demand (that safety stock could not handle) would occur before the item came into stock. The fact that this was totally out of touch with reality occurred to some people, and the "critical ratio" approach was developed in 1964. (4) The idea of this technique (which will not be explained here, but can be referenced in any standard text on production control) was that each week the status of each order point item would be reviewed to compare the stock on hand with the order point and to compare the amount of scheduled work remaining on the job to the original lead time (which represents, of course, the total original scheduled days of work). An item where inventory was being depleted faster than the job was moving through production was an "expedite" item. An item where the job was moving through production at the same rate as inventory was being depleted was an item in equilibrium. An item with inventory being depleted less rapidly than the job was moving through production would move to the bottom of the priority list. The principle behind critical ratio was a fundamental that has become part of the ground work of modern scheduling of manufacturing and distribution; _due dates will not remain correct because things will change. They will have to be reviewed continuously._

Unfortunately, the critical ratio technique had very little success in practice. At first, it was "glued on" to the order point. The order point didn't establish valid need dates for most items anyway since most demand is really dependent. Updating invalid need dates with critical ratio was of little value.

When MRP came along, it included a rescheduling function to move need dates in or out as actual needs changed. Critical ratio was no longer a requirement with MRP since all it could possibly add to MRP would be to express need dates in terms of ratios rather than dates. Dates are always more significant in a manufacturing operation than ratios.

So critical ratio was an attempt to add on to the order point a way to keep due dates correct. But the fundamental order point concept didn't even recognize this need. It assumed that due dates, once established, would remain correct.

The order point assumed stock replenishment. When material is below a given level, it must be reordered to replenish stock. The steel needed to make a product that is ordered twice a year by a customer does not need to be replenished because it is below order point. There are many items in inventory like this where order point simply does not apply.

"When to order" was assumed to be the burning issue of inventory management because inventory management was an outgrowth of order launching and expediting. Before it was recognized that the main value of the computer was in enabling manufacturing companies to do that which they could not do before, it was assumed that the primary value would be in enabling them to enhance what they were doing before. The natural reaction was to try to improve on the order launching which was the function of inventory management at the time. Whether or not inventory management should have been performing this function was not considered. The important question is, "When is the material needed?" "When to order" is easy to determine when the important question has been addressed. Moreover, "when to order" is a "one-shot" question. "When is the material really needed" is a continuing question because of the environment of constant change in manufacturing and distribution.

The theory of scientific inventory management revolved around the precise computation of safety stock. That was the "one number" that was assumed to be the most important. In fact, all that computation did was change the order release date. In a world where lead time was highly variable and very much a dependent rather than independent variable, the precision of the safety stock computation was purely imaginary. If an item can be made in one week rather than six weeks, the amount of safety stock required is not particularly great and the precision in the computation is an illusion.

The order point inventory model didn't look beyond the current order cycle. The objective was to trigger a reorder at the order point inventory level and have enough safety stock to cover any above average demand during the replenishment lead time. Little thought was given to the fact that when an order to replenish inventory is released, there must be material and capacity available within a plant or at the vendors to produce this order. The order point inventory model did not look into the future in order to provide plans for material and capacity availability.

Does this mean that the order point inventory model has absolutely no applications in the real world? It must be recognized that a model is a representation of reality. If it represents reality, it is valid. If it does not represent reality, it is invalid and will not function properly. The only place the order point inventory model can be applied is where the assumptions discussed above actually exist in the real world; if there really are any!

Section 4
The Time Phased Order Point

As material requirements planning came into more popular use, it was recognized that the order point could be set up in a material requirements planning format. This was originally called the "time phased order point" - but that was just a term to help people who had learned that "order point applies to independent demand items" bridge the gap in learning, and understand that MRP applies to independent demand items too! The fact of the matter is that the MRP format applies whether demand is independent or dependent. And time phased order point is merely a synonym for material requirements planning - for independent demand items.

Today, the use of time phased order point for independent demand items at distribution centers is called distribution requirements planning, DRP. Anything that is going to be distributed has to be made, and today, distribution requirements planning is seen as simply an extension of material requirements planning. The two examples of a "time phased order point" shown below illustrate how it solved some of the problems of the classical order point format.

The Order Point — Time Phased

SS = 250 FORECAST = 100/WEEK LEAD TIME = 6 WEEKS		Week							
		1	2	3	4	5	6	7	8
Projected Requirements		100	100	100	100	100	100	100	100
Scheduled Receipts									
On Hand	1000	900	800	700	600	500	400	300	200
Planned Order Release									

Figure A4 – 4. The Order Point Time Phased

Figure A4-4 shows an example where the lead time is six weeks, the forecast is 100 per week, and the safety stock is 250. If this were shown in the order point format, it would say:

$$100 \times 6 + 250 = 850$$

Since usage is 100 per week, there are 1000 units on hand, and the order point is 850; material would have to be ordered in week 2. The time phased order point projects the inventory being reduced by 100 units per week and backs off over the lead time to determine when the planned order must be released. In Figure A4-4, it must be released in week 2. If demand is continuous, the time phased order point answers the "when to order" question just as the classical order point did. But the time phased order point also has a significant advantage: an export order for 2000 in week 5 can be shown properly.

Time Phased Order Point — Rescheduling

SS = 250 OQ = 800 FORECAST = 100/WEEK		Week							
		6	7	8	9	10	11	12	13
Projected Requirements		100	100	100	100	100	100	100	100
Scheduled Receipts				800					
On Hand	700	600	500	1200	1100	1000	900	800	700
Planned Order Release									

Figure A4 – 5. Time Phased Order Point Rescheduling

Figure A4-5 shows the "time phased order point" used for rescheduling. There is a scheduled receipt in period 8, but that scheduled receipt is really not needed until period 10. (Ignoring the scheduled receipt for a moment, the inventory in Figure A4-5 would be projected at 400 units in week 8, 300 in week 9, and 200 in week 10. The 200 is below the safety stock, thus the 800 should be rescheduled into period 10.) Showing the order point in the time phased - or MRP - format allows it not only to determine "when to order," but also when to reschedule. Using MRP for independent demand items allows the system to tell people when to:

1. Order material (this is all the traditional order point technique was designed to do).

2. Reschedule material already on order to earlier or later time periods.

3. Generate planned order releases for:

    a. Lower level material requirements planning.
    b. Capacity requirements planning.

4. Handle "lumpy demand" (promotions, export orders, or any kind of lumpy demand can be put into a time phased MRP system as opposed to an order point system that assumes continuous demand during every time period).

Section 5
An Invalid Model

The order point inventory model was built around a number of false assumptions, the most important of which was that inventory management in the computer age would simply be an extension of the order launching that was done before the computer was available. Once the computer was available, manufacturing and distribution companies had the massive data manipulation capabilities to keep schedules up to date. Then it became apparent that inventory management was a by-product of scheduling, that inventories were not "managed" by manipulating lot sizes or safety stocks, but indeed by making the right products at the right time.

There are two key questions in scheduling: "When do we _really_ need it?" and "How much do we _really_ need?" The classical approach to inventory management did its best to obscure the answers to both of these questions. The safety stock changed the need date by moving it forward. The lot size increased the quantity needed to an "economic order quantity." Today, with MRP, safety stock can be used, but as discussed in Chapter 11, it can be shown without obscuring the real need date. Lot sizes can also be used, but with the "pegging" in an MRP system (see Appendix 1), the actual requirements can be determined to find the answer to that important question, "How much is really needed?"

The order point as an inventory model is a theoretical anachronism that has little value in the real world of managing a manufacturing or distribution company.

Footnotes

1. The theory of scientific inventory management has been discussed in many books which contain these statistical tables including <u>Production and Inventory Management in the Computer Age</u>, Oliver W. Wight, CBI Publishing Company, 1974, <u>Production and Inventory Control: Principles and Techniques</u>, George Plossl and Oliver Wight, Prentice Hall, Englewood Cliffs, New Jersey, 1967, <u>Decision Rules for Inventory Management</u>, Robert Goodell Brown, Holt, Rinehart, and Winston, 1967.)

2. By Joe Orlicky at IBM.

3. There have been some attempts to calculate the statistical interaction of demand and lead time variability Little has been done with this in practice because it makes the false assumption that lead time is an "independent variable." Lead time is very much a dependent variable - as any expeditor knows!

4. By Arnold Putnam of Rath and Strong, Boston, Massachusetts.

**Appendix 5
Glossary**

Appendix 5
Glossary

This is a very brief glossary of the terms most commonly used in manufacturing resource planning. Some of them are production and inventory management terms. (1) Others refer to areas encompassed by the entire MRP II system.

ABC classification Before computers came along, practitioners found that if they would rank the inventory items by annual usage in dollars, it would tell them how to best use their scarce resource - manual posting of inventory records. The low value items were typically put on a simple visual review system of some type to avoid having to make all the necessary inventory entries. With computers, the scarce resource is no longer clerical posting time, but instead the time people would use for planning and controlling. The ABC classification is still used to determine which items should be cycle counted most frequently, which items should have the largest lot sizes, etc.

The basic principle involves breaking the Inventory down into three categories where typically the top 20 percent ranked by annual usage in dollars are called the A items (they will normally account for 80 percent of the dollar activity). The next 30 percent are called the B items, and the next 50 percent are the C items which usually account for about 5 percent of the annual dollar usage.

Accumulation Staging.

Aggregate inventory management In the days when the order point inventory model was assumed to be a legitimate representation of reality, aggregate inventory management was based on safety stocks, lot sizes, etc. (See Appendix 4, The Order Point Inventory Model.) Today, MRP II can be used as a basis for costing out actual inventory by product line (or commodity if desired), costing out the requirements, costing out the scheduled receipts and planned orders, and generating a realistic projection of inventories. If the master schedule is met - generating the anticipated requirements - and the scheduled receipts come in as planned, the actual inventory levels will match the planned levels generated by MRP II very closely.

Alpha factor   The weighting factor that is applied against the most recent sales to compute the exponential smoothing average.

Anticipated delay report   A report usually sent to the planners daily from the factory and purchasing telling them of any shop orders or purchase orders that are anticipated to come in later than their required date.   The closed loop system requires this type of feedback and takes the stance that "silence is approval."

Back order   When a required item is not in inventory, an order created to withdraw it when it becomes available is called a back order.

Bill of material   (See also Planning bill of material, Indented bill of material.)   A listing of the components required to manufacture a product in product structure format.   A bill of material is similar to a parts list except that it usually shows how the product is fabricated and assembled, i.e., it would show that raw material is used to make fabricated components, the fabricated components go into subassemblies, the subassemblies then go into an assembly, etc. This is usually done by showing the bill of material in an indented (or multi-level) format.

Blanket order   A long-term commitment to a vendor for material against which short-term releases will be generated to satisfy requirements.

Branch warehouse   Distribution center.

Bucketless system   The original MRP systems time phased material requirements, scheduled receipts, the projected available balance and planned order releases into time periods, usually monthly or weekly.   These time periods were called in data processing slang, "time buckets."   In this type of system, the number of time buckets had to be determined as the system was designed.   If planning was to extend out a year in the future, every item had to have 52 weekly time buckets allocated to it.   Modern computer systems that maintain files of requirements, etc. by date do not require buckets and are called bucketless systems. The advantage of these systems is that one item with a very long lead time might need a planning horizon of two years while another item might not need a planning horizon beyond six months, and computer file space would not have to be tied up needlessly.

Buckets Data processing slang for the time periods used in time phased MRP.

Business plan The overall plan for the amount of dollars to be shipped, the amount planned to be in inventory or order backlog, and the amount to be produced. This is the basic business plan in a manufacturing company. The complete business plan would probably also include other planned expenditures like research and development, etc. not directly connected with the production functions.

Capacity control Monitoring actual output against plan for a work center or centers. The input/output report is usually used for capacity control.

Capacity requirements planning A time phased MRP system not only releases orders, but it also generates planned orders that are used to create lower level material requirements. Capacity requirements plans can be generated then by taking into account the hours by work center by time period needed to produce both the open shop orders and planned shop orders.

Capacity planning Capacity requirements planning.

Cash flow The comparison of the cash coming into the company versus the cash going out. See also projected cash flow.

Closed loop MRP A term used to describe a system built around material requirements planning that also includes production planning, master scheduling, capacity planning, means for executing the capacity plans such as the input/output report for monitoring it, means for executing the material plans such as the dispatch list and the vendor schedules. Implicit in the concept of a closed loop system is the feedback from the vendors and the shop floor using the input/output report and the anticipated delay reports.

Component inventory The word component embraces any inventory item that is used to make another. Thus, a raw material, a part, or a subassembly can be a component of another product.

Computer model Model.

Critical ratio A dynamic priority technique originally conceived in an environment of order point inventory control.

The idea was to review the inventory and the progress of the job periodically, usually weekly, and to revise the priority accordingly. As it became more and more apparent that order point inventory control was an obsolescent technique, critical ratio was adapted to be used with MRP. It expresses the priorities that MRP regularly updates in a ratio form.

Cycle count   Regular daily counts of the items in stores. Typically, a cycle count approach would be to count some items each day so that all items were counted at least once a year. Cycle counting should be viewed as a quality control function. Its major purpose is not to correct inventory records that are wrong. That's just a by-product. The major purpose is to monitor the process through sampling to make sure that inventory record accuracy is at or above the required level.

Demand filter   A technique for signaling any extraordinarily large demands. Usually a quantity that is a function of the average deviation is established, and if demand for any given period is greater than this quantity, an exception message is generated.

Dependent demand   Demand on an item is called dependent when it can be calculated from the need to manufacture or replenish inventory for a higher level item. A part that goes into a subassembly has dependent demand. If it is also sold directly to customers as a service part, it has independent demand as well. A raw material that is later converted into semifinished inventory has dependent demand. Demand on the semifinished inventory is likely to be dependent demand unless that semifinished inventory is sold directly to customers. Dependent demand requirements should be calculated using techniques like MRP rather than forecast using order point techniques.

Deterministic demand   Dependent demand.

Discrete lot sizing   Lot sizes in an MRP system that are equal to the unsatisfied requirements for one time period.

Dispatching   The selection and assignment of jobs at an individual work center.

Dispatch list   A schedule for a work center usually generated by computer, usually issued daily, showing the priority sequence of jobs to be done at that work center.

Priorities on the dispatch list are kept up to date by the material requirements planning system.

Distribution by value   ABC classification.

Distribution center   These are the warehouses where companies with finished goods inventory carry their inventory so it is close to their customers. A typical company, for example, might have a manufacturing facility in Philadelphia and distribution centers in Atlanta, Dallas, Los Angeles, San Francisco, and Chicago. The term distribution center is synonymous with the term branch warehouse, although it has become more commonly used recently. When there is a warehouse that serves a group of satellite warehouses, this is usually called a regional distribution center.

Distribution resource planning   DRP. Material requirements planning (MRP) was originally developed as a way to order material to support assembly operations. After it had been in use for a number of years, people began to recognize that distribution inventories also have levels. Branch warehouses draw inventory from a distribution center which, in turn, replenishes its inventory by ordering in lots from factories. DRP is simply the term given to MRP when it is used to properly time phase these dependent demands on finished goods inventory and plan production at the manufacturing facility to include the distribution system. Just as MRP was extended into areas other than material requirements planning, the same thing happened with DRP. Distribution resource planning includes planning cubage for traffic requirements, converting the distribution requirements plan into dollars, using it for planning manpower requirements at warehouses, etc.

DRP   Distribution resource planning

Economic order quantity   The mathematical computation for finding the least total cost lot size. The EOQ formula solves for the lot size where ordering cost and inventory carrying cost are equal.

EOQ   Economic order quantity.

Executing the material requirements plan   Done via the dispatch list in the factory and the vendor schedule for the vendors. The anticipated delay report is the feedback to signal when there is a problem in executing the plan.

Expediting Trying to get jobs rushed through to cover shortages or to meet shipping requirements. Expediting is a bad word in most companies because the entire system has often degenerated into an expediting system. The expeditor typically finds out what material is needed too late, and thus is chronically causing disruptions in factory schedules and in purchasing.

Explosion An extension of an assembly or subassembly bill of material into the total of each of the components required to manufacture a given quantity of the assembly or subassembly.

Exponential smoothing A rather pretentious name for a moving weighted average.

Exposures Dividing the lot size into the annual usage determines how many times inventory will have to be replenished per year. Each of these replenishment periods "exposes" the inventory to the chance of a stock out, thus large lot sizes require less safety stock, small lot sizes require more.

Extrinsic forecast A forecast based on external factors such as basing forecasts of automotive parts sales on automobile registrations.

FAS Final assembly schedule.

Final assembly schedule The schedule for actually putting an assembled product together into its final configuration as opposed to the master schedule which, in a make-to-order environment, would be stated in terms of the major components or groups of components. The master schedule in an automobile company, for example, would be stated in terms of engines, transmissions, and body types; while the final assembly schedule would specify a particular automobile with a specific engine, transmission, body, etc.

Finished goods inventory Product that is ready for shipment and is carried in inventory in anticipation of customer orders.

Finite loading Conceptually, the term means putting no more work into a factory than the factory can be expected to execute. This is a function of master scheduling. The specific term usually refers to a computer technique that involves automatic shop priority revision in order to level the load operation by operation. Finite loading requires that the arrival of jobs at each operation be predicted very accurately and also assumes that the computer can be accountable for the shop schedule and people don't have to be. It has had a very poor track record. Companies trying to use finite loading have gotten some benefits from the prerequisite capacity planning, but usually have discarded - or ignored - the automatic load leveling very quickly.

<u>Firm planned order</u> In material requirements planning, a planned order explodes material requirements to lower levels and is rescheduled automatically, as opposed to a scheduled receipt (released order), which does not explode material requirements and is not rescheduled automatically. The firm planned order <u>does</u> explode material requirements to the lower levels like a planned order. But, like a scheduled receipt, it is not rescheduled automatically. Thus, the firm planned order is a planned order that can be frozen in quantity and time so that it does not change without human intervention.

<u>Gross requirements</u> Material requirements that have not been reduced ("netted") by deducting the on-hand and on-order quantities.

<u>Horizon</u> Planning horizon.

<u>Indented bill of material</u> A bill of material that is printed with the top level (or level "0") items shown in the left-most column, level-one components indented one column to the right, etc.

<u>Independent demand</u> Demand for an inventory item is considered independent when it is unrelated to any higher-level item that the company manufactures or stocks. The demand for a service part that is shipped directly to customers would be considered independent. On the other hand, if that service part were shipped to a branch warehouse, the demand on the service part would be a function of branch warehouse replenishment, and thus would be considered dependent. Generally, independent demand items are those that are carried in finished goods inventories, although not all finished goods items are necessarily independent demand items, because much of their demand might derive from branch warehouses, for example. Independent demand items can be replenished using stock replenishment systems like the order point, although MRP or DRP (if branch warehouses) would give superior results.

Infinite loading Showing the work behind work centers in the time periods required regardless of the capacity available to perform this work. The term infinite loading is considered to be obsolete today, although the specific computer programs used to do infinite loading, when they take into account planned orders as well as released orders, can be used to perform the function now called capacity requirements planning. Infinite loading was a gross misnomer to start with, implying that a load could be put into a factory regardless of its ability to perform. The poor terminology obscured the fact that it is necessary to generate capacity requirements and compare these with available capacity before trying to adjust requirements to capacity.

Input/output control A simple technique for capacity control where actual output is compared with planned output developed by capacity requirements planning. The input to a work center can be monitored to see if it corresponds with plans so that work centers will not be expected to generate output when material is not available.

Intrinsic forecast A forecast based on internal factors, such as an average of past sales, is called intrinsic.

Inventory accounting Maintaining inventory balance records; what used to be called "perpetual inventory" records.

Inventory control A rather nebulous term sometimes used to refer to inventory accounting, sometimes used to describe order point based replenishment systems as distinguished from MRP systems; properly used, it means having the right material in inventory to meet needs. In an MRP-based system, inventory control is a by-product of priority planning. The term is also used as a name for a department that used to be responsible for inventory ordering in the days of order launching and expediting. See also Planning department.

Inventory management Another somewhat nebulous term for inventory control. When order point and economic order quantity were assumed to be the techniques for controlling inventory, inventory management was used as a term to describe the use of these techniques to achieve an "optimum" level of inventory.

Inventory turnover Turnover rate.

Item master record A computer term for the inventory record.

Lead time The time it takes to obtain an item. The overall lead time starts from the moment it is determined that the item is needed until the time it has been received into inventory and is available for use.

Lead time offset Time phased MRP shows planned orders in their proper release time period - the lead time "offset" - based on the lead time.

Levels A bill of material must be properly structured to represent the way the product is made. In the United States, the final product is called the "0" level. The subassemblies that go into the final assembly are at level 1, their components are at level 2, etc.

Load center Work center.

Loading Measuring the backlog or "load" behind work centers. Loading has been superseded by capacity requirements planning, which puts the emphasis on forecasting capacity requirements rather than just adding up backlog.

MAD Mean absolute deviation.

Machine loading Infinite loading and Finite loading.

Management science Synonym for operations research.

Manufacturing resource planning MRP II. Material requirements planning evolved into the closed loop MRP system which then evolved into manufacturing resource planning. Technically, MRP II includes the financial planning as well as planning in units; it also includes a simulation capability. From a management point of view, MRP II means that the tools are being used for planning the activities of all functions of a manufacturing company.

Master production schedule Master schedule.

Master schedule The build schedule, stated in bill of material (or bill of material module, or planning bill of material) numbers, that drives the MRP - and consequently, the capacity planning - systems.

<u>Materials management</u> An organizational concept that in-
volves putting all of the functions concerned with the
movement of materials, i.e. production control, inventory
control, traffic, stores, materials handling, purchasing,
etc. under one manager. The rationale is that this avoids
conflicts among groups with different objectives.

<u>Materials planning</u> Obsolete term for MRP.

<u>Material requirements planning</u> Computers were used short-
ly after their introduction into manufacturing companies to
explode material requirements or do "requirements generation." With the introduction of time phasing, these material
requirements could be expressed in detail in specific time
periods, usually weeks. By this time, netting out gross
requirements against on-hand and in-process inventory had
become a well-accepted technology. Modern MRP, therefore, is an approach for calculating material requirements
not only to generate replenishment orders, but also to
reschedule open orders to meet changing requirements.
Today, it is thought of more as a scheduling technique than
an inventory ordering technique.

<u>Mean absolute deviation</u> An approximation to the standard
deviation (MAD times 1.25 approximates the standard deviation). It is more convenient to work with, since there is
no square root calculation involved. This makes it particularly convenient to update the MAD using techniques
like exponential smoothing. The mean absolute deviation is
calculated by averaging the difference between the forecast
demand and the actual demand. "Mean" means average,
"absolute" means regardless of whether the deviation was
plus or minus, "deviation" refers to the difference between
the forecast and the actual demand.

<u>Model</u> A representation - usually done by computer - of
the relationships that exist in a real world situation. The
advantage of the model is that it can be used to manipulate
information and simulate the "what if" questions to see how
the model will react under various circumstances, or to
provide answers that the real world situation can't provide
readily. Material requirements planning is really a model of
the fundamental manufacturing equation. ("What are we
going to make, what does it take to make it, what do we
have, what do we have to get?") The advantage this model
has over the real world technique - the shortage list - is
that it can be used to predict farther into the future and
in very small time increments, over and over again, what
the shortages <u>will be</u>.

<u>Modular bill of material</u> A bill of material used for master scheduling that expresses the material requirements for a product without showing the final configuration of the product. Modular bills of material for an automobile, for example, would list the engines, transmissions, body styles, upholstery options, etc., rather than attempting to show the final configuration of a specific automobile. Modular bills of material are particularly useful for material requirements planning where the final configuration of the product is extremely difficult to forecast.

<u>MPS</u> Master production schedule.

<u>MRP</u> Material requirements planning.

<u>MRP II</u> Manufacturing resource planning.

<u>Net change MRP</u> Material requirements planning on a true exception basis. In a net change system, a partial explosion will be triggered by a change in inventory, requirements, open orders, or product structure status. A scrap ticket, for example, reducing the quantity of material on order, would generate a new net requirement, thus triggering a partial explosion down through the lower inventory levels. The net change system is a transaction-driven system. While, theoretically, the net change system would be a continuous processing type of system, in practice net change is usually done in daily batch mode.

<u>Net requirements</u> The amount of material that needs to be ordered to cover the difference between the current on hand and on order status, and the gross requirements.

<u>Netting</u> Deducting from the gross requirements the amount on hand and on order to generate the material needs or net requirements.

<u>Offset</u> Lead time offset.

<u>Operations research</u> The attempt to use statistical and mathematical techniques to quantify business decisions. The techniques of statistical inventory control such as exponential smoothing, the use of techniques like the mean absolute deviation to quantify forecast error, and the use of simulation are all generally considered operations research techniques. Synonym: management science.

Operations scheduling This means putting the dates on the individual operations on a routing in the computer (they <u>do not</u> appear on the shop paper) to show when each operation needs to be completed to meet the schedule. A similar term, operations sequencing, is sometimes used as a euphemism for finite loading.

Optimization Coming up with the one right answer. Compare this with simulation.

OR Operations research.

Order backlog In a make-to-order company, this is the booked customer orders. Backlog is the opposite of inventory in a make-to-stock company. The order backlog represents sold products not shipped.

Order point A quantity that is established for reordering purposes. When the total stock on hand plus on order falls below the order point, a new supply is ordered. The order point is computed by extending the estimated demand over the replenishment lead time and adding a safety stock to account for forecast error.

Parts list A simple listing of the parts that go into an assembled product, usually without any product structuring shown.

Pegging Showing what items at higher levels caused specific requirements in an MRP output report.

Physical inventory A count of actual inventory on hand in order to reconcile it to the book figures. Usually this is done annually for auditing purposes to be sure that the financial records accurately reflect the assets of the company.

Picking Collecting material from a stores area to satisfy a shop or customer order.

Planned order release In a time phased MRP system, "gross requirements" are deducted (by time period) from the inventory on hand and on order (scheduled receipts) to project an available balance. When requirements exceed the amount on hand and on order, a negative balance or net requirement results. The net requirements are converted to a lot size if necessary, and the lot size is then offset by the lead time to create a planned order release. Planned orders at one level in the product structure become gross requirements at the lower level.

Planning bill of material   A bill of material that is used in the master schedule to plan requirements before actual customer orders have been received. It will typically show the percentage of various options that are normally required.

Planning department   In an MRP II system, this is the group that plans material and capacity, and converts this information into dollars.

Planning horizon   The amount of time, as measured from today's date forward, that is planned in the master schedule and material requirements planning system.   The planning horizon might be one year, two years, etc. depending upon the lead times down through the product structure and the time required for capacity planning beyond the material lead times.

Priority planning   When MRP was first developed, it was considered to be an ordering system.   Then people recognized that it could also handle rescheduling.   Today, we recognize that the most serious planning deficiency before MRP worked was the inability to schedule properly.   The inventory system launched orders while the production control system consisted primarily of expediting.   As MRP was used more and more, it became evident that the real power of the technique was its ability not only to order material at the right time and to establish the correct due dates on the shop and purchase orders when they were issued, but also to keep these dates correct and in line with the latest requirements.   The term priority planning was coined to describe this function.

Production control   The old term used for the department that was responsible for "scheduling."   See Planning department.

Production and inventory control   Production control.

Production plan   Setting the level of manufacturing operations, usually by product group or in some other broad terms.   Production plans are established in units, dollars, or hours.

Product structure The way materials go into the product during its manufacture. A typical product structure, for example, would show raw material being converted into fabricated components, components being put together to make subassemblies, subassemblies going into assemblies, etc.

Projected available balance In an MRP output report, the amount on hand is projected into the future by deducting each period's requirements and adding scheduled receipts.

Projected cash flow A projection of the dollars that will be going out of the business and into the business in the future.

Purchase commitment report Projection of the dollars that are committed to the vendors based on costing out the open purchase orders by time period.

Purchase order An order going to a vendor authorizing the vendor to deliver one or more items.

Purchase requisition A document usually generated by production and/or inventory control personnel authorizing the purchasing department to buy material.

Regeneration A form of MRP where the entire master schedule is periodically re-exploded down through the bills of material, usually once a week, and netted out against on-hand and on-order inventory to determine what the net requirements are. At the same time, open orders that are out of phase with requirements are identified so that they can be considered for rescheduling. Contrast with net change.

Regional distribution center Distribution center.

Reorder point Order point.

Requirements Gross requirements; Net requirements.

Requirements planning Obsolete terminology for material requirements planning.

Resource requirements planning When a master schedule is first being developed, a resource requirements plan is frequently made. In broad terms, this compares the demand on some of the manufacturing facilities, engineering facilities, etc. with the availability of these resources in order to determine whether or not the master schedule is reasonable. Resource requirements planning implies that resources other than manufacturing capacity will be planned. This is the only difference between resource requirements planning and a rough cut capacity plan.

ROP   Reorder point.

Rough cut capacity plan   Frequently, it's a good idea to make a rough cut capacity plan directly from the production plan rather than going through the entire material requirements planning and capacity planning cycles to do this. This is done by having conversion tables for the approximate amount of capacity required for product families shown in the production plan.

Routing   A specification of the sequence of operations required to manufacture a product.

Safety stock   Stock replenishment systems are based on estimates of demand over lead time. Since demand in any particular lead time could exceed the estimates, extra inventory - called "safety stock" - is planned into the order point.

Safety time   Safety stock is expressed as a quantity, but the effect of safety stock is a change in timing. If the average demand is one hundred per week, for example, and the safety stock is two hundred, this means that the material is being brought in two weeks before it is really needed. Safety time is a way of expressing this safety stock in terms of time. In this example, it would be a two-week safety time. Safety time is a far superior method to safety stock for items with intermittent usage. A two-hundred unit safety stock would require the material to be brought in immediately to cover the safety stock even though there were no requirements in the near future. Using safety time, material would be brought in two weeks before it was required.

Scheduled receipt   An open shop or purchase order in an MRP output format. So called because the date the order needs to be received is especially important in view of the fact that much of the value of MRP is derived from its rescheduling capability.

Scheduling Establishing the timing for performing a task. There are various levels of scheduling within a manufacturing company. The master schedule establishes the overall logistics plan for supplying material to support production and sales. Material requirements are generated, and scheduled due dates are established for this material to support the master schedule. Shop orders may be broken down into more detailed schedules for each operation and desired completion (or start) dates for each of these operations established to show when they must be completed in order to get the shop order completed on time.

Scientific inventory control The name given to the use of statistical techniques for computing safety stock and mathematical computations of economic order quantities.

Semi-finished inventory Inventory that is stored before some final operations which will convert it to different products. Builder's hardware, for example, is usually stored before the finishing operation so that it can be plated or painted to meet specific requirements.

Shop order An order going to the factory authorizing manufacture of an item. Synonyms: work order, production order, job order.

Shortage list The list of material missing when the required material is staged; see Staging.

Simulation Representing the way a business works by manipulating numbers and logic in a computer. Simulation is a "what if" type of process as opposed to an attempt to find an optimum - one correct answer.

Staging When the formal priority planning system did not work, expeditors pulled material from the stockroom to see which components were missing to make the products in the master schedule. An expensive, confusing, obsolete practice. A synonym is accumulation.

Stock chasing An obsolete, yet still descriptive, term for expediting.

Time phased order point Material requirements planning for independent demand items where the independent forecast, rather than higher-level requirements, is put into the time periods.

Time phasing   A term frequently used as a synonym for MRP.   Modern MRP systems are time phased into weekly time periods - or smaller - by definition, thus the term is obsolete.   Strictly speaking, it refers to the practice of showing requirements, scheduled receipts, the projected available balance, and planned order releases in their proper time relationship to each other.

Time series planning   Synonym for MRP; obsolete terminology.

Turnover rate   A performance measure that is most meaningful within a company rather than comparing a company's performance with other companies. The turnover rate is calculated by dividing the inventory investment into the annual cost of sales to see how many times the inventory "turns over" during the year.   Frequently, turnover rate is calculated by dividing the inventory investment into the actual sales figure, which gives an inflated turnover rate since inventory is at factory cost and sales is at selling price.

Vendor schedule   Vendor schedules are being used in place of purchase orders for productive purchasing today.   The purchase order was a contract with a schedule in it.   The contract usually didn't have to be changed more than once a year.   The schedule should be reviewed at least once a week.   Consequently, modern MRP II systems use a "letter of agreement" which is really a contract between the vendor and the customer, and a separate vendor schedule that usually goes out once a week and shows the updated need dates for material.

Where used list   An inverted bill of material that shows where each component is used at its higher level.

Work center   A group of machines, or work stations, or people, which can perform similar operations.   A number of presses of the same capacity that can take the same dies could be considered one work center for capacity planning purposes

Footnotes

1. A comprehensive dictionary of production control,
    inventory control, data processing, and related terms
    is available from the American Production and Inven-
    tory Control Society; P.O. Box 219, Falls Church,
    Virginia 22046.

Appendix 6
Sources for Further Information on MRP and MRP II

Section 1
The Needs

Any company installing a closed loop MRP or MRP II system will need a number of types of professional assistance. Among these are:

1. Books on the subject.

2. Education in live classes.

3. In-plant education using video courses.

4. Reviews of commercially available software packages for MRP and MRP II. Companies using their own system rather than buying software should be sure that their system has the ability to perform the proper functions for MRP and MRP II. There is a <u>standard</u> system that will work. Very few deviations from the standard can actually work in practice.

5. Consulting services to help install the system or review it periodically after it has been implemented and is operating.

The following sections indicate a number of the services that are available in this field.

Section 2
Available Books

1. The Executives Guide to Successful MRP II, Oliver W. Wight, published by OWL Publications, Inc., Williston, Vermont, 1981. This brief, handy reference for the executive tells where MRP applies, the results to expect, what it costs, what has to be done to implement and operate it successfully.

2. Production and Inventory Management in the Computer Age, Oliver W. Wight, CBI Publishing Company, Inc., Boston, MA, 1974. This book, as its name implies, covers the subject of production and inventory management in the computer age with heavy emphasis on MRP. It also covers other areas like capacity planning, shop floor control, purchasing, etc.

3. Material Requirements Planning, Joseph Orlicky, McGraw-Hill Book Company, New York, 1975. This is an excellent technical exposition of material requirements planning and that is its basic emphasis as opposed to the entire closed loop system. This would be an excellent book for a systems designer who wanted to understand the detailed logic of a material requirements planning system.

4. Master Production Scheduling; Principles and Practice, William L. Berry, Thomas E. Vollman, D. Clay Whybark, American Production and Inventory Control Society, Washington, D.C., 1979. This is an excellent review of current master production scheduling practice at some of the best MRP users in the country.

5. Focus Forecasting: Computer Techniques for Inventory Control, Bernard T. Smith, CBI Publishing Company, Inc., Boston, MA, 1978. This is a detailed explanation of the focus forecasting system. A number of different forecasting strategies can be used within the focus forecasting system. The system tests each of these against

the most recent sales to see which works best, and then uses this strategy to forecast the immediate future. Focus forecasting has had great success at American Hardware Supply Company where thousands of individual items of virtually every kind have to be forecast.

6.   DRP - Distribution Resource Planning, Andre Martin, OWL Publications, Inc., Williston, Vermont, 1982. This is a description of the way distribution requirements planning and distribution resource planning can be applied in a company with branch warehouses and distribution centers. It is particularly valuable for those companies that have manufacturing which must be integrated with a distribution system.

7.   APICS Dictionary (Editor for 1980 edition; Thomas Wallace), American Production and Inventory Control Society, Washington, D.C., 1980.

It is fascinating to observe the lack of books on MRP and related subjects. There are several other books on MRP, but any books where there is little real information on MRP, or where there is a significant amount of misinformation about MRP, have been omitted. For example, books that discuss MRP strictly as an order launching technique, don't discuss master scheduling, etc. were not listed.

Section 3
Live Classes

These are classes run by consultants who teach MRP and related subjects. No attempt has been made to include classes taught by anyone other than the education professionals involved in Oliver Wight, Inc. and Oliver Wight Education Associates. A list that would appear to be "objective" would include a number of classes that the author does not consider to be professional because of the content, or the fact that the instructors don't have a track record for MRP success. Information on other classes is available from the American Production and Inventory Control Society, P.O. Box 219, Falls Church, Virginia 22046.

MRP II: Manufacturing Resource Planning for Top Management (two and a half day class). Instructors: Walter Goddard and Oliver Wight.

MRP II: Manufacturing Resource Planning (The Five-Day Class) is taught by the following instructors:

Roger Brooks and Al Stevens (West Coast)
R. D. Garwood (Atlanta)
Walter Goddard and Oliver Wight (Boston and Florida)

Other Related Courses

Subject	Duration	Instructors
Bills of Material	3 days	Dave Garwood
Capacity Planning & Shop Floor Control	3 days	Dick Alban
Distribution Resource Planning	3 days	Andre Martin
MRP II: Financial Management	3 days	Andre Martin
Inventory Record Accuracy	2 days	Roger Brooks

Master Production Scheduling	4 days	Dick Ling (East Coast) Al Stevens (West Coast)
MRP II: Successful Implementation	3 days	George Bevis & Tom Wallace
The Planner's Job	2 days	Tom Wallace
MRP II for Purchasing	3 days	John Schorr & Tom Wallace
MRP II for Service Parts	2 days	Dave Garwood

Most of these classes are also run in the United Kingdom in conjunction with our associate, Mike Salmon. Classes - taught in French - are also scheduled regularly in France.

Further information on these classes is available from Oliver Wight Education Associates, Inc., P.O. Box 313, Newbury, NH 03255. 800-258-3862 or 603-763-2061.

Section 4
Video Education Courses

Video education is an essential tool for educating enough people to really make MRP work. It would never be practical to send enough people off to live classes. Bringing in the "outside expert" to run classes has proved to be a very nonproductive approach for reasons discussed in the text of this book.

The following courses are available from Oliver Wight Video Productions, Inc., P.O. Box 278, Williston, VT 05495:

Managing Inventories and Production by Oliver W. Wight.

Managing a Master Production Schedule by Walter E. Goddard.

MRP II: Making it Work by Walter Goddard, Darryl Landvater, and Oliver Wight.

Bills of Material by Dave Garwood.

The Key to MRP Success: A New Set of Values by Oliver Wight.

MRP II. Manufacturing Resource Planning by Oliver Wight.

MRP II: Unlocking America's Productivity Potential by Oliver Wight.

Section 5
Software Reviews

At one time, there was one computer program available from a computer manufacturer or software supplier for doing MRP. This program was the only one for many years. Today, there are over 100 different programs available and before a user gets involved with any set of programs, it would be well to know what is in the programs. Manufacturing Software Systems, P.O. Box 278, Williston, VT 05495, is the only known source for software evaluations. This is a kind of "consumer report" for software users.

The basic point of reference is a book called the "Standard System." It lists and explains the functions any MRP software must perform to operate properly. This book was developed based on the experience of successful MRP users. Available also are evaluations of the most popular computer software programs available from computer manufacturers and software suppliers. These evaluations compare the available software with the Standard System, indicating whether or not the software will perform the functions properly, and also indicating what modifications will have to be made to the software if it does not perform these functions properly.

Even a company with its own in-house computer program for MRP and MRP II would probably be well advised to get a copy of the Standard System to make sure their programs are properly designed.

Section 6
Consulting

There are many consultants who claim to have expertise in MRP. Some of them known to the author have experience, but only in seeing MRP installations fail. As MRP has become the recognized approach to running a manufacturing business more professionally, every consultant that can explain what the letters stand for is offering services in the field. There is a group of people endorsed specifically by the author, people who are involved in Oliver Wight Education Associates. (A list of endorsed consultants is available.) There <u>are</u> other consultants in the field. A list of MRP consultants is available from the American Production and Inventory Control Society (APICS, P.O. Box 219, Falls Church, Virginia 22046). Anyone engaging a consultant should <u>check the consultant's references</u> to make <u>sure</u> they have <u>current implementation experience</u>. The most successful installations have been the ones where a consultant came in once a month or once every six weeks to guide and be the catalyst rather than being on site every day, because that tends to take the initiative for developing a system away from the users.

INDEX